.R.P.

Valentines & Vitriol

Books by Rex Reed

DO YOU SLEEP IN THE NUDE?

CONVERSATIONS IN THE RAW

BIG SCREEN, LITTLE SCREEN

PEOPLE ARE CRAZY HERE

REX REED

Valentines & Vitriol

DELACORTE PRESS / NEW YORK

Manufactured in the United States of America

First printing

Designed by Ann Spinelli

Library of Congress Cataloging in Publication Data

Reed, Rex.
Valentines and vitriol.

1. Entertainers—Biography. I. Title.
PN1583.R4   790.2′092′2   [B]   76–53002
ISBN: 0–440–09336–8

For
Linda

Contents

THE HEROES

THE SURVIVORS

THE NEW BREED

Picture sections follow pages 102 and 198.

Introduction
by Liz Smith

They used to say the definition of a true celebrity was someone identifiable by name only—in other words, you didn't
have to amplify: Michelangelo, sculptor . . . Elizabeth Taylor, actress . . . Sigmund Freud, analyst.

In my own gyrations through the upper stratosphere observing the famous, no phenomenon has been more fascinat-
ing and satisfying to me than the emergence of the dynamic
and dramatic name, Rex Reed, as it grew into celebrity in
its own right. It is even more satisfying that Rex Reed is a
celebrity whose claim to fame is backed up by talent, guts,
compassion, wit, just a soupçon of sardonic overkill, and the
warmth of a real person behind the image.

There *is* a Rex Reed image, of course. It is the one seen
on the TV screen, sleepy-eyed, slickly tailored, blue-black
hair sometimes falling in a forelock over a boyish face. This
Rex bites the inside of his cheek and thinks a moment before
answering the talk show host, who is leading him on to
commit merriment and mayhem. Then, from those full baby
lips falls a silver stream of biting invective, savage criticism,
and mouth-watering simile. (In Rex's world a certain sensu-

ality reigns—people are always edible; their hair swirls like buttercrunch ice cream, their skin is pitted like an orange rind . . .)

Is this image on a flickering screen the *real* Rex Reed? People sincerely want to know, because it is the question most often asked me. They don't ask what Robert Redford or Barbra Streisand or Liz Taylor is *really* like. They ask what Rex Reed is *really* like. And because he is smart, sassy, successful, and opinionated, many of the questioners are hanging on for a bitchy answer. They want me to confirm that there is only the one image—that Rex Reed kicks his cat, hates his mother, mistreats his secretary, indulges in secret high-wire acts with transvestite midgets, cheats on his expense account, and doesn't like women.

How disappointing I must be. The real Rex Reed is only a human being like you and me—his faults, foibles, prejudices, intelligence, and charm made larger than life and exaggerated by TV. In actuality, he is a man who loves animals and adored his late mother; is worshipped by his helpers and friends; maintains an almost stoic indifference to any interest in his private life (I sometimes think he is indifferent to any private life himself); is scrupulously honest; and prefers the company of women to the company of men.

Others asking about the real Rex Reed are already true believers. They are the people who shove aside stage and screen stars at Broadway openings to ask for his autograph: mumbling CPA's who hold out scraps of paper and pencils, or lovely older women in carnation corsages who want to kiss him. Once I was with Rex in Russia and his hotel room was besieged by squealing American teenagers on tour. They had heard that their idol was behind the Iron Curtain. These kids were unimpressed that Elizabeth Taylor and Ava Gardner were down the hall. Rex invited the fresh-faced girls in for tea, exchanged autographs for their precious U.S. periodicals, and asked them the same kind of questions he puts to Faye Dunaway or Natalie Wood.

Rex always treats noncelebrities exactly as he treats glamorous stars. Every encounter for this Texas-born, Louisiana-bred writer is as important as any highly paid interview. It is life—life for which he has the insatiable curiosity, the nose for truth, the will to make contact with that characterizes so many fine reporters. And if you want to know one urgent reality about Rex, it is that he hasn't got a snobbish bone in his body. While he name-drops with the best of them (after all, many of his best friends are famous), he is unerring in his feel for people, for ordinary life drama, for what is in the human heart or withheld from it.

A glamorous time sitting on yachts in view of the Cannes Film Festival, eating among the fluttering white doves at Colombe d'Or, or drinking Dom Perignon with movie queens is just the maraschino cherry on the Rex Reed career. To him it isn't real, and he'd never be dumb enough to try to live on such poisonous Red Dye No. 2 fare. Rex's real life is among ordinary people, just as his tastes are for black-eyed peas, fried chicken, gumbo, and chocolate chip cookies made in his own kitchen, or sitting around down in Baton Rouge with his daddy, Jimmy Reed, cracking open "craw-dads" (crayfish).

Thus, if he isn't so all-fired glamor-ridden and unique, what is the secret of Rex Reed's infallible interview technique? Why do the famous tell him everything—and then more? Why do they, almost eagerly, tick off their vulnerabilities, disappointments, frustrations, and feelings? Why do they go deep into personal and professional problems that usually remain off-limits to the press? And how is it that Rex Reed unlocks the persona they keep reserved and worms out their secrets as well?

In the Rex Reed interview, we seem to experience the actual person rather than the public relations plastic wind-up so often served up to and by reporters. "Rex Reed is either at your feet or at your throat," Ava Gardner was quoted as saying after he had met her, admired her, observed her, and gone away to write the truth. Did she expose herself so openly because she thought Rex was just a vulnerable young kid, because he touched some wellspring of Southern sympathy, or because he was interesting to her and interested *in* her?

Some of Rex's success comes from his quality of never having met a stranger. He is instantly there. He doesn't require getting used to. Rex is himself open and the subject becomes open as well. He expects to love or like the interviewee, so woe betide the subject who doesn't measure up, play fair, open his life to the old Rex Reed Bullshit Detector.

Over and over, common themes emerge in Rex's writing. Time and again we see him fascinated by people who have survived some truly hideous and disabling setback. He is not just obsessed by the great, the famous, the starry ones; he also wants to know, to show and tell how they have learned to cope. He is pulled by the same life force that is so strong in Elizabeth Taylor, in Lillian Hellman, in Bette Davis, in Sylvia Syms, in Hildegard Knef. He analyzes and empathizes with their loneliness, their struggle, the happenings that beset them in their journey to the top, their attempt to stay there. Rex is attracted to profiles in courage.

Another of Rex's almost unnerving areas of expertise is his understanding and analysis of the actor and his work. It is striking, for instance, how often male actors reveal their professional ambivalence when they talk to Rex. Giancarlo Giannini finds that acting is not proper work for a man; Robert Redford obviously is uncomfortable in his shoes as a star; William Holden has no respect for what he does for a living and longs to get back to African adventuring. Most of the men Rex interviews seem to say they are not happy in their profession as actors, while Rex's women—ah, his wonderful women—can hardly imagine doing anything else.

Rex Reed has an essential quality that brings color and vitality to his work. He is a frustrated ham, a sometime actor himself, and an unselfconscious performer all the time. So Rex is drawn to actors, actresses, singers, artists, creators. He admires their nerves, their guts, the strengths they must summon to express pain and joy in a catharsis for all of us. He respects their craft and shows us the source of their strengths while illuminating their weaknesses.

Rex's writing is vivid and full of spicy specifics. He conveys the feeling to the reader that someone has finally gotten inside the interviewee for a closer-than-usual unique examination of their viscera, their brain, their heart. The pieces in this book, originally written under terrifying deadline pressures for magazines and newspapers, speak for themselves.

The incredible thing is that they take on such a timeless quality.

But if I could add one word to any portrait of Rex Reed, it would not concern his creative talent, his way with words, his unusually successful technique, his professional abilities, or his engaging and controversial personality. The single and best feature distinguishing Rex's work is his courage.

I have seldom known anyone as brave as Rex. I've never known him to weasel as many of us do, to be too flattered or overwhelmed by charm or position to be objective by his own lights. I have never known him to fail to try to tell the truth or to back off from an important issue or an unpopular verdict. He plunges on without reservation, aware that his candor will get him barred, dropped, spat upon, ignored, attacked, and held up to ridicule.

Rex Reed has written things about Frank Sinatra's unsavory public image, private behavior, and arrogant performance that would make a Mafia hit man flinch. He has attacked unfairness and bigotry, race hatred and prejudice. He has taken dramatic and brave stands against government censorship of the arts as well as interference with first amendment rights. While his detractors like to characterize him as a lightweight dandy who is only interested in the cut of his sartorial tweeds or what wine to order with fish, I have to laugh. I think Rex is a heavyweight humanist who has been on the right side of most of the important issues of our day, and I know he'd rather order Dr. Pepper with catfish than anything else.

One measure of any journalist's courage is how often he is fighting right down to the deadline with editors who want to emasculate his copy, play it safe, or bend over backward not to offend. I doubt there is a writer for the Chicago Tribune–New York Daily News Syndicate who is in there sweating to keep his work *as written* more often than Rex. He is the gadfly of the copy desk.

In a celebrated battle with conservative opinion, Rex attacked Columbia Pictures for burying their own shocking documentary about Vietnam. Though sixty newspapers refused to carry this article on "Hearts and Minds," Rex refused to withdraw it. And he carried his fight to the talk shows. As a result, his piece was read aloud in Congress and Rex is now the only film critic in history whose review is an official part of the *Congressional Record.* In a recent contretemps where another might have knuckled under to the power of big business, Rex took on a major movie press agent. His fellow critics, who have often disagreed with Rex in their own internecine manner, rallied to this fight because Rex was doing it so all of them might have the right to say what they honestly think without fear of reprisal.

Hemingway said that guts was grace under pressure. John Kennedy amended this to say that courage was grace under pressure. I understand the concept, but I think there is most often nothing graceful about the process. Having guts and courage means being lonely, ostracized, badly used, pushed around, misunderstood, and paying for your integrity. Some of Rex Reed's fights with popular opinion have been bitter and ugly, but he has never given ground. Under the Bill Blass suit is really a "down home" champ who won't wait and take the count, who keeps getting up again, who ignores the bell. There is no neutral corner in Rex Reed's life.

Reader, aren't you glad?

THE
OBSERVER

Pages From My Diary

1.

There's only one thing that makes me angrier than the question, "What is Barbra Streisand really like?" That's when people come up to me and dreamily say, "Gee you're lucky —you don't have to work." Hopefully to destroy that erroneous illusion forever, I've decided to publish these pages from my diary. The week went something like this:

MONDAY—The George Gershwin birthday craze is in full swing in New York. To honor his seventy-fifth year as a deity, there is a beautiful eight-cent Gershwin stamp, pretty as anything in the National Gallery. Frances Gershwin, his sister, threw a lovely party at "21" with player pianos and hot-and-cold-running Ziegfeld girls. New Gershwin book called *The Gershwins* published by Atheneum. Beautiful book, with thousands of photos, correspondence, anecdotes, song lyrics, and complete chronology of his shows. Did you know the Gershwins used to run a Turkish bath and George was allergic to champagne? Just folks, really.

   More Gershwin over at Lorna Luft's nightclub act at the St. Regis. She sings sweeter and softer than sister Liza, and

Dustin Hoffman and Ethel Merman clapped a lot. There's a spot in her show when she sits on a stool, catches her breath, and half-whispers her mother's old arrangement of Gershwin's "Do It Again." It made Tony Bennett cry. A man came up to me after the show and offered me $5,000 to interview his wife as a Christmas present.

Topped off the evening with a visit to Lainie Kazan, who is torching it up at the Waldorf. The act was so good Alexis Smith said she might steal it. Best part comes when Lainie sings about her past year's troubles (being fired from two Broadway shows, among other plagues) to the tune of "I'm Still Here" from the defunct Alexis Smith show *Follies.* Alexis loved that. Stephen Sondheim, the composer, didn't. His lawyers visited Lainie next day and she had to cut the number. Some people have no sense of humor. Got to bed at 3 A.M. after somebody called to tell me Candy Darling, the Andy Warhol transvestite superstar, was in the hospital with cancer. Only twenty-seven years old. Sex hormones and the good life don't mix. I understand Andy Warhol is bringing in top specialists, trying to find a cure, and Candy is propped up in bed with candy and flowers in a pink Rita Hayworth feather boa, saying, "My whole life has been a miracle—maybe I'll be saved by a miracle, too." Fans can send cards to Columbus Hospital, New York City. So much for Monday.

TUESDAY—Lunch with my publisher to discuss title of my new book. Heard another Gershwin tribute by two of New York's most stylish singers, Ronny Whyte and Travis Hudson. "We Like a Gershwin Tune" (Monmouth-Evergreen Records) is a taste thrill. If you like obscure Gershwin show tunes, this one is a must. Ronny has a collegiate, scrubbed, Harold-Teen-with-white-tie-and-tails approach. Travis gives her songs a soft, vulnerable "I've been around but I'm still unspoiled, boys" treatment. Together, they've assembled a rich and versatile tribute to Gershwin, including waltzes, tap dances, lullabyes, Charlestons, rags, blues, I've been down songs, I'm feelin' up songs, I'm in my cups songs. My favorite is a lost ditty called "The Real American Folk Song." Since it's a Gershwin folk song, it's more sophisticated than you might imagine. I'd like to challenge the dirty-haired, long-toenailed folk singers of 1973 to try this one on their flat guitars. Ronny and Travis are wunderkinds. It's a terrific album.

Now I hear Bobby Short is putting out a double Gershwin album on Atlantic. It's a veritable Gershwin festival. He would've been seventy-five this year. With all these new albums and books, it's living proof that he's never really been away.

Saw a horrendous movie this morning—Roman Polanski's *What?* Miss it if you have any regard for your sanity.

Saw a horrendous movie this afternoon. I've been feeling guilty about snubbing the New York Film Festival in last Sunday's column. Went over to Lincoln Center to give them another chance. First saw an animated cartoon about a butterfly that gets squashed out of a meadow when an ugly housing project springs up. Then I saw an interminable short about Yellowstone National Park that showed geysers erupting while a woman's voice moaned sexily on the soundtrack. Then came the main attraction—a new psychological drama by French director Claude Chabrol, called *Just Before Nightfall,* about a dull suburban businessman who murders his best friend's wife. Guilt overcomes him and for two hours he tries to confess, but nobody will believe him or even punish him. It drives him mad. His wife finally poisons him so he won't worry so much. It sounds like a comedy, but audiences don't snore in comedies. I go away with my opinion reinforced. The New York Film Festival is a pretentious, antipublic disaster. I go home and throw away my invitation to meet François Truffaut.

WEDNESDAY—I skip the Bill Blass fashion show to attend writer Barbara Goldsmith's dinner for Frank Perry. Good group. Sue Kaufman, who wrote *Diary of a Mad Housewife,* complains because she can't grow radishes on a rooftop because of the fallout. Richard Benjamin laments the demise of MGM. Everyone agrees James Aubrey has leveled the greatest movie studio in the world (and a symbol of perfection that made most of the people in movies go into the business in the first place) to a rubbish heap in record time.

I make a note to write an epitaph, then tear it up, figuring nobody cares. Woody Allen makes funny faces across the room. Larry Peerce tells fabulous stories about directing Elizabeth Taylor in Rome in *Ash Wednesday.* He says it's the first movie she's made in years in which she doesn't look like a drag queen. This I gotta see. Dan *(How to Be a Jewish Mother)* Greenburg says he just returned from Scotland where he followed the Japanese research team around looking for the Loch Ness Monster. He says he has photos of the Loch Ness Monster. Looks something like Elizabeth Taylor. (My remark, not his.) I go to bed happy. Seventy-five business phone calls on the answering service go unanswered. Before sleep takes over, I watch the end of Katharine Hepburn on Dick Cavett. He was a disaster; she was Katharine Hepburn. Did you know she used to break into houses when she was twelve years old? The only thing she stole was a stuffed alligator.

THURSDAY—The day starts with a delightful quote from Mrs. Daniel Berrigan. "Why did you steal all those things?" coyly asks *The New York Times.* "Because I wanted them," answers Mrs. Berrigan.

I give a speech at noon to a group from the Television Academy of Arts and Sciences. Nobody asks what is Barbra Streisand really like. Bette Midler calls to wish me Happy Birthday two days too late. Somebody tells me the Pointer Sisters are men. Hall Bartlett invites me to a private screening of *Jonathan Livingston Seagull* next week. I write a note of apology to Alice Faye, begging forgiveness for missing her "Welcome to New York" dinner party last Sunday. Somebody asks me to do a rice commercial. I receive forty-five pieces of hate mail on my review of *Jesus Christ Superstar.* Half of them are typed on the same typewriter. One unusual letter, from Grosse Pointe, Michigan, threatens suicide if I don't print Robert Redford's unlisted telephone number. This worries me until six o'clock.

The evening begins. I head for the Seventy-ninth Street Boat Basin, where Pauline Trigere is throwing a cocktail party. Mostly fashion plates. Carrie Donovan, the chicest fashion editor in New York, tells me she's going to bring back good taste. Geoffrey Beene and Arnold Scaasi say they'll help by burning all the Carmen Miranda heels.

I barely make it to the opening of *A Streetcar Named Desire* on Broadway. Faye Dunaway was a disaster in Los Angeles, Rosemary Harris was a sorry disappointment at Lincoln Center. Now they've taken Ellis Rabb's sets from the Lincoln Center production, moved it to the Big Time and employed Lois Nettleton as Blanche DuBois. I approach with trepidation. What unfolds is sheer magic. Except for Elia Kazan's movie with Brando and Leigh, I've never seen a first-rate production of this greatest of Tennessee Williams plays, but the new Broadway production comes delightfully close. Jules Irving has pruned away all the ridiculous clutter from Ellis Rabb's overproduced folly, fired all the nuns with umbrellas and French Quarter traffic, and the play comes alive without gimmicks. Lois Nettleton is a shatteringly brilliant actress and her Blanche made me cry. We have stars without talent coming out of our ears, but Lois Nettleton is that rare discovery—a magnificent actress with star quality who turns the dwindling theater into a shrine. The standing ovation was truly deserved. This is a triumphant *Streetcar* that anyone planning a visit to New York cannot afford to miss. It revives my faith in Broadway.

At 11 P.M. I rush to the quite different ambiance of the Continental Baths to see Eleanor Steber's concert. The invitation says "Black Tie or Black Towel." Some people wear a black tie and nothing else. Miss Steber appears from the steam in a lemon chiffon gown, loaded with diamonds, with a black towel draped around her formidable waist. Mrs. Leonard Bernstein, Suzy, Patrice Munsel, a lot of Metropolitan Opera stars and half of New York society love it. Miss Steber is in good voice, singing everything from *Tosca* to Strauss waltzes while naked boys yell "Brava!" Somebody bends over and whispers in my ear: "Art embraces everyone!" At midnight, half the group heads for Henry Kissinger's party for himself, the other half heads for a party thrown by Francesco Scavullo, the photographer who photographed Burt Reynolds nude for the *Cosmopolitan* centerfold. I choose the latter, where boys in jockstraps serve champagne to everybody you ever saw on the cover of *Vogue,* and a naked cowboy falls into a forty-pound cake. New York is beginning to look like Berlin before the fall and all the girls look like Sally Bowles.

Four A.M. finds me writing three movie reviews, four record reviews, and a letter of apology for not being able to plan a James Cagney Film Festival at San Quentin.

FRIDAY—I spend the day in bed with the hangover of America, filling out my visa application for a trip to Russia after three hours of bureaucratic red tape on the phone with the Russian Embassy in Washington. I turn down an offer to write a biography of Frank Sinatra. I call Gloria Vanderbilt to cancel my weekend trip to New Orleans with her. I read half of Truman Capote's new book *The Dogs Bark,* and forty-five pages of Lillian Hellman's *Pentimento.* I accept three lecture dates and look over next week's itinerary: a screening of Joanne Woodward's new movie, three art gallery openings, a party for Lillian Gish, a trip to Rhode Island to review a play, dinner with Jacqueline Susann, five movie openings, and an appointment to get the vision in my contact lenses adjusted before I lose my eyesight. Somewhere between, I have to write two columns. I turn off the phones and go to bed for the weekend.

And that's just what I do for a living!

2.

Critics, like everyone else (but not as often as everyone else), occasionally take a day off. So, figuring I've been spending entirely too much time lately in movies, at plays and in nightclubs, I decided to devote one entire day last week to reality instead of make-believe. I went to three parties—and this is how it went, on a lazy Sunday in New York.

PARTY NO. 1 was in full swing at noon when I arrived at Elaine's, that kissy-poo restaurant that is the private hangout for everyone from Elizabeth Taylor to members of the SLA disguised as Jewish playwrights. Elaine's is so inside it's not even listed in the *Guide Michelin* because you can't get in anyway unless your obituary has already been researched and filed at *The New York Times*.

Elaine didn't plan it that way. It's just that everybody she knows—and she knows them all—is famous, talented, powerful, interesting and also hungry. Elaine is mother–analyst–cook–public-defender–baby-sitter to each. She's a cross between Golda Meir and Perle Mesta, but inside beats the heart of a ballerina. If you are on the scene in New York and don't know Elaine, you might as well move to Keokuk.

Today's brunch honors Joan Hackett, the dizzy but monumentally gifted actress who is giving up New York and moving to Hollywood—but not, one shudders to think, to the oblivion that usually implies. Bobby Zarem, the supersonic press agent who gets written about almost as often as his clients, has decided to pull in a few friends to say good-bye. He's one of the few press agents everybody likes. So much, that even the critics hate themselves when they have to pan one of his projects. He threw a party for the TV special "The Entertainer" recently. It wasn't very good, but everybody raved about the popcorn.

Elaine served Bloody Marys, quiche with sausages and spinach, french-fried zucchini, and garden salad. Liz Smith, the ace columnist and everybody's favorite social detective, took notes while Carrie Fisher told about how Debbie Reynolds, her mom, was mugged in Beverly Hills. Then Andrew Sarris and Molly Haskell, who are critics married to each other and not Comden and Green, said they were mugged in Palm Springs. A man wearing a Ronald Reagan button said everyone was getting mugged in California because all the rich people are moving out of New York and all those muggers are following them. Pat Newcomb, the most beautiful press agent in New York, said she didn't care who moved to California as long as it wasn't her.

Peter Finch said he loved New York so much he had applied for U.S. citizenship and was busily learning the preamble to the Constitution. Andy Warhol took everybody's picture. Charles Michener of *Newsweek* said he had just seen *Robin and Marian* and it was awful. Pat Newcomb said she had just seen the first rough-cut of *The Bluebird* and it was terrific, if only people would give a charming, whimsical fantasy film a chance instead of anticipating blood, violence, carnage, and rape.

Tout le monde said they abhorred violence. Nora Ephron of *Esquire* said she hated violence more than anyone else but didn't sign the petition of complaint sent to the district attorney trying to close down *Snuff,* the vile South American porno film that allegedly shows the disembowelment of a woman, because if there was anything she hated more than violence it was censorship. Joan Hackett said she was voting for Jerry Brown. Everyone stared in horror, as though she had just emptied a bottle in the middle of Elaine's containing plague-carrying rodents from Madagascar.

Nothing fazed Hackett. "I'm into California all the way," she said. "I just bought a Tudor mansion in Hancock Park, just the other side of the La Brea tar pits, and I'm ready for the Big Sleep."

"Hancock Park," gasped Nora Ephron. "How *nice.*"

"Does anyone actually live there?" asked Dena Kaye, Danny's huggable daughter.

"Oh, yes," said Hackett. "In the old days Buster Keaton and a lot of politicians. Now, the only person I know is Jerry Brown's sister. I moved because I got mad when *New York* magazine did a story on movie stars who live in New York, and they didn't name me. They named Barbra Streisand. She hasn't been here in three years."

New York's loss is Hollywood's gain. For starters, there's a new Western called *McIntosh and T.J.* starring Joan Hackett and Roy Rogers. "Are you McIntosh or T.J.?" I asked.

"Neither one."

"Are you a good person or a bad person?"

"Oh, for a change, I'm really good. But I look bad." She filmed it in Lubbock, Texas. "Just a hundred and seventy-five men and me in a Howard Johnson's motel on a deserted highway. It was amazingly boring. Everyone in town carried a gun, and there were twelve murders the day I left town. It was so dull that to relieve the tedium the entire cast went to a hog-callin' contest. This is what you have to do to be in the movies."

Marisa Berenson never showed up, but Carl Bernstein, of the Watergate sleuth Bernstein-Woodward team, did. He said their new book is ready, and there is absolutely no truth to the rumors that Bernstein and Woodward are no longer speaking. They are currently seeing Comden and Green.

PARTY NO. 2 was for Ginger Rogers, who tapped her way into New York's posh Empire Room at the Waldorf to so much applause they heard it in New Jersey. The setting was Privé, a *très chic* watering hole that looks like an Art Deco set from a black-and-white RKO musical. When I arrived, Ginger was on her third plate of scrambled eggs, bagels, cream cheese and watermelon.

Ruth Warrick brought along some of her soap-opera children from *All My Children,* and Ginger said she'd like to do a cameo like Carol Burnett did, maybe as a tap-dancing tennis player soda jerk? No sign of Marisa Berenson, but Sylvia Miles was there. She just returned from London, where she did twenty-five interviews in two days, and had a terrible case of laryngitis.

"For the first time in my life, I can't talk," she whispered.

"Oh, good," smiled Alexis Smith.

Everyone was talking about Truman Capote's tattletales in *Esquire.* Jackie Rogers (no relation to Ginger, but the most outspoken tongue in fashion) said, "It's a comment on society. There's nobody left to write about." Sylvia Miles said nobody was tired of writing about her. "I even got reviewed at Ginger Rogers' opening. When I got nominated for Best Supporting Actress this year, I said, 'Quick, book me at the Beverly Hills Hotel.' I always stay there when I get nominated. Isn't that a good line? Write that down. Listen, only the untalented can afford to be humble."

Jackie Rogers said the No. 1 person she was tired of reading about was Frank Sinatra. A man with a butterfly tattooed on his forehead said he was tired of reading about Cher's navel. Practically everybody said they were tired of reading about the Burtons, and Ginger Rogers said she was having second thoughts about seeing *Equus* after she discovered it was about a boy who blinds horses. Alexis Smith said she'd like to read about herself for a change, and almost got the chance when Howard Koch asked her to be a presenter on the Oscars telecast. She flew to New York, shopped for clothes, then Koch, for whom she made *Once Is Not Enough*, dropped her because she's appearing on another special about the Oscars with Douglas Fairbanks, Jr. "Doug's father inaugurated the Oscars, and he's never been asked, either. Wouldn't you think they'd want style and glamour instead of the same old rock stars and people on TV shows?"

"What do they know about glamour in Hollywood?" piped Ginger Rogers. "The whole town is run by get-rich-quick artists who have short memories. They've burned or lost so many old films they're now calling me for prints from my personal collection. I gave everything to Texas Christian University. I have the only complete, uncut version of *Roberta* in existence. Don't tell me about Hollywood!" And nobody tried.

PARTY NO. 3 was so elegant you almost needed a blood test to get in. It was a birthday extravaganza for Anne Slater, a beautiful Southern blonde who wears blue-tinted sunglasses and lives in a Fifth Avenue penthouse in a style that would make Marie Antoinette commit suicide. There's chile on the stove, a red Christmas tree in the den and a silver bathroom. It makes Versailles look like a Girl Scout tent.

Nobody was talking about Truman Capote's articles about the rich and famous because everybody in the articles was there. Joshua Logan told wonderful stories about his first job as dialogue coach on Marlene Dietrich's movie *The Garden of Allah*, way back when you and I were somebody's imagination. ("It's twash, ain't it?" said the million-dollar kraut.) Bobby Short told Adele Astaire to thank her brother Fred for sending him the songs he'd just written for Bobby to sing. Anita Loos told me if I had ever met Dorothy Parker she would have eaten me for breakfast.

Ahmet Ertegun, Arlene Dahl, Kitty Carlisle Hart, Peter Glenville, Suzy and a lot of dashing roués you only read about in the newspapers were there. Charles Addams forgot his drawing pen. Somebody said isn't it just awful that Kay Thompson has covered Liza Minnelli's grand piano with red contact paper? Adele Astaire said no matter what people think, Fred's favorite dancing partner was always Gene Kelly and they'll both open the Cannes Film Festival with the sequel to *That's Entertainment!* for which they have both filmed a new dance number that will rock the world.

Somebody else said that Jacqueline Kennedy Onassis had no heat or hot water for three weeks, and if you told that to anybody in Kansas they'd think you were crazy. A man in a leather dinner jacket said it was the third party he'd been to that day, and he still hadn't seen Marisa Berenson. "Everybody's down in Key West," sighed a millionaire too rich to mention. "I went to a convent in Key West as a child," recalled the daughter of a retired navy officer. "It was called St. Mary of the Sea and I fell madly in love with a nun who looked exactly like Humphrey Bogart."

They sipped white wine and danced into the night. On my way home, I saw Marisa Berenson in blue jeans rushing from a taxi into Diane von Furstenberg's apartment building. I slept like a baby.

THE
GODDESSES

Elizabeth Taylor

Elizabeth Taylor Hilton Wilding Todd Fisher Burton has
survived the perils of Job. She can survive *The Bluebird.*
She's always been a fighter. When she was twelve years old,
she marched into Louis B. Mayer's office at MGM and announced: "You and your studio can go to hell!" Two Academy Awards and fifty films later, she's survived two broken
engagements, five husbands, a couple of international scan-
dals, a broiled finger, a broken foot, an ulcerated eye, a
twisted colon, a locked cartilage in her knee, three ruptured
spinal discs, acute bronchitis, chemical thrombosis, phlebi-
tis, sciatica, double pneumonia, a tracheotomy, three Cae-
sarean sections, and several nervous breakdowns and alleged suicide attempts. "I've been through it all, baby," she
says. "I'm Mother Courage."

Well, sort of. At forty-three, she opens the door of her suite
at the luxurious Dorchester Hotel in London looking more
like a creation dreamed up by the gods on Olympus. It is
impossible to imagine any living creature more beautiful. In
person, with the freckles on her neck and the silver strands
of hair zig-zagging through the lustrous ebony mane, she

manages to be what the Technicolor screen can only suggest teasingly. Yes, she is gorgeous. She has been asleep, and she is in a wretched temper because her doctor will not let her drink her beloved Jack Daniel's on the rocks or anything else stronger than apple juice, but she makes amends by just standing there. It is, upon meeting her for the first time, rather like climbing to the top of Cap Haitien and getting a first breathtaking view of the Citadel. It's impossible to keep from staring.

She looks even better after losing seventeen pounds from a near-fatal case of amoebic dysentery contracted while trying to film *The Bluebird,* a $15 million musical fairy tale that is being made in Russia. Simply everything has gone wrong, and now, in the midst of rumors about actors quitting, interminable delays, soaring costs, miserable conditions and low morales that might force the film to shut down, she is taking it all in valiant stride like a finely tuned race horse who has been in a few canceled races before. She's wearing lime jello green pajamas by Valentino and yes, her eyes are truly a legendary lavender. Since she never gives interviews, we pace each other like two strange Maltese cats, settling for positions on opposite sofas. The initial suspicion soon wears off after a couple of apple juices on the rocks and before long she's bringing out her granddaughter, a fat, healthy baby who has just traveled five hours from her son Michael Wilding Junior's hippie commune in Wales. In one elegant bedroom of the suite where she's recuperating while two hundred photographers line the driveway outside waiting for a glimpse of her famous profile in the window, her son and his girlfriend and their new baby are sleeping in sleeping bags on the floor.

I break the ice by asking about *The Bluebird.* It looked good on paper. First American-Russian co-production filmed on authentic Russian locations with American stars (Taylor, Ava Gardner, Jane Fonda, Cicely Tyson, James Coco) and directed by the legendary George Cukor. Now it was going down the toilet. What happened? "Well," she sighed, playing with a diamond ring the size of an Easter egg, "I have never been involved in such a disaster. I'm waiting any moment for the phone to ring telling me it's all been canceled. I arrived in Russia in January, worked two days on the witch sequence and did some bits and pieces on the mother sequence—I play five roles in all—and I did some wardrobe tests. In five months, I did about a week's work in all. The rest of the time I just sat around and got sick."

"Do you attribute the delays to the Russians, who work at a much slower pace than we do?" I asked.

"No, I found the Russians helpful, enthusiastic, and really looking forward to the whole operation. Before I got there, everyone said 'Look out!' and 'Your room will be bugged' and the usual warnings. But I was very excited about the whole thing and I figured that would be the wrong attitude to go in with. And after I got there, I was totally surprised. I found no signs of surveillance or wire-tapping or anything. The first thing that went wrong was that nothing was ready when we arrived. Edith Head wasn't allowed to do the costumes in America, and the producer, Eddie Lewis, told her she would have to get all of the materials and accessories after she arrived in Russia. So she came over with a costume that had a collar that looked like a pancake flapping around my head and it made me look like a pregnant penguin. We recut it and it took a week of delays just to take it in and fiddle around with it and it got worse and worse and finally we discovered the Russians had expected the costumes to be ready when we arrived. They couldn't provide the jewels or the shoes or any of the accessories. The costumes all looked uncompleted because they *were* uncompleted. Ed Lewis finally coughed up three hundred dollars for some fake costume jewelry to tack on the dress but by that time they had recut it so many times it was just a wreck, so we had to start from scratch."

Edith Head went home disgusted and Elizabeth ended up spending $8,000 of her own money for costumes for which she was never reimbursed. At one point, the producer sent a wire saying if she didn't like her jewelry just wear her own diamonds. "That," screamed Elizabeth, "will be the day."

The next thing that happened was the Russian cameraman had to be fired because he had only worked in black and white before. "Every day we went in to see the rushes and you couldn't see anything because it was so dark. So he had to be fired and then we sat around waiting until Freddie Young, the man who shoots all of David Lean's films, could arrive from London. You must remember none of these Russians have ever done anything approximating the kind of major film we're doing. Nobody told them how to do anything. It's not their fault. They don't, for example, know how to build sets realistically, with fly-away walls. So we'd get into these tight little sets and you couldn't move the camera around. It was like shooting in a tiny hotel room. But that is the fault of the people who designed the sets, not the Russians who built them."

The second day she was there Elizabeth came down with the flu and had a temperature of 104 degrees for six days. "Which left my stomach very weak anyway. Then I caught amoebic dysentery from the ice cubes. When I go back I'll boil everything. You are forbidden to take your own distilled water. I did get some from a Russian pharmacy and it tasted like cyanide. Even if you get a doctor's permission to bring in special food for your own survival, the Russians hold up everything for three days in the Moscow airport and it spoils. That happened to Cicely Tyson, who is a vegetarian, and it happened to all the meat I had sent from London. You can't eat the meat they sell in Russia. The chickens look like they've had every last egg squeezed out of them and you're getting them to eat just before terminal cancer sets in."

"It sounds to me like the whole thing should've been better organized before anyone arrived in Russia."

"From the American producer's point of view, baby. We are there because we need their money and the Russians have plenty of it. They have invited us because they want to learn something from our technical expertise. But they're at a disadvantage because we haven't provided them with our best equipment. But every time the technicians ask for something the American producer says it's too expensive. He is the biggest cheapskate I've ever heard of! The Russians are slow but they've lived up to their part. Ava and I have a song to do in the movie. We're not singers. I haven't sung on the screen since *A Date With Judy*. So we asked to hear the song on a cassette. Do you know there isn't one tape machine in Russia that can duplicate a cassette tape? And nobody could get an OK to have one sent over from California. All of this causes delays. It's not lack of enthusiasm that has kept us there five months. It will take a miracle to finish this picture."

I asked her what she did to pass the time when she was sitting around watching the gunboats on the Neva River. "Well, for five months I went to the Hermitage . . . and I went to the Hermitage . . . and I went to the Hermitage [chuckle] and I read a lot. Excuse me. Russia's calling." She went to the bathroom, flushed loudly, then returned. "I've lost tons of weight and I've never looked so good, but what a hell of a way to diet—to flush it all down the toilet."

"Where is home now?"

"Wherever I am. [More laughter.] Actually I have a real house in Gstaad, Switzerland, for tax purposes. All those places in Hampstead, Mexico and Beverly Hills were with Richard. They're all just sitting there empty now."

The mention of Burton reminded me of the last time I saw them together, on the David Frost program. Everyone said she was drunk. "Well, I'm always being asked to do television and I keep saying wait till I'm dead. They did some kind of special on me in America recently. I didn't see it, but Richard Brooks and Roddy McDowall were on it, so I can count on them. It was probably so nice it was a goddam bore."

"But why don't you do more interviews? You are very natural and very warm in person, yet nobody ever gets to see you this way."

"It's not my medium, television. I get terribly nervous. I don't think I'm any good at ad-libbing. I've been suckered into a few of them. I mean, literally. I was sitting in the sound booth watching Richard being interviewed when David Frost came in and dragged me out and I made a fool of myself as usual. I always hate myself in interviews."

She's still the queen of the screen whether her films make money or not, yet practically a mystery woman when it comes to interviews. Why? "I just think it's extraordinarily boring to sit down and talk about yourself. I don't have anything to hide. There's no way I could keep my life a

secret even if I wanted to, in this business. But I'm actually
very shy and I have a big thing about being a private person.
I don't think I've ever been considered an enemy of the
press, except maybe a few members. I'd like to kill Ron
Galella, that slimy photographer who hounds me all over the
world. But he isn't even a member of the press. He's just a
creep."

Even in Russia, where they never heard of Ava Gardner
or anybody else connected with *The Bluebird,* Elizabeth
was mobbed by peasants. I asked her how it is possible to
guard privacy in the kind of life she lives. "Isn't it a bore
always having to look glamorous in white fur in case a photographer might be lurking nearby?" She laughed that combination fishwife howl and velvet mule chaser that has become her screen trademark.

"Baby, you've got it all wrong. I don't live in a shell. If I'm
pounced on wearing white fur it's because I like white fur.
I do what I damned well please. The press is so silly anyway
I can smell them a mile off. When I was in the hospital in
London last week they found out which wing I was in and
the nurses were having a giggle opening the windows so I
could see. I looked out and there were these silly jerks hiding
in a building opposite my room, peeking through the vene-
tian blinds with their cameras. You have to have a sense of
humor about it or else you'd go insane. I learned to accept
and live with public adulation and invasion of privacy when
I was fifteen years old. Now I just go through the back door.
My father also taught me how to tune it all out and ignore
people who stare at me. If I let it get to me I get claustrophobic and an inner panic sets in because I am so shy. So I
put on blinkers. It just clicks into place now. Oh, there have
been times, though, when I wanted to punch some rude
bastard in the face, let me tell you. It's cost me. It's cost me
my guts!"

She has been ill so much I decided to break a taboo and
ask her if she'd ever talked to a doctor to see why, out of the
whole human race, she was selected to suffer so many physical ailments. She didn't throw her apple juice at me. "Yes,
I have," she answered bluntly, taken aback. "Because I
thought at one point it might be psychosomatic. I've had so

many serious illnesses that I'm not terribly strong, so the doctors all say I'm prone to other sicknesses because of all the previous ones. If there's a germ in the air or in the food, I'll get it. I don't take any special vitamins or take care of myself in any special way. I'm just lucky. I pull through somehow. Otherwise, I'd be dead."

"Well, it doesn't seem fair for someone to be so sick who is considered a cherished natural resource." She roared. "I don't mean to make you sound like a waterfall . . ."

She shrieked even louder. "I felt like a waterfall last week. No, the point is that if you start to worry about it you become a hypochondriac. I've had to fight that. Consequently, I don't give in to the symptoms and I let things go on too late. I always say, 'I'll fink myself out of this one' and all of a sudden I'm in the hospital. I've got doctors spotted throughout the world, my dear. When I woke up at six o'clock in the morning in Russia with a temperature of 104, I must say I thought I'd passed on. About six doctors walked into my room all dressed in white from head to foot—little white hats, white face masks and white aprons that looked exactly like butcher uniforms and they wanted to take me to a hospital. I was clinging to the bed yelling 'No, don't take me! Help!' It was like a comedy routine. They told me to take yoghurt with mineral oil. Fortunately, I had brought along my own CARE package with antibiotics. So I got over that by using my own noggin. But it was later, when I developed the amoebic dysentery, that I had to get out of there. Then it took me four days to get a visa just to get to my own doctor. Once you get into Russia you can't get out. That's another reason everyone there is so miserable."

"Have you been in contact with the producer?"

She frowned. "Yes, I've had that experience. We had rather sharp words the last time we spoke."

"At least you've met him. Ava Gardner says she's never laid eyes on him."

"She hasn't missed much. Listen, this is absolutely absurd. I have never heard of a producer who wasn't on a difficult location like this one every day. He has only been there three days in five months. Naturally there are going to be problems. The first Russian-American co-production. I

mean, he's not shooting a car commercial. The questions
these poor people are asking are not irrational. Like, 'When
are we going to get paid?' There's nothing irrational about
that. Everyone gets twelve rubles a day, which is about
twelve dollars a day. Try living on that. That covers everything—your food, your postcards home, your drink, your
mittens—*everything!* It's cost me a fortune personally. I've
turned down three films to do this film. It was supposed to
start back in September 1974 and I was ready then. I sat
around from January to May getting sicker and sicker. The
place obviously does not agree with my stomach.

"I don't know how I got into this mess in the first place.
I was told Shirley MacLaine and Jane Fonda were doing it.
Meanwhile, they were being told I was doing it. So I was the
first sucker to sign. I have never worked with anyone as
devious as this producer in my life. I didn't think it was
necessary on a production of this importance to check on the
man's credentials. But nobody is getting any money and I
want to make a percentage on this picture and that's why
I'm not walking out. The days of getting a million dollars a
film are over. If this film doesn't come out and isn't a big
success, I've wasted a year of my life and spent my own
money instead of the usual expense money I get when I'm
working. That's why it's to my interest to see that it's made,
so maybe I'll see some money out of it. The first time anybody got a million dollars was when I got it for *Cleopatra*.
I didn't want to do it, so I just said, 'Oh, tell them I'll do it
for a million dollars!' and they said yes. [Large shriek of
laughter at the joke on herself.] I was left with a large portion of egg on my face. That film took forever, but they paid
nice overtime and we were in Rome, for god's sake. If you
were sitting around with a lot of stupid delays, you could at
least order a Jack Daniel's. It wasn't like Russia, where you
can't even afford the vodka, or you can't get a visa to get out.

"Listen," she said, eyes narrowing. "It doesn't seem right
that Ed Lewis should be lunching every day at the Polio
Lounge [her euphemism for the Polo Lounge of the Beverly
Hills Hotel], lording it up telling everyone what's done on
this picture when he hasn't done anything but cause a lot of
strife and misery for people. He's taking a lot of credit and

patting himself on the back for something that may not even be completed. And if it isn't completed I'm sure he'll have everyone else to blame except himself. And it's his own damned fault, nobody else's. The Russians have tried and certainly we've all tried. Now I'm just sitting around like everyone else, waiting for a miracle."

She looks in the mirror, I look at her; we both see one miracle. Why not two?

SATURDAY. The plane from Paris to Leningrad lands. I don't know what I expected. People with horns, marching around like Martians with guns pointed at their heads from control towers, I guess. Bleak, cold and colorless as a test tube, yes. But it's nothing like the spy stories. I have CARE packages from Fauchon for needy friends: magazines, tropical fruit, perfume, Kleenex, chewing gum, a script and a portable Scrabble set for Jimmy Coco, a bottle of Dom Perignon for Cicely Tyson. Nobody searched my luggage, although they did go through the reading material. The sight of a helmeted Russian cossack holding the *Hollywood Reporter* upside down was something out of a Billy Wilder movie. They kept one passenger's *Time* because it contained some unfavorable remarks from defected Russian dancers Valery and Galina Panov. My Bloomingdale's shopping bag falls apart and rolls to the feet of a severe-looking Peter Lorre type carrying a machine gun. He keeps the papayas from Fauchon, gives me back *Playboy*. Clearing customs was unusually fast and not at all what I expected from descriptions I had read of bureaucratic red tape. The entire process might have taken twice as long had they searched everyone's bags. The group I was traveling with had packed all sorts of forbidden goodies regarded as symbols of western capitalist decadence: peanut butter, cheese, Ritz crackers, Jefferson Airplane albums, English newspapers, silk stockings, chocolate bars. The only thing they ask is if I'm carrying any pornographic or religious literature. All in the same sentence.

On the way to the hotel, my interpreter—Igor, a bearded young man who looks like an intense, blond Dennis Hopper —strikes up a conversation about literature. He reads and speaks English fluently and buys his books from a store where lucky Russians who travel abroad dispose of their bounty. His proud collection includes Faulkner, Vonnegut and Hemingway (all banned) and he says he once spent two weeks' salary on a contraband copy of Nabokov's *Lolita*. How I wish I had brought books instead of Kleenex. He says it is a federal offense to mention Solzhenitsyn but talks about him anyway, ignoring the angry glares from the driver. These guides and interpreters are always being watched, and although most tourists form attachments to them and write them letters from home, they are usually very careful about what they say. Igor is different. He's highly opinionated, very curious about Democracy, says the worst thing about Russia is censorship. I give him my copy of *Newsweek*. He says the last thing he's read is a year-old copy of *New Republic*. One of the first things you learn in Russia is that the government and the people are two completely different things. As one Russian friend commented slyly: "Just like America."

The road leads, like a strip of gray velvet, to the 1,300-room Hotel Leningrad, which looks like a gigantic filing cabinet. My room isn't ready, so I spend an hour looking at the warships on the Neva River. "In Russia, time has no meaning," says the reception clerk. When I finally do get into the room, it smells like old gymnasium socks. There is no soap, the toilet is broken, and there is one frayed towel the consistency of sandpaper. On TV, there's a Russian Ninotchka doing calisthenics, a soccer game and a blackboard covered with algebra equations. So much for entertainment. The actors were not in their rooms, so I wandered around the hotel looking for excitement, remembering Woody Allen's famous line: "I read *War and Peace* in ten minutes. It's about Russia." On Ava Gardner's door a sign was posted: KEEP OUT—DO NOT DISTURB—I WANT ABSOLUTE PRIVACY —THIS MEANS YOU! If privacy is what you want, Russia is the place to get it.

Back in my room, there's a knock on the door. It's Jimmy Coco, who plays the mythical Dog in the film. Jimmy is not one of your sylphlike creatures. Fat is his middle name and he's made a career of it. After spending thousands of dollars slimming down for the role, he's gained twenty pounds because the only thing he can eat is the bread and butter. "It is impossible to get served in the dining room because it is set up for tourists," he explains. "Mona Washbourne, the English character actress, was here for three days' work. It led to three weeks of sitting around. During that entire time, she lived on vodka. The rest of the company has gone on hunger strikes. I solved the problem by purchasing a two-burner hotplate only to discover the only thing you can buy worth eating here is cabbage. So far I have developed six different ways to cook cabbage. Have you ever tried cabbage à la mode? It's not bad."

Everyone has been sick. In addition to Elizabeth Taylor's amoebic dysentery, the rest of the cast has had various stomach disorders from the terrible food. Edith Head lost all of her luggage including the costume sketches for the film. Jane Fonda loved it when she first arrived, spent three weeks saluting and calling everyone "comrade." Then when the delays dragged into six weeks, she couldn't wait to leave. There were no fresh vegetables, her child broke out in a rash, and her husband, Tom Hayden, was arrested for getting locked out of the hotel and standing in the middle of the street yelling his wife's name until he was taken away for interrogation by the secret police. At one point, the entire company tried to mutiny, but Elizabeth Taylor said, "I stand to lose two million dollars, so I'm not about to do that for anybody." The actors have tried everything to get out of the film. Jimmy Coco even invented a lump in his breast, hoping they'd send him back to America for a cancer checkup. Instead, the Russians sent a woman doctor with fever blisters who recommended mustard plaster. Cicely Tyson has been retiring to her room each each night to practice voodoo. Each morning she arrives on the set asking, "Is he dead yet?" (Meaning George Cukor.) One day Cukor had a violent argument with Cicely. The following day she asked for a photo of him. The day after that, he complained that his leg hurt. "Oh?" asked Cicely. "What *time* did it start hurting?" Cicely and her alleged Haitian voodoo got to be a joke on the *Bluebird* set. But more than one observer secretly hoped there was some truth to it. With each new crisis, Cukor seemed happier. "He's determined to finish this film, even if it kills us all," groaned Coco.

No wonder George Cukor is enjoying himself. To the hungry anger of the rest of the company, he has all of his meals sent in by air express through the American Embassy from Fortnum and Mason. While the others face each night's new peril in the dining room, Cukor feasts on ham, parsley potatoes and chocolate cake. Dinner in his suite, decorated with framed photos of Katharine Hepburn, produces a fine meal, but little else. He is the model of diplomacy. While Coco cooks on a hotplate and two directorial assistants wash dishes in Cukor's bathtub, the grand old man of film magic tries to hide the mountain of problems caving in on his elderly head by giving the kind of interview that makes press agents dream of Cadillacs.

"I'm curious how an old-timer comes to such a remote place to try to make a fifteen-million-dollar musical . . . "

"Who's an old-timer?"

"Well, a young-timer, then. You've always been surrounded by the very best technicians who freed you for the important work of dealing with the actors. Here, you are having to be your own lighting man, your own script coordinator, your own carpenter . . . "

"A lot of that is the Tower of Babel. It's a different country and they don't speak the language. But I'm adapting nicely. What is wrong here is not the fault of the Russians. It's because we were not organized to begin with. I only speak to the producer through my lawyers. Now we are all very spoiled in America. We have a successful tradition of seventy-five years of movie-making that touched the imagination of the world. They don't have the same skills here, but that's why we're here, to teach them."

"But how can they learn anything if we don't bring our best technical know-how and they are providing every-thing?"

"Now you are asking embarrassing questions. They don't have the knack. They work very slowly and they quit after eight hours. There is no such thing as working overtime. If you're in the middle of a shot, they go home. And they have a notorious way of disappearing when you need them most. However, I've seen nothing but warmth and courtesy. I scream at them, but never rudely or offensively. There's a lot of complaining going on here and I am getting very bored with the bellyaching. No white slavers forced me to come here. I knew exactly what I was getting into. I just didn't know for how long. Nobody forced a single actor to come here and it's very impolite to the Russians to show how unhappy we are. Actors are a pain in the ass anyway."

"But if this film is ever finished, you will have been here a year . . . "

"Hell, I did *My Fair Lady* for a year. I was at Universal a year before that."

"Are you comparing Russia to Universal?"

"All movie locations are the same. Nothing goes like clockwork anywhere. Elizabeth Taylor has been very ill, but a darling. Ava Gardner is a newcomer, unnecessarily nervous and press-shy. We are all doing the best we can. These actors have made pictures on much worse locations than this. This is not a difficult location. I don't know what the hell they're talking about. I think they should stay home with their society friends and go to the White House or whatever it is they do."

A lovely man, a great raconteur, hopelessly over his head in a situation recklessly out of control, occasionally falling asleep in mid-sentence.

After dinner, everyone gathers in Coco's room because he owns all the games. The walls are decorated with letters from home, valentines, Easter cards ("We've seen all the holidays come and go—Elizabeth Taylor is having Christmas cards printed up") and a box that once held a McDonald's hamburger somebody smuggled in from Stockholm. Now I begin to learn some of the real problems. The dry cleaning has to be sent to Helsinki. It takes three weeks. There is no press agent on the film because the one they had was fired when the Russians learned he could speak fluent Russian. Now the press is all being handled by his secretary, a young English girl who cries herself to sleep every night. Every day there is a new problem. One day, the entire crew didn't show up. It was their day to devote a full day's work to the state. The grips and electricians were all outside raking dirt. Filming had to be canceled. The weather is also unpredictable. One sunny day Elizabeth Taylor went to be photographed at the Hermitage and came back drenched with snow. Incoming mail takes three weeks. It goes to Moscow, where it's opened, translated, then sometimes thrown away. Some of the actors go for weeks without working in front of the camera but they can't run away because Cukor puts them on automatic call every day to make sure they stick around. The usual evening schedule is dinner at six, Scrabble at eight, cards at ten.

Tonight after cards we're in the ballroom listening to a Forties' dance band play a Russian version of "Marie." George Cukor's complaint about the gaping tourists who take up all the space in the Hotel Leningrad ballroom and dining room seems to be true. Everyone seems to be on a cut-rate tour from Akron, Ohio. One man, learning about the *Bluebird* company, tried to scale a wall and climb into Elizabeth Taylor's window, falling instead to his death. At 11 P.M. George Cukor's assistant appears, rubbing his eyes. He's been awakened from a sound sleep by Ava Gardner's maid. Seems Ava is missing and he's been sent to search for her. She consumed six bottles of wine on the set, requiring ten retakes on one line, and now she's flown the coop. Cicely Tyson's secretary says she saw her at six o'clock in the parking lot searching for one of the Russian drivers. Now they don't know where she is. "Try Madrid," says Jimmy Coco. Everybody laughs. Here is a woman who was thrown out of Spain for defiling the bullfighters, an international femme fatale who has made headlines in every country, and they're worried because she's not tucked in bed at 11 P.M. "I mean, we're not talking about Tatum O'Neal on a school night," I said jokingly. Everybody laughed some more.

Back in my room, the radio plays Glenn Miller's "In the Mood." It goes off at midnight and comes on again at 3 A.M., waking me with bells and a military parade. Welcome to the steppes, buddy.

SUNDAY. 6 A.M. Everyone is up already, watching the rain fall on the bombed-out lots behind the hotel from the coffee bar. A third of the city was destroyed by Nazis in 1941 and more than a million people starved to death. Most of them starved to death behind the Leningrad Hotel. Here there are bleak ruins with a yellow trolley clanging through the middle. "It's 'Meet Me in Pittsburgh,' " laughs Jimmy Coco. Since it is impossible to get served in the restaurant downstairs, the cast and crew gather for hard-boiled eggs in the bar. When you slice them, they run all over the plate. Ever tried a cold, runny, soft, hard-boiled egg at 6 A.M.?

"They found Ava," says Cukor's assistant wearily. "She couldn't find her driver so she took a taxi to the Astoria Hotel and was up all night dancing with the cab driver." They draw up the bridges on the Neva River at midnight to let warships through, and if you have to get from one side of town to the other you have to swim or stay out all night. Today there is no filming so I take a trip to the market to see if it's true about the Russian inflation. It's true.

Most of the city of Leningrad is a work of art. Designed by the same man who worked out the architectural plan for the city of Paris, it is a scenic jewel built on forty-two islands in the Neva River with eighty-five rivers and canals, twenty-nine winter and summer palaces built by former czars, and the streets are clean as eggshells. Scenic splendors abound, but the market is not one of them. This is like a gigantic slaughterhouse. You step over trenches in the dirt floor running with the blood of newly killed animals. The prices are unbelievable. Four tomatoes cost $15. A head of lettuce costs $7. One woman was selling a cow's head. Another woman was selling a box of dirt. Wilted flowers cost $5 apiece. Chickens are of a color not yet invented. One night Ava Gardner's maid cooked fried chicken for everybody. The cast went crazy. It was the first time in three months they had eaten anything vaguely American. Jimmy Coco called up to thank her and asked her where she found such wonderful chicken. "I bought it in that market," was the reply. "Didn't it look strange?" he asked suspiciously, rubbing his stomach. "Oh, I soaked it in vinegar for twenty-four hours to get rid of the stench." The company spent the next three days on the john. I bought two apples for $10. They both had

worms in them. On the way out, a man offered me $55 for
my $7 blue-jean jacket.

Back at the hotel, Cicely Tyson has returned from a forbidden trip to Hollywood with a Ouija board, Mille Bornes,
Probe, Monopoly, a bicycle, peanut butter cookies and a
Lhasa Apso puppy, purchased at the Farmers' Market. "Pee
on the call sheet, darling," she instructs the dog, who obeys
on cue. "You think what you've been hearing is incredible?"
she asks me. "You ain't heard nothin' yet. I signed to do this
thing for fourteen weeks. I haven't worked since February
26. It is now May, and I'm told I'll be here another three and
a half months. They were worried about the ten-year-old
boy in the film looking too old. By the time we finish, he'll
be entering college. Listen. I went to California to regain my
sanity. Without permission. What are they gonna do, fire
me? I'd give anything to get fired off this thing. It's not the
deprivation or the suffering. It's the waiting around. All you
want to do is get it on, do your work and go home. Everything I've shot has to be refilmed because they switched
costumes on me in the middle of the picture and now nothing matches. Don't tell me what a great director Cukor is.
He didn't even notice I wasn't wearing the same costume.
Now are you ready for this? I have a white stand-in. No
dresser, no makeup man, but a white stand-in. They light
everything for her and then I'm expected to go through the
same paces with the same lighting. Naturally, my black skin
disappears on the screen. You can't see me at all. And sup-
pose I don't want to do what my stand-in does? And they say
I'm the biggest complainer of all. Listen, Dad. When I did
The Autobiography of Miss Jane Pittman I had to get up at
four A.M. every morning in the swamps of Louisiana, spend
three hours having forty pounds of glue and rubber put on
my face to look a hundred years old in that hundred-degree
heat and I thought that was rough. But when I went home
at night I could order a fresh salad and make a long-distance
phone call. That only took seven weeks and we created
something we were proud of. Here you can't get out of the
country and I'm starving to death and there isn't even a
telephone operator in Leningrad. Every time you pick up

the phone a voice answers in Moscow and sometimes it takes two days to make a phone call.

"Don't forget I arrived in midwinter and there was nothing to eat but cabbage. I had diarrhea for three weeks. Then I switched to boiled fish. For four months we were not even allowed to go to Helsinki for the weekend. Then Jimmy Coco said, 'I want an answer so I'll know what to tell the press,' and we had visas in twenty-four hours. We went wild. We stepped off the plane in Helsinki and saw bananas, Coca-Cola signs, a McDonald's hamburger stand . . . it was like Robinson Crusoe arriving in civilization after being shipwrecked for twenty years."

Before turning in, I run into Ava Gardner's hairdresser, Sidney Guilaroff, flown to Russia at her own expense, having a late coffee. He is manicured, elegant as a Bill Blass ad, sitting in Palm Beach tweeds at a table with two Russian truck drivers. "Ava's just about to throw in the towel," he says grimly.

MONDAY. The entire company leaves for the Leningrad studios at dawn except me. Ava Gardner has made it clear that if I show up she'll not only leave the set but Russia as well —a difficult feat even for her, since she has no passport. At ten, I'm having a coffee when Jimmy Coco, Cicely Tyson and music arranger Irwin *(Sound of Music)* Kostal come in looking bewildered. They've been sent home in full makeup because one of the Russian cast members has a cold and shooting has been canceled. Kostal says, "This is the most abusive waste of talent I've ever seen." Most of Kostal's songs have been scrapped. The lyricist has walked off the picture. "I've been here four months and we haven't recorded one song. We have no equipment and Fox, the American distributor, won't pay for anything to be shipped in. The whole company is ready to walk out."

At lunch, I'm cornered by Carl Kress, the brilliant young film editor who won an Oscar for *Towering Inferno*. "I'm working on equipment that is prehistoric, man," he says. "You won't believe it but this picture is being edited on a 1921 Movieola like the one they used on *Potemkin*. Everyone agreed to do this picture because we thought it would be another *Wizard of Oz*. With such big stars and George Cukor, who is a legend, why wouldn't it be a great adventure? Man, it's the worst piece of junk I've ever worked on." We are joined by Coco, who says, "The first indication I had that things were going wrong was when I saw my costume, which consisted of a mohair sweater and mohair trousers. 'That doesn't look like a dog's costume to me,' I said. 'It looks more like a gorilla suit from some bus-and-truck company. So then they got a group of Russian delegates together to decide whether I should have fur. Then they gave me an aviator's cap and I looked like a bear from outer space. I made ears myself by sewing two powder puffs together. The original designer of all the costumes, sets and magic for the movie was a very talented man named Brian Wildsmith. He left when they lost his sketches and the Russians tried to take credit for everything. We didn't even have a script girl until eight weeks ago. We were running around on the set holding pieces of film up to the light to see where we were standing the day before because there is no such thing as a Polaroid camera in Russia."

"Cukor has never made a setup, never looked through a lens, never worried about matching," says Kress. "He's seventy-six years old and now he's got to do his own matching, his own continuity, his own lighting. He doesn't know what he's doing. And Eddie Lewis sent word from Hollywood that we have to use Russian equipment. There is no money for anything. And we are working for nothing, man. There are a hundred and twenty-two pages to the script. In five months, we've shot twenty pages. Figuring a minute a page, we've got another hour and forty minutes left to shoot and we haven't even got the sets built yet for the difficult scenes. Everything we've done so far has to be shot all over again and nobody wants to come back. When Jane Fonda left she looked at her rushes and said, 'You can't release this crap!' It's the most unbelievable movie-making experience I've ever been involved in, and if you write all of this nobody in America will believe you."

That night, I'm invited by Jonas Rosenfield, head of publicity at Twentieth Century-Fox, to a dinner that turns out to be a kangaroo court. I'm in the witness box. "We're trying to change the publicity image here and now we hear you've been asking a lot of negative questions," he says.

"I haven't had to ask any questions at all," I reply. "Everyone on this film is so unhappy they're asking me if they can talk to *me.*"

"Well," he said, "there are a lot of complainers who should be proud they're pioneers involved in a great adventure."

"If it's such a great adventure," I answer, "why isn't the producer here sharing it?"

He has no answer. "Well, you don't hear Elizabeth Taylor complaining."

"Elizabeth Taylor isn't even here. She flies to London every time she isn't needed and stays there. Everybody else has to stay here because if they travel they do it at their own expense. If you want a different kind of story, then show me a different kind of story and I'll try to be fair. I haven't seen the sets or costumes, I haven't been invited to the studio, and your caviar and smoked sturgeon, which I don't eat anyway, are diversionary tactics to keep me from seeing the truth of what's going on here."

"Well, you only have one side of the story."

"Okay," I said, taking out my pen, "tell me the good things and I'll write them down."

"Well," coughed Rosenfield, "you couldn't get the Moiseyev or Kirov Ballet in America."

"You don't have them either. They pulled out months ago and you've got the Jacobsen Ballet, which I never heard of. Now you expect me to tell millions of readers in America we are here spending fifteen million dollars and wasting the time and talents of some of the most famous people in the world just so we could get the Jacobsen Ballet? They'll laugh me out of the country. We've got better dancers at home in the New York City Ballet, but the real truth is they'd cost more."

"I can't deny that. But you wouldn't get Maya Plisetskaya in America. She's dancing one of the leading musical roles."

"You don't have Maya Plisetskaya either. I happen to know she came to the set one day, did a slight turn, fell down onstage and had her period. She's out of the film."

He couldn't believe it. "You've done your homework," he said, rising from the table. Nor could he deny that the whole undertaking has been naïve and poorly organized from the beginning. As a publicly owned corporation, Fox is in it to make money. Negotiations began in December 1973 between the Russians and Eddie Lewis, an independent producer. It was considered a great coup, an opening for a new cinematic frontier. But what it still boils down to is money. It would cost $10 million minimum to make a Maeterlinck fairy tale on the sound stages in Hollywood and nobody would back it anyway. The Russians are putting up more than that, but it's all rubles, which can't be traded in or taken out of the country. They have nothing to lose. All Fox has to do is pay the stars' salaries, which is a minimal investment since everyone is working for percentages, and provide the Russians with technological know-how. In return, they get the distribution rights to a major film at practically no cost. Talk about cultural détente all you like. It still boils down to profit and loss. The question is: is it worth it to go through so much agony when the film, if it's ever completed, could very well still be a financial disaster at the box office? We'll have to wait and see.

Meanwhile, I am promised a visit to the studio tomorrow when Ava Gardner isn't around. The dinner is charged to American Express. I wonder if the bill will register with the credit card computer back home in less time than the six months it takes to get a postcard.

TUESDAY. Today is Lenin's birthday. Red flags wave from every building. A flame burns in front of the Lenin museum, where the clock is always set at 6:50 P.M., the hour he died. The city is drenched in a blinding blue rain. The Lenfilm studio is a series of tiny cottages with a central courtyard beyond which stand grim sound stages, drab and smelly as shoe factories. Inside one of the stages, a circus tent is set up. Into the circus ring Ava Gardner rides a white horse. She doesn't know I'm there. I hide behind a curtain. The entire backdrop is the same color as her costume. It is a symphony of rotten pomegranate red. The whole thing looks like the set of a Soupy Sales TV show for Saturday morning shut-ins.

Tempers are flaring. A conglomeration of flotsam is wandering everywhere: Hollywood movie set grips, Russian crones with their heads in rags, sinister Russian executives in shabby suits which they all bought at the same store, extras in ball gowns wearing sneakers and white socks beneath the satin trains, sweet little Russian men sweeping the floor who look like Khrushchev. Cukor is talking about how lovely Ava Gardner looks. Her face, masked in three tons of grease paint, looks like the map of China.

Another nearby set where the Cat and Dog in the film show the children the bluebirds (played by pigeons painted blue) is a surreal dream of papier-mâché mushrooms. Some of the blue pigeons have gotten loose and are seen flying past the commissary windows. Lunch on the set is abominable—greasy fried fish and muddy-looking brown peach juice. The cast and crew have to pay for this swill. Most of them have stomach cramps. "How's it going?" I ask Cukor. "Haltingly," he grumbles.

I spot Freddie Young. "Do you think this will take as long as it took you to shoot *Ryan's Daughter*?" "The rate we're going," he glowers, "it'll take five years." The script supervisor adds: "It takes ten days just to fill out all the requisitions to get a ladder to mount a light. I've been here eight weeks, I was told it was an eight-week job, and we haven't even started."

Back on the set, Cukor is still pushing ballroom extras out of the way. The deposed Russian cameraman stands on the sidelines steaming. Jimmy Coco, in his mohair dog suit, says, "I feel like I'm wrapped in Saran Wrap." Cicely Tyson looks like something out of a Las Vegas chorus line in her cat suit. The Russian with the cold finally shows up for work in the middle of the scene. "She's an absolute bitch," whispers George Cukor. Diplomatic relations have finally come to a crumbling, ruinous standstill. And so it goes for the next three days, with one horror story mounting on top of another, until one wonders if the domino theory will hold. Will the clashes of egos, the frustrations and the impossible sophomoric working conditions finally explode into a Vesuvius of screaming, erupting lava? I run away to the circus, where a bear walks a tightrope in tennis shoes while an orchestra plays "Liebestraum." I dine at the only restaurant in town recommended by Igor, my friendly guide, who has mysteriously disappeared for being too friendly, and suffer through a dinner of smoked fish, cranberry juice and a piece of meat with ketchup and dill pickles on it ($25) while a singer who looks like Ilona Massey dances to balalaika music and a Wagnerian soprano sings in a helmet with horns, a low-cut velvet gown and a white turtleneck sweater.

I interview Victor Blinov, the Louis B. Mayer of Russia, who blames everything on Svetlana Stalin's ex-husband, who introduced him to Eddie Lewis in the first place. "The first version of *The Bluebird* had strikes in the streets, tanks, guns and a rock score," he says with horror. "We changed it back to a fairy tale. Now the capitalist egos are creating problems. We must help each other, not eliminate each other." But will they buy it in Peoria?

I spend two days trying to get out. Ava Gardner has taken to her bed with a stomach virus. Jimmy Coco and Cicely Tyson have spent one whole day shooting close-ups of a scene filmed three months earlier against a black curtain because the Russians have torn the set down. It is all turning into a Marx Brothers movie and I have the flu. How will it all look on the screen? Does anybody care?

On the night before I'm to leave, all hell breaks loose. The cast learns by telegram they have been on suspension for the past week. All salaries have been suspended. All this time, they have been reporting to the studio daily. Cicely Tyson and Jimmy Coco finally get their agents on the phone at 6 A.M. They are informed Eddie Lewis has just told them everything is fine and George Cukor is rehearsing the musical numbers. Elizabeth Taylor will be back on the set Tuesday. "How can this be when she has just checked into a hospital in London?" yells Coco with something resembling delirium tremens. "Everyone is leaving Leningrad. What songs? What dances? How can you be on suspension if you've been reporting for work? We're dealing with a mental case!"

On Friday night, the cast had a meeting to decide what to do. Tempers flared, mothers were in tears. Will the rooms be reserved if they leave? Who will pay for overweight luggage? How much luggage should they pack? Who will pay for the transportation? Will the film be resumed after the hiatus? Ava Gardner ventured forth from her Garboesque sanctum sanctorum long enough to hear the wails and the cries of gloom and doom. She had been a lady long enough. She punched the production manager, John Palmer, in the nose. Throughout the hotel, you could hear that Cinemascope and stereophonic sound voice booming: "I will not be quiet! I will not behave! Get me outta this town, get me outta this picture. I want my visa and I want my passport and I'm getting the hell outta here *tonight!*"

SATURDAY. My week ends in glorious Leningrad. Members of the *Bluebird* company sit around in various stages of suicidal despair on pieces of luggage strewn throughout the lobby, waiting for passports that might never arrive. As the baffled, unhappy cast prepares to depart at their own expense for places unknown, wondering if the *Bluebird* will ever fly again, there's a new sign on Ava Gardner's door that says: ENTER PLEASE—WELCOME ONE AND ALL!

Since I am willing to take anything that flies, I somehow manage to get onto an Aeroflot heading for London. There is no pressurization on Aeroflot, and as you lift above the ground an arrow shoots through your head like you've been attacked by Apaches. I looked at the little pale people down below in their Salvation Army clothes with nowhere to go and nothing to do but wait, and the pain didn't matter. The arrow in my head was small potatoes compared to the arrow through the hearts of the people left behind.

Sophia Loren

Caramba! They look like giants on the screen and turn out to be dwarfs in person. Or their beauty masks turn out to be pimples. Or their lustrous, gumdrop eyes turn out to be contact lenses. Or their dimples turn out to be dewlaps.

Not Sophia Loren. She doesn't disappoint. If anything, she lives in Panavision splendor, her olive-sunny skin kissed by her own Technicolor. For a girl born forty-one years ago, illegitimate, in a ward for unwed mothers, she has become the richest actress in the world. For a child who scavenged for food in a wartime Naples slum with dreams of becoming a movie star, she has endured as one of the few film queens of international stature. For an ugly duckling whose chin was too short and whose mouth was too big, with the neck of a swan and bosoms like pumpkins, she has emerged as beautiful as Aphrodite rising from the Aegean. For an actress who began as one of ten thousand slave-girl extras in *Quo Vadis*—with no talent, no training, no range—she has developed into an Oscar-winning artist of the first rank. She has sung duets with Noel Coward, dined with Queen Elizabeth and shooed President Tito out of her kitchen for sticking his finger in her spaghetti sauce. Elizabeth Taylor credits her for saving her marriage to Richard Burton. She has beaten Taylor, Burton and another friend, Peter O'Toole, at both Scrabble and poker.

For a woman who has spent most of her life in the headlines, been threatened with excommunication by the Roman Catholic Church, jail sentences by the Italian government, rape by German soldiers, robbery at gunpoint by thugs, scandal and sometimes even death, she is sane, natural, and unpretentious as a lemon pie. But she's no pushover; although she rarely displays temperament either in public or private, she once called her co-star Frank Sinatra a "mean little SOB" in front of a hundred cheering film technicians when he called her "a broad"—and when Marlon Brando slapped her fanny she slapped his face. "Well," said her biggest fan, Charlie Chaplin, "what else can you expect from a girl who was raised halfway between a gun factory and an erupting volcano?"

The story of how frightened, desperate little Sophia Scicolone pulled herself up by the shoelaces and fought her way to fame, comfort, and respectability has been told many times. The point is, she no longer has anything to fight for. She has achieved it all. The Sophia Loren I face on the silk-damask sofa in her sumptuous Paris apartment on a rainy afternoon is a study in serenity and repose. When she moved there from her two-thousand-year-old Villa Ponti in Rome with her lawyer-producer-multimillionaire husband of eighteen years, Carlo Ponti, and her two sons, Carlo Jr. (she calls him Cipi because Ci Pi are the Italian initials for C.P., pronounced phonetically) and baby Edoardo, everybody said she was afraid of Italian kidnappings. Scarcely a day passes without some gossip columnist heralding the gloom, doom, and dissipation of her marriage. One newspaper account said she'd lost a leg, another said she had suffered a stroke and that her face was paralyzed. "If I go to a nightclub with a friend while Carlo is out of town, I'm cheating. If I visit a relative in a gynecology clinic, I'm pregnant again. If I stay home and enjoy my family, I'm fighting to save my failing marriage. If I don't feel like working and Carlo hires another actress, I suddenly read that I'm crying myself to sleep because my husband is having a torrid affair behind my back. So I have stopped reading what they write about me and I almost never give interviews."

This is a rare one, and she is in a talking mood, anxious to get the record straight and put all the balls neatly in all the right pockets. We have the afternoon to ourselves. Cipi, seven, is in school. Edoardo, three, has been sent to bed after pulling the lid off the toilet. Carlo Ponti is upstairs in his office doing what he always does—making á transatlantic call to Hollywood. "Every time Carlo picks up the phone," Sophia says, "he makes another million." She isn't joking.

The Pontis live in a palatial residence across the street from the George V Hotel. They need so much space that they've taken over three floors. They can afford it. They also have the Villa Ponti in Rome and a penthouse in New York, where Sophia, in her nightgown, was knocked to the floor by muggers and robbed of $500,000 in precious gems. The money they spend is almost as unimaginable to ordinary mortals as the money they make.

Sophia serves tomato juice swimming in Baccarat crystal. Her closets bulge with Balmains, Diors, Balenciagas, but she seldom wears them. The frescoed ceilings, the Louis XV furniture and the Picassos and Rembrandts on the walls are admired only by the nanny and the cook. The engraved invitations to fashionable parties and premieres remain unopened, like unwelcome bills. She has become a recluse in Paris. There are three unreleased films—*Poopsie & Co.*, a farce with Marcello Mastroianni (her favorite leading man and close friend), in which she plays a happy-go-lucky prostitute involved with the Mafia; *The Journey*, the last film directed by the late Vittorio DeSica and co-starring Richard Burton (she plays a woman who dies of a heart attack); and *Cassandra Crossing*, an all-star epic with Burt Lancaster, Ava Gardner, Ingrid Thulin, Lee Strasberg, and Richard Harris, about a train sealed off from an epidemic of bubonic plague. But she isn't interested in talking about movies. The old days of being a sexy siren are snugly behind her. (On a recent trip to America, a chanting hippie broke through a police blockade and shoved a religious book into her stomach, shouting, "Read it, Sophia—it'll tell you you're not just a body!" Carlo threw the book into a garbage can and roared over his shoulder, "She already knows that.")

It is obvious that such things as career, success, and money are no longer the driving forces in her life. She shrugs away any mention of the words "glamour" and "stardom." "All it takes to look the way I do is a simple regimen headed by a minimum of ten hours sleep each night. I turn off the phone at nine P.M. and I'm asleep by nine thirty. Women who live for the next miracle cream do not realize that beauty comes from a secret happiness and equilibrium within themselves." Strange words from the woman who used to feed the press such pap as, "Everything I am I owe to a diet of spaghetti and Coca-Cola." Today, she says simply, "Everything I am I owe to Carlo Ponti and my children."

She has wide penetrating eyes, like black raisins, which she paints into an almond shape with her own pencil. She does her own hair, rarely wears makeup, sips an occasional white wine and has given up cigarettes. "I gave up smoking twice, each time my sons were born. I went back each time. Then I did *Man of La Mancha* with Peter O'Toole, who smokes like a chimney. He said, 'Don't be chicken, take one' —and I said, 'Sure, why not?'—being very strong. And I started all over again and smoked very heavily. I haven't had one for a year now." She does nothing, in fact, that calls attention to her status as a movie queen or disrupts her family life. "I hate the word *star* but sometimes you have to use it. Anyway, that's one word we never use at home. With my children, I am an anonymous mother like all other mothers. The worst thing is the photographers. They follow me rudely in the streets and wreck my privacy, but I go to the school with the other parents whether the *paparazzi* are there or not. Listen, I have to live my life. If it gets too bad, I call the police."

The villa in Rome is guarded by vicious Alsatian dogs and men with walkie-talkies who pop out of the shrubs if you so much as bend over to smell a camellia. In Paris, the security seems minimal. The downstairs *concierge* lets anyone go up in the elevator. Anybody can ring Sophia Loren's doorbell. Yet it's a deception. "I'm more protected than you think. We have bodyguards everywhere, but their guns are discreetly hidden. I'm surrounded by very reliable people in the house who would never betray me. Cipi has a bodyguard who takes him to school. I worry about the children every moment, but what can I do? We have to live like normal people." In 1972, an escapee from an Italian insane asylum broke into the grounds of the Villa Ponti waving an axe, chopped his way into the house and demanded possession of Cipi. It was one of the most terrifying experiences of Sophia's life. "He claimed he'd had sex with me and Cipi was his son. He was someone I once gave an autograph, obviously very ill. He's in and out of asylums all the time. He writes me letters. We keep a very watchful eye on his whereabouts. But these things happen to all people in the public eye. There are so many people out there who are out of their minds. I get threatening phone calls. There is nothing I can do. If there was something I could do, I would do it. You just have to learn how to protect yourself. These lunatics will not go away, so the best I can do is raise my children to feel loved and secure under the circumstances. That's all any mother can do."

Sophia says she does not live in Paris because of safety. She had already become a French citizen in order to marry Ponti. (Yes, Virginia, the most famous Italian since Columbus is no longer Italian.) "You have to decide where you want to bring up your children. Three years ago, when I came to Paris to do a film with Jean Gabin, I enrolled Cipi in the École Bilingue, a very good school where they speak both French and English. He loved it and was so happy every day that I decided to keep him there. We already had the apartment and nobody was using it, so we moved here. That was actually before all the kidnapping started in Rome. Now they will kidnap you for fifty dollars. It's so bad that I'm glad we don't live there anymore. But the real reason was that I wanted my child to speak more than one language properly. The schools in Italy are terrible. You should see my nieces. They had to have private English lessons just to learn how to read a menu. It's ridiculous. Now Cipi speaks better English than I do. He also speaks French like a Parisian, and Italian and German. He swims, he does judo. I don't like karate; it's too violent. But judo is good exercise, and psychologically, it's good for children, too. It never hurts to learn self-defense." Cipi has already been enrolled at Eton when he grows up. Baby Edoardo already babbles in German and English.

"They are completely different," beams Sophia, "but I'm already seeing character beginning to develop in my children. They are simple, kind, generous children. Cipi is a dreamer. Edoardo is very aware of everything. He also knows how to get his way, like his father. If he doesn't get it with charm, he tries screaming. He's very clever. Maybe I do mother them too much, but I worked all my life to have children and they are gone all too quickly. They belong to their school, then to their wives, then to their jobs. I want to share their lives as long as I can." They know their *mama* is more *mia* than most, but she tries to hide them from any unnatural spillover from her spotlight. "My only philosophy to them is: 'Learn to respect yourself and then you can respect others.' I don't want them ever to feel they must prove or achieve anything because their parents are famous. This is a burden on them I do not permit."

The children are not allowed to see many of their mother's films, although one of her biggest flops, *It Started in Naples,* with Clark Gable, is their favorite. They have never seen her best film, *Two Women,* or the original Oscar she won for it. (Thieves stole her cherished statuette, although she has since replaced it with a $60 replica.) She has sheltered them from her film work ever since they saw *Sunflower.* "I let Cipi see it because he was in it when he was six months old and I wanted him to see himself. Just after the scene he was in came a very powerful scene on a train, where I screamed and and cried and threw myself on the floor. The effect was so traumatic that he still has nightmares about it to this day. After that, no more Sophia Loren movies for my children until they are older and can understand that it is only make-believe."

Despite the nagging rumors of storm clouds that constantly threaten to pour water on her marriage license, Sophia insists that her marriage to Carlo Ponti has never been more secure. "For me, it's a beautiful thing. When you find the right person to have children with, it's the *most* important thing in life. Otherwise, you don't have to get married. I always wanted children and I was determined they should have a father. I didn't want them to feel the same shame and torment I felt as a child. I met Carlo when I was fifteen, and I never looked at another man after that. We didn't start going together until I was nineteen, and the press called us terrible names because he was married with two children of his own. But it's true when I say that there has never been anyone else but Carlo for me. I guess it's true that he has always been a father image to me, the father I never had, but from the first moment I met him I felt I had known him all my life, ever since I was born."

Few people understand the attraction of a voluptuous Galatea to a sixty-one-year-old man who might, in another setting, pass for her bachelor uncle. Short, paunchy, balding in his stuffy suits and purple socks, he looks like an apple vendor on the streets of Milan. But to know Sophia is to understand the compulsive need for security, prestige, and fame that has driven her throughout her life like an apocalyptic rider. Her father was a construction worker who refused to marry her poor, pregnant mother, leaving her in a war-ravaged factory town near Naples with two daughters to raise. His name was Ricardo Scicolone, and to this day Sophia's mother curses him for destroying her life. Sophia is more forgiving, though her childhood left scar tissue you can still find today if you probe with a scapel. "I always knew who my father was, but we never spoke," she says quietly. "It bothered me so much as a child because the children teased me cruelly and I would hide in the back of the schoolroom with the orphans. I once spoke about him to a reporter and my father sued me for libel. He dropped the charges, but I hated him at the time. Now I am older, I have children of my own, I understand more. As time goes by, you learn to forgive and forget. I don't forgive easily, but I do forgive. Now my father is old and very ill and very lonely. He sits in dark cinemas and watches my movies. I often wonder what goes through his mind. But it's water under the bridge now."

She was seven years old when they bombed Naples. The children called her *stecchetto* (the stick) and *stuzzicadenti* (toothpick) because she was so frail from malnutrition. "I never had enough to eat. At the age of six, I already knew well the meaning of the word deprivation. I was brought up with hunger and fear. My mother tried to provide what she could, but there was nothing around to provide. Everyone was desperate. We lived on sour bread and rainwater.

"Naples was the first bomb target because of the harbor and the railroad stations all around the port. It was really the city that suffered most in Italy. They only bombed Rome once and the Pope stopped it. But we were bombed five times a night in Naples. My earliest memories are of always being hungry and sleepy. The air-raid shelters weren't safe, so we would go at ten P.M. and sleep in the railroad tunnels and get up before the first train passed by at four thirty in the morning. It was never enough sleep for a child. My house was bombed only once. The walls were damaged, but it's still standing today. My aunt lives there over a vinegar factory, and the tourist buses drive by and point out Sophia Loren's house. The humor in that is incredible. I once won second prize in a beauty contest and they gave me fifty dollars and some new wallpaper. That wallpaper is still on the walls of my old room. It's very good paper." She laughs that little-girl Neapolitan giggle that radiates on the screen, pours me another tomato juice, then settles down again, discreetly cupping one manicured hand over her breast to hide the no-bra look.

She becomes reflective again. "It's sad when I go home to visit now. I have such nostalgic feelings about that house. I never tried to block out the memories of the past, even though some are painful. I don't understand people who hide from their past. Everything you live through helps to make you the person you are now. I even have nostalgia for the German boys who marched by my house in the mornings on their way to kill people. Such handsome youths with blonde hair and blue eyes, pretending to be men. Whoever thought they'd do what they did later on? I didn't know anything about war or politics, so I didn't hate those men. Children don't know how to hate. When you're a baby, you have no social conscience. Also, don't forget the Germans were not our enemies in the early part of the war. They were supposed to be our friends. When the Americans came, it was like a big carnival. They were a symbol of liberty and food."

Those early stories of how she worked as a prostitute on the streets of Naples, seducing GI's for money to buy food, make her eyes flash with anger. "Well, that is typical of the things they've said about me. In 1944, when the Americans arrived, I was ten years old. I was a rather mature child, but I wasn't *that* mature. In every house we used to sell drinks to soldiers—to make money. The bars were all closed so the only way they could buy beer was in people's homes. That was the only contact I had with soldiers. They used to call me 'Little Chicken.' But I liked them very much. They were always very homesick, very unhappy, and very drunk. When I was in America recently, I got a letter from a man who told me he met me when I was a child. He even remembered I had a wound on my head from a piece of shrapnel. I remembered him very well because he came to our house often and loved our family. It was a memory coming back to haunt me. Some faces you never forget if you're an impressionable child."

The beauty contest money got her to Rome, where she and her mother boarded with relatives for three months. They both got jobs as extras in *Quo Vadis,* but her mother had to return to Naples when Sophia's younger sister, Maria, became ill. Sophia stayed on, posing for topless comic strips called *fumetto.* She entered another beauty contest and didn't win, but she met Ponti. It was a day she will never forget.

"I went to see him wearing a red dress with white polka dots that I borrowed from a friend because I did not own a decent dress of my own. I made a screen test, but I was very skinny and very ugly and everyone said I looked like a giraffe. Mr. Ponti said I would never be an actress because I didn't photograph well, so I left in tears. But even then, I was in love with the movies. After the liberation, I devoured the Hollywood movies that came with the GI's. I adored Yvonne DeCarlo and Rita Hayworth. They were part of another world. I never dreamed one day I'd be one of them. Who knows about success? You start with great faith, know your limits, and if you have temperament and drive you will eventually get somewhere. I didn't know how far, but *somewhere*. Every time I have wanted something badly, I have had to wait. But eventually it came. I found you really have to concentrate, especially for marriage and children. I've been lucky, of course. Meeting Carlo was the thing that changed my life. But I worked hard to change from an ignorant, unattractive peasant into a real actress. Nobody will ever know how determined I was."

Ponti made ten more screen tests. There was something about her. She made a movie of *Aïda* with Renata Tebaldi's voice. Her publicity flowered. In her first American film she was so much taller than her co-star, Alan Ladd, that she had to stand in a ditch during the love scenes. The press crucified her, but Ponti was powerful. Without him, there might never have been a Sophia Loren. He was called a "pizza Pygmalion," but it didn't matter. She provided the sex appeal a man of his position craved; he provided the financial security a frightened, insecure waif sought desperately. They were married by proxy in Mexico in September 1957, but it wasn't the end of a dream. It was the beginning of a nightmare that led to an interminable stream of legal, religious, and emotional complications that have made Ponti bitter about the Catholic church to this day. "That quiet wedding in Mexico was blown out of proportions by a reporter," he says saltily, "and that is when our problems began. The Italian government charged me with bigamy because they didn't recognize my divorce from my first wife, so I was forced to become a French citizen rather than go to jail. My first wife became French and Sophia also became French. Then my first wife and I divorced a second time and Sophia and I were married again, in 1966. All this because of the connection between the church and Italian government. It's very bad when the priest tries to become a politician. The result is they are never very good priests *or* very good politicians."

Sophia is less emotionally charged. "I told you, I forgive. We wouldn't have to go through the same problems today because the church is making reforms—and the divorce laws are changing, too. My husband could have his marriage

annulled now, but we had a civil ceremony and the children
have a name and everything is okay. If some day Carlo wants
to marry me in the church, too, it would make me very
happy. If it doesn't happen, it doesn't matter. It wouldn't
change anything. I will not live in guilt or sin."

"Are you religious now?" I asked.

"I don't practice Catholicism. I don't go to church every
Sunday. I don't go to Mass, I don't take communion. But I
believe in God and myself and the people around me. I pray
sometimes, but I believe now in relating directly to God
instead of through a priest." Privately, she has donated ru-
bies to a church in Llano, Texas, and paid for the expensive
heart surgery that saved the lives of two total strangers.

She does not ask for publicity, but it follows her around
like a hound dog sniffing bacon frying. Once she became
fodder for the cynics when she attended her sister Maria's
wedding to Romano Mussolini, son of the Fascist dictator.
Sophia says she never approved of the marriage, but it was
her duty to attend. At the ceremony, the widow of Benito
Mussolini led the wedding procession to the discredited *Il
Duce*'s tomb, where she proceeded to give the Fascist salute. Sophia was so unnerved that she drove away in tears
and collided with a motorcycle, killing the twenty-four-year-
old schoolteacher who was riding it. She was questioned by
police for two hours in a local grocery store while the flash-
bulbs popped. (Years later, after Maria divorced Romano,
Sophia once told a biographer, Donald Zec, that she was
baby-sitting with one of her sister's children by young Mussolini when Peter Ustinov paid a visit. While they were
chatting, the baby wandered onto the balcony. "That's just
how her grandfather started, crawling out onto balconies,
and look what happened to him!" cried Ustinov. Sophia
rushed out and dragged her bawling niece back inside.)

"These things just happen to me," she sighs. "And I rarely
ask for publicity unless I'm doing a film. If my chauffeur
drives me to a *trattoria* where I buy a delicious meal for two
dollars, they say I'm cheap. When I gave a vintage Rolls-
Royce to Joseph E. Levine's son for his car collection, they
say I'm looking for publicity. I don't care anymore what
anyone says. I have worked all my life to be the woman I am

today, and there is nothing I am ashamed of. I deserve to live the way I please. I make no apologies to anybody, including the Pope."

Her mother, Romilda, and her sister, Maria, do not fly, so they rarely visit her in Paris. "I miss those family reunions, but when I see them in Rome none of them treat me as an important person. They love me and scold me and treat me like I'm a little girl and I love that. We all say whatever we feel; there are no secrets in our family. I've made over sixty films, so they've seen a lot of movies. More than I have seen. I hate seeing myself on the screen. Once the job is over, I don't think about it again. I never go to daily rushes. I avoid premieres. Sometimes we show them at home, but the fun is making them, not seeing them."

"If you dislike yourself so much on the screen, why do so many others feel just the opposite?" I asked.

"Well, I don't know, but it is true that even though I don't live in America I am one of the foreign actresses who have a great market abroad. Who else is there? Name one." It is a rare outburst of ego in a woman who works overtime to be humble. I egg her on, nefariously, but she deals with my candidates one by one. "Ingrid Bergman? She's practically an American. Audrey Hepburn? Her whole career is based on Hollywood. Simone Signoret? That was ten years ago. Anna Magnani had it for a brief time. But at the moment, I am the only one. It's a very mysterious thing why you are liked and others with great talent are not liked. It depends on the characters I play on the screen, I guess, and the identification people have with my personal life. What I am as a private person has got a lot to do with it, too. Nowadays they know everything about everybody. It interferes with the psychology of the public. I'm always very honest with myself so maybe they feel that. I can't put on an act. What you see on the screen is me. I've had no formal training. I learned everything from working and from living. Life is the best school if you are perceptive, if you absorb."

"But there are a lot of people who have experiences with life and they don't show on the screen."

"Well, they have no talent." We both laugh at the statement. "I mean, maybe they're shy or they don't know how to let out that little treasure inside of themselves. Acting is a gift." She says she has never been disappointed in any of her films—a statement that could only be made by someone who hasn't seen them all. She's made some stinkers. "I've always been treated well by the critics; even in bad films I was always saved because I believed in what I was doing at the time." (In truth, she's the one who saved the films.) "And," she adds, "because Carlo was there to help me."

Of her marriage, she insists that it is "getting stronger every year that goes by. I had the good fortune to find the man I was looking for, and when people show surprise that we've been married eighteen years I always laugh. What could be more natural than to love the same man forever? Isn't that what every woman wants? For a marriage to last, you have to want it and work at it. You must know what you want in life. You must know what you need to make you happy, serene, tranquil. If you really know what you want, you will find it. A woman becomes mature only after she finds the right balance between herself and the life she wants to lead. Carlo doesn't have to worry about me losing interest in him. I see men every day who are more handsome, but they are cardboard compared to my Carlo. I am the one who worries about him. As a producer, he is surrounded by beautiful women every day."

It doesn't make sense. Here is a ravishing creature, adored by mankind, devoted to a chunky little man twenty years older and three and a half inches shorter than she is. He could be the grandfather of her sons. Yet she is jealous of him. "What can I do?" she laughs. "The truth is, I never found any other man who captured my attention. He has given me everything no man ever gave my mother when I was a child. I don't want to give that up. Jealousy is a human emotion I understand very well. He might one day be unfaithful. I don't know how to prepare for that. Even with everything I have, I am never totally secure. I know what it is like to be without, too. Before I was fifteen, I never in my life slept in a bed with less than three people in it. Everything you have you can also lose. If people saw what Carlo represents to me, they would understand. I love him as a man, as a person, as a provider, as a lover, as a friend.

I even love the negative things about him—he travels too much, he's too distracted by his work, he talks on the telephone and it drives me crazy. But I have my faults, too. He likes to go to parties and I prefer to stay home. I hate to talk business. I never socialize with actors. If they happen to be in town and they call me, I whip up some *pasta* and have them over, but not often. I socialize more when I'm working because I have to be friends with my leading men. To walk on the set first thing in the morning and have to get in bed with a man is the most horrible thing I can think of. With Richard Burton and Marcello Mastroianni, I feel nothing because I've kissed them so many times. But if you have to kiss somebody at 7 A.M., you better be friends."

Ponti was off the phone now and Cipi was bounding noisily in from school. Sophia and I had talked the afternoon away and it was time to go. One last look. The slave girl from *Quo Vadis* had come a long, long way. "Only one complaint," I muttered. "I flew all the way to Paris and you didn't even offer me lunch."

"Well," she said, her Gioconda smile erupting into a sulphurous Vesuvius of laughter as she led me to the door, "nobody's perfect."

Audrey Hepburn

She came and went, breezing softly through New York like the petal from a cabbage rose, carried aloft on a moonray. And for a short time, in her presence, the city went mad, touched by her magic. Audrey Hepburn is still the kind of star marquees light up for.

She flew in a snowstorm from her country house in Switzerland, first to Hollywood to pay tribute to William Wyler, the director who made her a household name in her first big picture, *Roman Holiday*, then to New York to open *Robin and Marian*, her latest picture after an eight-year absence from the screen. "It's not a comeback," she blushed shyly. "I had no idea I would be away so long. It's just that I remarried, had a baby and found a new life. Those things take time, and you just have to decide what's important in life."

At the premiere, the photographers blinded her. Somebody stuck a fountain pen in her eye. And eager autograph hounds spilled ink all over her clothes. "It's not so funny when the clothes are by Givenchy," she grinned. But Audrey Hepburn is that rarity among stars—unpretentious, unspoiled, realistic and wise, with her priorities in the right place. She's rare as a blue giraffe.

On the morning after the premiere, she met the press for breakfast, answered a thousand boring questions between muffins, and when it was over, she met me in a private suite at the St. Regis, breathless and exhausted, but still smiling in Technicolor. She is more beautiful at forty-seven than any other star imaginable, and warm as a kitten's tongue.

In a long-sleeved silk blouse under a Renaissance jumper, her lithe body is fresh and slender as a new spring tendril popping through the ground for a look at the sun. It's the shape that made her the envy of a million women on a million diets, and there's nothing she can do about it. She eats plates of pasta every day and can't gain weight. And the uncreased face gives no indication that there's ever been a day or an hour of unhappiness. It might be an illusion, but the illusion works.

To be truthful, she is going through an anxiety attack even as she kicks off her shoes and curls up on the sofa for a chat. Her husband, Dr. Andrea Dotti, was assaulted by kidnappers in broad daylight a few weeks ago in Rome. They forgot their chloroform, so he screamed until they ran away, but he was badly injured, requiring seven stitches in his head. "I tell you, it's a very anguishing period in Rome. They're even kidnapping tourists for fifty dollars apiece, ransacking apartments and breaking into cars. There are so many different groups—some do it for political reasons, some for money, and others are just delinquents who do it for kicks. If you're a famous person, it's especially worrying, but I can't let fear dominate my life. I get up in the morning, do everything like everyone else, and it's second nature, really."

Sean, her son by Mel Ferrer, is fifteen, six foot three, and away in college. Lucca, the baby, is six and in a very safe village school in Switzerland near the country house. "I worry less now. But two years ago, the joy of Rome was to walk around in the streets at night, enjoying the charm. Not anymore. The whole world has changed. Now I shuttle back and forth between my husband and his work in Rome and the children in Switzerland. It's not an ideal way to live, but it seems the best thing to do for the moment."

All of which has kept her away from the screen and the fans who love her. "It's all geography," she sighs. "I only work if I can combine my family's holiday with the shooting schedule. Acting is something I love to do and will do again, but I'm not having a career. Movies will always be an occasional thing now. It's hard to say this, but I am sincere when I tell you I really haven't wanted to work. For many years, ever since I was a child, and all through my first marriage to Mel, I was always traveling around making films. So I wanted and needed a rest. I hated the idea of leaving the children once they started school, and my husband must be near his clinic. I had to rearrange my life."

She's returning to Hollywood for the Academy Awards, and her husband and youngest son will accompany her. Givenchy has designed a knockout for her to wear, which will be a change from the blue jeans she wears at home. But even then, she says, "there will be no movie-star talk. I'm not a movie star to my family. Far from it. Not that I've hidden it from them. The children know what I do for a living. Lucca was with me in Spain during *Robin and Marian,* and it was a grand experience for a little boy, watching Robin Hood come to life. He kept saying 'Why isn't Daddy playing Robin Hood?' I told him that was impossible and he said, 'I know why—because Daddy doesn't have the right suit.'

"Sean's friends know more about my career than I do, and they're always coming around for a photograph or something, but I think it amuses him. They don't think of it in terms of having a famous mother because I don't think of it that way. They're very natural children. I think I worry more about their future than they do. They'll take their period the way we took ours. All you can do is give them affection and what you hope is a background with the right values."

If there's any negative reaction to her appearance in the lushly romantic *Robin and Marian,* it's seeing Audrey Hepburn playing her age. "Well, I am forty-seven, and I think it's silly to play younger parts. People have been youth worshipers too long. This is by far the happiest period of my life, even with all the tragic changes in the world. I'm less restless, and I no longer look for the wrong values. If I only knew then what I know now. I've had so much more than I ever dreamt of. It's not as though I've had great disappointments or unfulfilled hopes that didn't work out. So much more has happened than I ever thought possible. I didn't expect any of this. I am the most un-bitter person in the world.

"I decided ages ago to like life unconditionally. I've never expected life to do anything special for me, yet I've accomplished more than I ever hoped for, and most of the time it just happened without my even seeking it. I was asked to act when I couldn't act, I was asked to sing in *Funny Face* when I couldn't sing, and dance with Fred Astaire when I couldn't dance, and do all kinds of things I was not expecting and was not prepared for. Then I tried like mad to cope with it.

"Now I make a real division—when I'm at home, I'm really at home, and I don't do anything. I haven't done any interviews in the past eight years. Of course, I can't do anything about the photographers who follow me around in the street and wait outside my door. I don't have a secretary. I don't have attack dogs. My dog is a gorgeous mutt my father-in-law picked up in the street, and she's madly sentimental and gushes all over everybody. I don't go to parties or official functions, and I answer my own telephone. I cope."

It seems impossible, for few stars have ever achieved the kind of supersonic international stardom Audrey Hepburn has. Yet she honestly does not view herself as anything special. (She must have removed all the mirrors from her house.) "Truly, I've never been concerned with any public image. It would drive me around the bend if I worried about the pedestal others have put me on. And also I don't believe it. I've never thought of myself as glamorous or anything. I think Ava Gardner and Elizabeth Taylor are glamorous, but I don't fit into that category at all, at all.

"There's never been any question of my not being me. I'd be schizophrenic if I worried about makeup or evening gowns. Maybe that's why I suffer double when I do have to do something like the Willie Wyler tribute or the New York premiere of *Robin and Marian*. My knees were shaking, my hands were clammy, it was terrifying. I'm an introvert. You'd think after all these years I'd be accustomed to all the fuss, but it never gets any easier."

Women everywhere think she possesses some magic formula for staying young, beautiful, and perfect. "It's all in their minds. I use creams because I have dry skin and I'm a nut on sleep. If I go without sleep, I feel like I have the flu. But I have no pattern or routine. In Italy, I get up early to get Andrea off to the clinic by seven thirty, and he doesn't come home until after 9 P.M. So we don't eat until ten and midnight is an early night, but it ain't early for me. I have to make up for it by taking afternoon naps. I take care of my health, and the world takes care of my thoughts.

"I never read articles about me because it makes me nervous to know what others think of me. I used to suffer so from gossip columns. There's never been a helluva lot to say about me, but they make it up anyway. Only last week a San Francisco columnist printed that I was in America because my marriage was over. I don't care, but there's always some obliging soul who sends these things to my mother. I'm afraid I'm very dull copy. I haven't anything unpleasant to tell, and I can never remember anecdotes."

That doesn't mean she is empty-headed. Looking back on her career, she doesn't regard all of her films with pride. "I'm not so sure I would've done any better with a second chance, but some of my films were bloody awful. *Green Mansions* didn't come off at all. I'd like to have another crack at the new one. I don't think Richard Lester gave me enough time to do the love scenes with Sean Connery. I felt a bit rushed. And why did they have to show those rotten apples at the end? Were they supposed to represent Sean and me? I could've done without that last close-up of fruit turning rotten."

The Oscar from *Roman Holiday* is in a bookcase in her playroom next to the other prizes. "The children don't seem too impressed. They just want to know if it's real gold. It isn't."

As for the future, she says, "You're going to think I'm so corny, but my wish is not to be lonely. And to have my garden. I grow everything—flowers, herbs, vegetables. I'm not a city person. That's the basic and only disagreement between Andrea and me. He's gregarious, and he loves the noise and hubbub of a city. I love the country, dogs, flowers and nature, and I'm very bored by cement and skyscrapers.

"Don't get me wrong. I've enjoyed the klieg lights, the sound stages, the camera and the hard work making films. But if you ask me what I want from life, it's not glamour or money. I don't know what I would've done in the movies during the past eight years, anyway. It's all sex and violence. I don't like guns, and I can't strip because I don't have the body for it. I'm too scrawny. So I don't know what the future holds. We'll have to wait and see what happens to Rome. Will there be a new election or will there be a revolution? Will we move to Switzerland or to Timbuktu? We're playing it by ear. But whatever happens, the most important thing is growing old gracefully. And you can't do that on the cover of a fan magazine."

Then she put her shoes back on those dainty feet, and was off to the airport, clutching and sniffing a bouquet of spring flowers. And for a brief moment, I knew what spring was like in the middle of March. Audrey Hepburn's radiance and spirit are contagious fevers for which there are no known or desirable cures. If they ever discover an antidote, God help us and the movies.

THE HEROES

Sylvia Syms

She did it the hard way.

Today, Sylvia Syms is a legend who deserves the label in the competitive world of singers where everybody else tries to be one. She earned it, and when she opens tomorrow night at Buddy Rich's great jazz club, Buddy's Place, all of New York will get a rare opportunity to see what a legend is like in action. If they only knew what she went through to get there.

As a singer, she's incomparable. As an actress, she's in a class by herself. Everything else is redundant and always has been. In a world where good taste is as hard to find as good music, she's carried a bloody but unbent banner for both and she's never compromised. She's often had to do it alone. She's been ripped off through the years by bad agents and bad managers. She's been through some bad marriages, once to Bret Morrison, star of radio's *The Shadow* ("and, baby, let me tell you—the Shadow knows!," she laughs). She always laughs. Even when the world kicks her in the face. It's her sense of humor that has catapulted her through seas of adversity and into the hearts of the people who know her

and hear her sing. And a lot of people care. She is blind in
one eye and must undergo another operation on the other
eye in January. She went into Mt. Sinai Hospital in 1969 for
a checkup and they said, "She'll never make it. This lady is
dead already." They removed one lung, her spleen, and a
portion of her intestines. She was in the hospital three and
a half months, and now she lives with a respirator every day,
a wildly expensive Byrd-Mark 7 paid for by Frank Sinatra,
who is her biggest fan.

Then, on Aug. 5, 1970, when she was finally on the road
to recovery, she broke both of her legs in an automobile
accident and spent one whole year in a wheelchair, losing
a part in the *Bridget Loves Bernie* TV series. Even then, she
had a sense of humor, when others gave up hope that she'd
ever walk again, and instead of dwelling on the long hours
and days and months of agony lying in the hospital, she tells
of the time Hedy Lamarr threw glasses and eggs at the wall
in the room next door because Sylvia received flowers from
Frank Sinatra, and Hedy, who thought her flowers were also
from Sinatra, discovered from the nurses that they were
really from the Frank Sinatra Funeral Parlor down the
street in Yonkers.

Sylvia Syms is back on her feet again and singing her heart
out, and everybody who knows anything about good music
will be cheering her on at Buddy's Place, not knowing what
a climb it's been to get there. She was always, like Porgy,
determined to make the trip. When she was seven years old,
a fat little Jewish girl from Brooklyn, she changed her name
from Sylvia Blagman to Sylvia Black, then to Sylvia Syms
because "it would look good on a marquee. I never wanted
to be a nurse or a ballet dancer or a typist. Certainly not a
housewife. I made a bargain with myself a long time ago,
baby, about which room in the house I would excel in, and
it wasn't the kitchen.

"No, I always wanted to be a singer. I was the only kid with
a professional name and no place to go. My mother says I
sang before I talked. I knew all the lyrics and all the melodies
and sang right out of my baby carriage to all the folks on the
front steps in Brooklyn. Today, they call that a gifted child.
In those days, they just thought I was bananas."

Her father was a clothes designer on Seventh Avenue who thought people in show business were bums and hookers. "He fought my ambition all my life and never gave me any formal training. I learned everything I know from other singers. First, I listened. Then I lived. Now I've got wrinkles in my face and wrinkles in my soul and I sing better than I ever did when I was young. I still don't know what keys I sing in. Nobody reviews my voice, they review my style and my feeling. Mel Torme and Jackie Cain have great voices. I don't. My singing is acting and emotion and interpretation. If you want to hear my voice after I leave, baby, go home and tear up a rag. But I can't sing anything unless I know and care about the lyrics. It drives me crazy to hear some fourteen-year-old kid sing 'I did it my way.' They don't have a way. They haven't lived. I've paid my dues."

She started out listening to the radio in bed at night, after the house was asleep. She sang along with the big bands they broadcast from the hotel lounges. Then, at seventeen, she started sneaking out of the window after her folks went to bed, creeping down to the subway with a dime in her purse, and heading for Manhattan. She was a regular at the old Café Society Downtown and the night spots on Fifty-second Street and in Harlem, where the doormen knew her and let her in even though she was a minor. She'd watch the shows from the hat-check room. Mildred Bailey adopted her. Billie Holiday called her "my little girl" and one night, when Billie burned a hole in her hair with a hot comb, it was Sylvia who grabbed a gardenia from the cigarette girl, stuck it in Lady Day's hair, and started a trend. Count Basie let her sing with his band. Duke Ellington used to tease her: "Baby, I don't know what you're gonna do, but save a dried-up bone for me."

The jazz writers of that period started comparing Sylvia to Billie Holiday, Ella Fitzgerald, Lee Wiley. "I didn't have a direction of my own. I just imitated the people I loved. It wasn't until years later that the real Sylvia Syms emerged."

She's made a dozen great albums that are collector's items today, and hundreds of singles through the years, but she hasn't kept any of them. She cut her first records with Stan Kenton and Shelly Manne in 1948, but they were destroyed in the famous International Studios fire on New Year's Eve. She cut her first album in 1951 with Barbara Carroll playing an out-of-tune piano in another little studio for no money. "I didn't know I was supposed to get paid. I was just grateful to be able to sing. That album was for Neshui and Ahmet Ertegun at Atlantic records."

Her Decca recording of "I Could've Danced All Night" sold more than a million copies in 1956, the closest she's come to the big time and the big money. She doesn't cry in her beer. "The business of getting on with it is more important than hanging on to the past. I live for right now, baby. Every time I hear my old records I can tell you fifty million things wrong with them. I'm glad in a way that I never became a superstar because I don't have to worry about topping what I did yesterday. If God is good to me, I'll do it all over again tomorrow without having to prove anything to anybody. Look at me at this time in my life. I'm fifty-two years old and I haven't even touched the surface of who I am or what I can do."

She's already done it all. After she was heralded all over the world as a singer's singer, they discovered she could act, too. She was singing in a Greenwich Village dive called the Cinderella Club with a drag queen called Rae Bourbon in 1948 when Mae West walked in and offered her a part in the revival of *Diamond Lil.* Sylvia had never read for a play before, so she read her part and everybody else's, too. "Mae West took me on the road for a year and was wonderful until I got my first rave review. Then she turned into a monster. I weighed over two hundred pounds, and Mae added forty more pounds of padding to my costume to humiliate me." But she stuck it out, went on to do *Dream Girl* with Judy Holliday, *Rain* with June Havoc, and *Camino Real* with Al Pacino and Jessica Tandy at Lincoln Center. On opening night, Tennessee Williams took her chubby face in his chubby hands and said, "I'm so glad to see my gypsy fortune teller come alive on stage at last." Since then, she's played an Indian in the Broadway musical *Whoop-Up,* a Pago-Pago native, a Hawaiian hula dancer, and Fanny Brice's mother in a tour of *Funny Girl.* Her Bloody Mary in *South Pacific* has become legendary (she's been in every company since

1951 to standing ovations) and her *Hello, Dolly!* ran for seven months in New England. "I've played everything because I look funny, I guess. Let's face it. I've never been Miss America. But my type is coming back. I don't care what anybody does in bed. I just wish they'd do it to me once in a while."

Sylvia doesn't do anything halfway. She works hard, she plays hard, and she cares hard. Plagued by her own physical handicaps, she suffers from emphysema and asthma and still undergoes occasional cobalt treatments, but she gives most of her money away to needy children and charities. People like Van Johnson and Tony Bennett phone her daily for advice. She lives in a candy box apartment on East Sixty-third Street with a bedroom painted lemon chiffon ("I wake up every morning and wonder how I can eat the ceiling"). She doesn't smoke and doesn't drink ("I gotta be in charge of myself in case somebody makes me an offer") and never complains about her illnesses. Recently, she went to a doctor for a painful cobalt treatment, and the only time she balked was when it looked like it was going to delay her for her next appointment.

Her sense of life comes out in her music. She has supernatural good taste in the songs she picks and the uncanny ability to dramatize them with a voice lush and cool and full of compassion. She's a lyric writer's dream, which is why songwriters like Cy Coleman and Jerry Herman try out their material on her first. She's developed a loyal following through the years, and if marquees don't always light up for her the way they should, it's because the world is at fault, not Sylvia Syms. "I'm happy. I have no regrets," she says. "When you're not sure you've got a lot of time, each day becomes important.

"Most people take living for granted because they think they'll be here fifty years from now. So I don't mind living day to day, because planning a lifetime is living a day at a time anyway. There are many people who prepare for death. I prepare for life."

The philosophy, like the woman, is simple but elegant. Through her songs, she affects the lives of others. That is the art of Sylvia Syms.

Hildegard Knef

Most books by celebrities should only be read between Oxydol commercials. Cocktail party chatter without the benefit of alcohol. That's because: (1) Most celebrities are interested only in themselves, a fact that poisons the stories of their lives with an air of self-indulgence that is about as relevant to mankind as wallpaper paste; (2) most show-biz autobiographies are not so much written as phoned in from a cabana at the Beverly Hills Hotel. Hildegard Knef is a noble, enlightening exception.

Her first book, *The Gift Horse*, an international best-seller to this day, was about her childhood under Hitler, the ravages of war, and how she got to America, where she eventually became the toast of Broadway in Cole Porter's *Silk Stockings*. Her new book, *The Verdict*, which has already been translated into eighteen languages, goes off like a grenade in your hands. After fifty-six operations for cancer, she has written a blistering saga of survival without the slightest trace of self-pity.

She's no Joan of Arc and there's none of that sad, mawkish sentimentality that makes martyrs out of mortals. Yet these two books form one of the most moving and involving chronicles of life I have ever read, combining a richness of style (Knef knows so much about the new journalism she could teach Tom Wolfe and all the rest of us a few things) with the emotional development of a hypnotically structured novel. This gorgeous woman with bottle-green eyes that see through everything has lived through Hell and written about it clearly.

"She's the best thing that ever came out of Germany," says Stuart Schulberg, producer of NBC's *Today* show, who has known her since he was a GI in Berlin after the war.

"She's Mother Courage," says Marlene Dietrich, the only other German who was ever in the same league.

But Dietrich was a creation. Knef is a reality. She is the perfect wedding of intellect and emotion, incapable of a dishonest response or a phony ideal. She's like a tree. No matter how many times you chop away at its branches, it stands proud and tall. No wonder so many men have loved her, from Cole Porter to Henry Miller. She came to New York recently to talk about her books and her life, and everyone who met her fell in love again. She turned winter to spring.

She shook all the hands, submitted to all interviews, wore lavish fashions, posed for thousands of photos, then wept like a schoolgirl when she heard Sylvia Syms sing love songs in the Hotel Carlyle bar. She's been pronounced dead so many times she has acquired a love of life we could all learn something from.

"There is only one capital of the world," she said, "and that is New York. I get very excited when I am here. But in the long run, I know New York eats you. Writing is a crocodile that eats up your time. It's an anaconda of the worst sort. A book takes two years out of my life. I can't do that in New York because I can't concentrate here. So I always go home. But America is always in my heart."

She has three completely different, successful professions. She is considered the greatest actress to emerge from the postwar German film industry. Author. Singer and writer of more than two hundred songs. A new book of poetry and a forthcoming novel. In Europe, she's one of the hottest recording stars alive. She doesn't have time to get sick, yet most of the money she's made has gone for doctor bills.

"I wrote *The Verdict* because we spend billions to fly to the moon just to bring back a little bag of rocks, yet with the illnesses that descend upon us like the plague we act like primitive tribes in Africa doing a rain dance. If only half the money we spend on weapons in the world could be spent on research, we would be much better off.

"I also find it disgusting the way doctors treat patients. Physical illness does not make you an idiot. They have no personal feelings. A breast or a foot is examined like a pack of cigarettes. They are responsible for the lives of others, yet they go on forever and nobody checks them out to see what they are doing, whereas a pilot, who is also responsible for the lives of others, must undergo rigorous tests every six months.

"Now why do we accept every man in a white smock who looks at us like a ham sandwich just because he is scientific about it? I don't think medicine is a science, because you go to two doctors with the same illness and you get two different verdicts. Our faces are different, and so are our insides. I didn't write the book as a revenge to smash all doctors, but as a hymn to life that might help others."

The Verdict is now required reading in some medical schools and hospitals. Knef knows what she's writing about. Infantile paralysis in childhood followed by malnutrition during the war led to "a snowball that turned into an avalanche": hepatitis, colitis, gallstones, rheumatic fever, a ruptured appendix, a hysterectomy and a mastectomy, among other ills.

"I have also had the misfortune to fall into the hands of doctors who would like to have a new house in Ibiza and figured I'm the perfect patient to finance it, forgetting totally that I have to work very hard for every dime I earn. I didn't inherit any money, and I'm not independently wealthy. Then they operated on me whether I needed it or not. I have never found one doctor who said, 'I took out your appendix, it was perfectly in order and I made a mistake.'

"A lot of things that had been in order have been put in disorder. For example, when my daughter, Christina, was

born, I was happy as a cow and looked like a bus and everything was marvelous. Then she came early, and the way they
handled it was so demented it started a whole series of
complications from which I still have not recovered. The
anesthetist was late so they let me lie there in agony, then
performed an unnecessary female operation that now pre-
vents me from having any more children. I didn't even
know what was happening. When you are lying there in pain
with the belly open, it's not the time to ask questions, and
this happens to thousands of women."

She has survived the perils of Job, yet it has not made her
cynical or apathetic. "I hate pity. Help helps, but not pity.
I have been so close to death that now just growing old
would be a luxury. I have learned the hard way to love life
each day." She knocks on wood. "I have a clean bill of health
now, so I live each minute at a time. I was trained and
computerized from childhood to fight for life. Sometimes,
with the bombs falling and my head bleeding and my jaw
broken, I would stay alive just by concentrating on a new
case of dysentery. At the blackest moments, when I've been
close to death, there's too much anger in me to give up. The
loss of a breast or a hip is nothing compared to the beauty
of living."

She never set out to write a book about an actress. When
she left *Silk Stockings* and her Hollywood film career behind, she decided to tell what it was like growing up under
a dictatorship. "You had no chance as a child in Nazi Germany to work in the resistance or emigrate or anything,
because you didn't even know what was going on around
you. Then, by the time it is over, you are held responsible.
Only then do you find out what really happened. I felt it was
time somebody told the truth. The former Nazis are becoming biologically extinct, and the young generation in Germany doesn't even know what Hitler looked like. So I wrote
The Gift Horse to explain why I innocently fell in love with
a Nazi and ended up in a Russian prison camp. And I was
ready to accept the consequences.

"Only through the profession of acting was I catapulted
into Hollywood, where I thought the war was over and
everybody loved everybody. I found out nobody loves any-

body, and the resentment against the Germans was so tremendous it made me absolutely speechless. I was put on ice and dragged out every time they needed a glamorous spy in a Darryl F. Zanuck movie. I went from a dictatorship to a dictatorship operetta."

No book has ever dissected Hollywood with the insight, brilliance or biting wit of *The Gift Horse.* She prunes away the clutter the way the best gardeners select the ripest flowers for the vase. Yet she has an amazing command of sophisticated English.

"Nothing is harder than knowing what to leave in and what to leave out. Most people writing autobiographies just write what happened to them in their lives. That does not make a good book. I always try to write in the style of the girl I was at the time. As I matured, so did my vocabulary. I write in German, and my husband, David Palastanga, translates it into English. I write two hours a day and then file it away and forget it. I have the illusion nobody will ever read what I am writing. Otherwise, I would not be able to write my own name."

She hates Hollywood movies about Nazis, she says, because "they are always shown as blubbering idiots, but they were there for twelve years and they were not clowns, and they brought the greatest horror the world has ever known and changed all our lives for generations to come, and I get absolutely furious when I see them treated like Keystone Kops, because they were much too dangerous." She has just completed her first film in nine years, about the German resistance.

"I said I'd never make another film. At a certain age you must face the fact that films are an idiotic profession and you can't be held responsible for the work of others. A film is made by the author, the producer, the director, the camera and the cutter. But in the end, it's the actor who gets the blame. So I got fed up.

"Now I break my 'never again' rule because this is the most honest, intelligent script I've read in years. I play a poor woman whose son was shot in the first days of the war. She wrote postcards saying, 'Hitler killed my son!' and 'We are following the Führer like a herd of sheep to the slaughterhouse!' and planted them all over Berlin. The Gestapo went insane. She succeeded to baffle them for a year before they caught her. It's called *Everyone Dies Alone,* and it's a true story—the first indication in years that the German film industry might be surfacing again."

She has "a criminal memory" for all that has happened to her. Also a deep, throaty laugh that moves sexily from her porcelain neck downward until it hugs her toes. She's so shrewd that she cuts through façades like a laser. She doesn't suffer fools easily, yet she's not tough. "I'm a goulash of emotions. I have a great capacity for friendship and laughter. But I'm terrified of stupidity because it's the stupid ones who are the most dangerous. My private life is chaos, but my work is very disciplined. I am totally unable to handle money. My finances are always in a muddle.

"I could probably have been a big American film star after *Silk Stockings,* but I detest playing the silly games that go on in Hollywood. If you go to this party, maybe you'll get the part. I hate the bickering with agents and the asininity of being a star.

"Yet I don't regret the decisions I've made. I don't censor my life. The things we do are there, they change us and it's these changes which make us what we are in the end, good or bad. I have paid a high price for my survival, but survival breeds optimism. Right now, I am more optimistic than ever. For years I went around being somebody else. They changed my name to Hildegarde Neff. I was an onlooker in the wrong vicinity. Now I am my real self again—Hildegard Knef, pronounced with a K. I know who I am, and the climate looks good."

It's not just the survival that makes her remarkable. It's the way she survived and what it can teach us about ourselves that makes her books and performances such rewarding experiences. We should be grateful that she cared. It's a better world when Knef is in it.

Louise Fletcher

Smart money in Hollywood is on Louise Fletcher, who has just won an Oscar nomination for Best Actress of the Year for her superb, chilling Nurse Ratched, the cold-blooded bitch who destroys Jack Nicholson in *One Flew Over the Cuckoo's Nest.* I look forward to interviewing her. It's not every day you come face to face with a monster.

But wait! Is this an April fool joke? The languid, lovely ladybug who opens the door to a dimly lit hotel suite is no starchy, steel-faced piranha. The dreaded Nurse Ratched, who gripped the men in the cuckoo's nest with cowering terror, has been sent back to studio wardrobe. The real Louise Fletcher speaks in the liquid molasses tone of her native Alabama. Her manner is warm as a kitten's paw. She has ice-blue eyes that flash with intelligence, a smile that offers friendly persuasion, short cinnamon-brown hair, and a shape that lounges in silk pajamas like a mermaid.

She has been up all night on a plane from Rome, where she busily promoted the film with Jack Nicholson, and has spent the morning shopping for a dress to wear to the Academy Awards. By sunset, she will be on another plane to Los

Angeles, where she lives with her husband of sixteen years, film producer Jerry Bick (he produced *Farewell, My Lovely*) and their two sons, John, fourteen, and Andy, thirteen. Her jet lag is understandable. So are the pajamas.

"It's unique what's happening to me, so I'm learning a lot about myself. I've never done publicity before in my life. I did twenty-two interviews in one afternoon in New Orleans. I'm not twenty-one anymore, so I'm exhausted. But I'm not bored." She sips coffee and pinches herself. The coffee is to stay awake. The pinch is to make sure it's still happening. And it is. Nurse Ratched has turned Louise Fletcher, retired actress, lazy housewife, and latent feminist, into what they call a "hot property" in movie lingo.

"I was the lady in the motel who turned in the young lovers to the police in Robert Altman's *Thieves Like Us* in 1973. It was the first time I had worked as an actress in eleven years. I gave it all up in 1962, when I was pregnant with my second child, and I never thought about it again until Altman came along. I didn't think it was a great picture, but it led to *Cuckoo's Nest*, and I guess you have to love acting to get through that. Ratched was horrible, grueling, the pits. But when the movie was over, I was sad. That's when I realized how much I had missed it."

She's had a strange life, so it's no wonder she was so effective in a strange role. Born in Birmingham, Alabama, one of four kids, with both a mother and father who were deaf mutes. Father an Episcopal minister, a "man of God"; childhood very traumatic.

"Most children with handicapped parents will tell you it's not easy," she says pensively, staring into her coffee cup and chain-smoking while she talks. "You want your parents to be like other parents, and mine were not. Every kid in our family had to have psychiatric treatment. I knew at the age of eleven I was not going to stay there. Still, the idea of doing something 'different,' like acting, was considered bad. So I went into psychoanalysis, and it taught me I didn't have to be the perfect Southern lady to please my parents. I found out it was okay to screw up. If someone doesn't like what I do, I no longer go to pieces or live to please other people. From now on, I come first no matter what anybody says.

"That was my key to Nurse Ratched. She thought she was helping the men in her ward. To do that she had to control her environment because she was afraid of experiencing real feelings. I played it with repressed sexual feelings and fear and took it all out on Jack Nicholson through control and hostility. It made me sick and unhappy to do that film, but at the same time it was the most joyful work in my life.

"I was the last person cast on December 27, and we went to work in the mental hospital January 4. I had one week to prepare, during which my house was robbed. I didn't know until two weeks after shooting began that Angela Lansbury, Colleen Dewhurst, Anne Bancroft and Geraldine Page had all turned down the role. All I knew was that I was scared. The fact that the whole company responded to me as a professional, and nobody acted like a star, helped me to cope with the changes I was going through. It renewed my self-confidence."

Ellen Burstyn, one of the actresses who turned down the part, recently appeared on TV asking members of the Motion Picture Academy not to vote in the Best Actress category on the basis that the nominees all appeared in supporting roles. There has been speculation elsewhere that Louise was elevated to Best Actress category because there have been so few starring roles for women this year, and she might stand a stronger chance than others. It all makes her furious.

"Those are sexist remarks, and I take total exception to them," she states with defiance. "If Nurse Ratched had been played by a big star, it would have appeared above the title in a co-starring position with Jack. So it's not the size of the part. Also, if I had not come off so strongly as the nurse, the film wouldn't have been the same success. If this had been a movie about the Marines, and a male star played the nurse, it would have been a starring part. Why can men play monsters, but not women?

"Ellen Burstyn's remarks are tacky. It's none of her business, and it's hurtful. I would never be presumptuous enough to criticize another actress's work. I didn't want to play Ratched like science fiction—with big breasts, red lips and smoke coming out of her ears. I played the truth. There's nothing feminist about that."

While she was making the film, she says, "everybody supported everybody. Jack could not and did not carry the movie alone. It was a total ensemble piece. We got so involved that some of the actors actually took on the psychotic problems of the patients they played. I insisted on remaining apart from the cast and ignored the actual patients who worked on the film in the hospital scenes. I wanted to maintain the nurse's aloofness. I isolated myself. It was lonely, lousy, and horrible.

"I never laughed or got involved with the actors' shenanigans. I was so wretched people started avoiding me on the set. It was very painful, but it worked. I wasn't permitted to see daily rushes, so I had no idea how I was being photographed. I was shocked when I finally saw the picture. Nothing was ever funny to me when we filmed it, so I was also shocked that it was so warm and funny. But basically, I was truly moved and pleased. And I don't think it's a depressing downer, either. How many men give up their lives for their friends? I thought it was a noble, uplifting story."

Movie-crazy in those years of escape from childhood reality, she dreamed of heading for Hollywood instead of New York, although when she graduated from the University of North Carolina in 1957, she did some stage work in summer stock playing Helen of Troy in a production of *Tiger at the Gates* in Bucks County opposite a young unknown named Robert Redford. Then she drove to Los Angeles with two roommates and $7 in her pocket, got a job as a receptionist in a doctor's office and studied at night with acting coach Jeff Corey. Jack Nicholson was in her class.

She appeared in TV assignments, but it was the time when seven-year contracts were dying out, so she "started having kids and went back to sleep. I wasn't aggressive, wouldn't go to parties. I just gave up. My family loved me, I didn't have to prove anything to them. It was warm in that role. Then in 1973 the Women's Movement crept in through my pores and made me crawl out from under my comfortable rock. I realized I could be a wife, mother, and actress at the same time. Other women were doing it. I had to prove to everyone who I was all over again. My major concern now is to find a director who will give me a part that isn't a heavy."

It almost happened with the Lily Tomlin role in *Nashville*. It was written for Louise. Much of it was written *by* Louise. It was the story of her life. Altman watched her with her deaf parents, created the role from her own experience, then gave it to a bigger name. Now they don't speak to each other.

"It's one of the things that happens," she shrugs. "People start hating you, and you don't even know why. You just have to ignore that pain and get on with your life. If I had done *Nashville,* though, I might be competing with myself this year in the Oscars in two different categories."

She has never been to an Academy Awards show, but she's been watching them all her life. "It's an arena I never thought I'd be in. The competition is fierce, the trade-paper campaigns and the pressures and the infighting—I thought I'd have a nice, quiet career. But it's thrilling, and I'd be lying if I said it meant nothing.

"I've watched those people with the cameras on their faces when their names are announced, and I know it's a terrible ordeal. But I'm American clear through, and I know about winning. It's like getting thirty thousand red roses at one time. I never won anything in my life except a beauty contest with eleven other contestants in Vicksburg, Mississippi."

She has no illusions. "Success breeds success. After *Cuckoo's Nest,* I got a big agent and a lot of big offers. Now they say, 'You've got twenty-four hours to read this script,' and the phone rings thirty times in one hour and sometimes I feel like I'm having a nervous breakdown. But I've been through a lot in my life, and I feel like I know real joy from make-believe. I just want to do good work.

"I think things are improving for women. I'd rather be an emotional optimist than an intellectual pessimist. We're going through a revolution, and women have no sense of humor while they fight the battle.

"When I went to California I was five foot ten, brunette, and flat-chested. I didn't fit into any category. Now there *are* no categories. So I think it's improving. At least everyone is beginning to recognize all types. My life is too important to spin my wheels worrying about some nonexistent role that might or might not be written. I'm not in it to wave flags. I'm in it for the joy I can get out of it."

If she wins an Oscar on March 29, she doesn't know who to thank. "There are so many people taking credit for getting me the role of Nurse Ratched it's like *Rashomon*. Milos Forman saw *Thieves Like Us* and called me. But Jack Nicholson says he suggested me for the part. Then there are those stars who turned it down. Listen, I've been having fantasies about Oscar speeches in my head since I was fifteen, but if I win I don't know who to mention." She grins, unashamed. "Maybe I'll just thank them all."

Pearl Bailey

Somewhere in her fifty-seven years, Pearl Bailey has scrubbed floors, dined with kings, danced with Presidents, slept in the Lincoln bedroom at the White House, been baptized in the River Jordan, stood before the wonder of the Pyramids, looked in the muzzle of Arab and Israeli guns as they faced each other, and brought joy to the hearts of a zillion people. Now, like the title of the theme song she's called her own for a quarter of a century, Pearlie Mae is "tired." To the shock and dismay of a legion of fans, she will throw in the towel after her current Broadway revival of *Hello, Dolly!* ends.

Nobody really takes her seriously, but Pearlie Mae says this is for real. It's good-bye to a career in show business, and hello to "bigger fish to fry, maybe in politics." Perhaps, for starters, as a member of the official U.S. delegation to the United Nations. She's been invited personally by Daniel Patrick Moynihan, the U.S. ambassador to the UN. Well, why not? As Pearl says, "I got things to do, sweetheart. I have passed the peace bridge and made friends on both sides. Most people can't even pass a peace pipe!"

If you think she can't lick 'em in a skirmish the way she knocks 'em dead onstage, you should have been in Sardi's a few Saturday nights ago. We were doing an interview over coffee, minding our own business. She was talking about the world crisis, saying, "War is easy, peace is hard," when suddenly, like an electric shock treatment, a hideous apparition loomed menacingly over our table like one of the witches in *Macbeth*. It was the drunken wife of a Broadway actor, ranting incoherently about some review I wrote two years ago about a short-lived gangster movie.

"This is *my* interview, *my* table, and *my* guest, and since nobody invited you to interrupt, I must ask you to leave," said Pearl with firm authority.

The intruder went berserk, spewing forth a spray of filth that stopped forks in midair. While everyone in Sardi's froze with horror, Pearl Bailey rose above the crowd with ten fingers high in the air, announcing: "This garbage has got ten seconds to get outta here on her feet, on her face, or in an ambulance!"

The diners cheered, the maître d' and an army of waiters dragged the screeching cow and her husband to the door and into the street with the other trash, the restaurant went up in a chorus of "Right on, Pearlie Mae!" and order was restored.

"I don't like scenes," she said, still fuming, "but if you make one, you got an Aries to deal with, honey. You are lookin' at the Queen of Sheba, and that broad was one of the handmaidens goin' stark ravin' mad. I don't care if I'm with Mister Gerald Ford or Mister Rex Reed or the janitor— nobody insults *my* table, sweetheart. I've scrubbed floors with better-lookin' mops than that broad. Now, where was I?"

"Something about peace."

"Oh, yeah. I sit in the gallery at the UN and I see it being used as a political body, not as a human body the way it was founded. We've lost sight of our origins in this country. The hate is *so* extreme. Sweetheart, the labels are killing us. Courtesy, decency, and class have left the world. That was just proven at this table tonight. There's a sickness in the world, and I would like to help cure it.

"I ride home from the theater at night, remembering what New York was when I was a girl, and it makes me cry. The politicians have milked this city dry, and the people have given up. This one's on welfare, that one wants somethin' for nothin'. Instead of goin' to work in the mornin', they're hanging around, waitin' for the bars to open, and while they're waitin', they grab some woman or child and either mug 'em or rape 'em or beat 'em. What is it with these people?

"If you don't get up in the mornin' and go to work, you have no sense of pride or decency, and we have got to find a way to restore decency to society. Honey, I did every kind of work that was decent in my lifetime, and I never asked nobody for no handout. I can look back on my life with no regrets.

"It's not just New York. Look at Philadelphia, Cleveland, Los Angeles—every city in this U.S. is based on the pride of its citizens, and they better wake up to the fact that the government does not run the people. The people run the government. I'm not a worrier, I'm a carer. Now if we don't all start carin', we are gonna destroy the world.

"It used to be that if you got on an elevator, and somebody stepped on your foot and you said, 'Ouch!' they turned around and said, 'Excuse me!' Now if you get on an elevator, first of all you may not live to get down to the bottom floor. Second, if you step on somebody's foot, he looks to see what race, religion, or creed you are before he kills you. And now I'd like to ask one question—what happened to the pain in the foot?"

She has a way of reducing things to a common denominator, understandable to all. She can be direct and simple as calico, sweet as brown sugar, or passionate as an uncaged lioness. But on the phone, on a talk show or on the dais with Henry Kissinger, she is never at a loss for words. "Before I go to each country I sing in, I learn to say 'Thank you' and 'I love you' in every language. We throw around the word 'democracy,' but we must start practicing it right here. Then when foreigners visit they'll say, 'Ah, *that's* what they mean!' We have to stop and look at life from two points of view. I took *Hello, Dolly!* to Boston for two weeks in the middle of the busing riots, and the same folks who were out there fighting in the streets during the day came to see me at night. Black and white, they all became friends in my presence. Now why couldn't they see things through the eyes of the kids on those school buses afraid to get out instead of just through the eyes of the kids who were waitin' to beat them up?

"Why doesn't anybody go to the library to borrow books anymore? Why do all the movies have to be pornographic? Ten minutes after the picture starts, before I get the popcorn open, they're in the bed. For every ten minutes in the bed, I'd like to see fifteen minutes in the shower gettin' clean again. Equal time for hygiene, that's all. The courts let the criminals go free, nobody controls the guns the maniacs are carryin' around—there are a thousand things we gotta change instead of worryin' about who's got the oil and who's got the wheat. Instead of sayin', 'What have you done for me lately?' the only way we can change things is for each human being to say, 'I care, it must be done and together we'll find a way.'"

Whatever she does, she has the support of her two adopted children, twenty-one and fifteen, and her husband for twenty-three years, drummer-composer-arranger Louis Bellson. "He was always secure as a man and never showed any sign of weakness because his wife was a star. When we married, he said, 'Honey, I can't ask an artist with the dimension you have to stop working, but the day you *want* to stop, you don't have to work.' The world may not know it, but my Louis has always paid the rent, honey. We have friends and relatives who say, 'You and Louis are always working,' and I laugh because work was our joy. But now, by the grace of God, I can sit on my fanny and live the life of Cindy Lou, can you? And I don't have to sit on a pot of gold, either.

"I always said I'd quit when I got enough money. But when is that? There's never really enough, darlin', and when there is, you're in the coffin, and the insurance people and the relatives only get into the argument over the will. There's no more money or fame for me to get. I've had diamond rings, chinchilla coats. What God gave me, man doesn't have enough money to pay for. I never thought I'd make a dollar. I just wanted to go on the stage. I never thought I'd write a book. Now I've published four, with two more on the way. One is called *Cross the Bridge and See the Other Side,* which is an American's view of how other people live, and the other is called *Hurry Up, America, and Spit!* —and it had better."

Publicity? "Don't need it. I make headlines no matter what I do, and I have never been able to understand it. I didn't go to the White House for publicity. I went because a friend was stuck. Mrs. Ford called and said Johnny Cash can't come, and I said I had two shows to do, but I'd try to help out. Only reason I reached out my hand for Sadat was because I thought, 'Gee whiz, they all dancin', nobody asked that poor man to dance.' I'm honest and I dig people. They made a fuss about me dancin' with an Arab, but they didn't bother to print that my musicians were Jewish, and, honey, we was *all* dancin' and havin' a ball."

Ill health? "Honey, in spite of my heart attacks, angina, and all, I have pulled blood transfusions out of my arms and walked out onstage to do a show. I spent last Christmas in intensive care. First time I did *Hello, Dolly!,* I only came for fifteen months. I stayed two years, three months, and four days, and people laughed and said, 'Well, there's nothin' wrong with her,' that was a joke. Okay, medically, I'm a member of the coronary club. But spiritually, I feel there's nothin' wrong with me. After my last attack, I woke up in intensive care and heard the doctor say, 'I wish I had a heart as good as hers.' I know this is God's way of sayin', 'I have much for you to do and you are misusing it, so I am gonna knock you down and make you rest.' I'm not on any medication, I don't take vitamins, I swim and do my own cooking and washing and ironing when I'm home. On tour, I do needlepoint and walk and meditate. Wherever I am, I do a full, eighteen-hour day. Everybody thinks Pearlie Mae got seventeen servants. I do my own scrubbing and mopping, and I enjoy it. It's *que será, será,* darlin'. "

The plain truth is, she wants to do something else with her life. "A lotta people say the word 'retire' because they're croakin' or their knees are bendin,' and they can't stand up straight. But how can I retire what God gave me? I can still sing like a bird. My feet move, I can strut around. I'm not a rich woman, but I'm rich inside. It's time to take off my mink coat and wrap it around the people who need it more than I do. I'm singing in Luxembourg for retarded children. I'll do benefits. I'm giving my clothes to Goodwill, for the handicapped. But I been around fifty-seven years, and I heard all the stories. A girl came up to me in the alley outside the stage door and said, 'I got a one-way ticket to Richmond, loan me fifteen hundred dollars.' Oh, no, darlin', I'm not playin' games, and I cannot be hustled. People say, 'Where are you goin', what is your plan?' I couldn't tell you. I'm gonna live from day to day. You are born, you live, and you die. I've done all three. For two minutes in 1972, during one of my heart attacks, I was pronounced dead. My heart had completely stopped. So I have come back from the dead, honey. I've cared about other people all my life, and I won't stop, but now I'm also gonna start carin' about *me.*"

George Burns

George Burns. Even the name makes me laugh. One of the comedy originals for sixty-five years, he'll be eighty years old in January and he's still going strong, like a baby hooked on Ovaltine. He's been a veteran of vaudeville, radio, TV, concerts, Las Vegas, and the movies, but he's not going down for the count. Not yet. The radio nostalgia craze has made him a legend once again, and right now he's wrapping up a starring role in Neil Simon's movie version of *The Sunshine Boys* for MGM. Clint Eastwood, move over. George Burns is back, full of vim, vigor, vitality, and vitamins.

Between scenes on *The Sunshine Boys,* he orders a martini, leans back in his Flo Ziegfeld dressing gown, and lights up one of his nauseating foot-long cigars with a mischievous grin on his pixie face, looking like a leprechaun who just won a race at Santa Anita. "I haven't been in a movie since Gracie Allen and I did *Honolulu* with Eleanor Powell in 1939. It's a completely different ball game. They used to use so much light you could get a suntan. Now they use natural light and hand-held cameras that can get into corners of a room we never dreamed of in the old days. When I did

Honolulu they had sets with four walls, and you had to shoot everything from one angle. Now they take out walls and shoot you from four sides at the same time. It's incredible.

"*The Sunshine Boys* is partially based on the old comic vaudeville team Smith and Dale, and we're shooting in an old folks' home in New Jersey for retired actors. Joe Smith is one of the people who lives there. Jack Benny and Red Skelton were supposed to do the film. Skelton wanted too much money and Jack died. Now they got me and Walter Matthau. They got the man who did Cicely Tyson's make-up for *Jane Pittman,* and now Matthau looks older than I do."

George Burns is one of the lucky ones. He always had a majestic career with a huge following, and, like his best friend Jack Benny, he saved his money. There's not much chance he'll end up like the old vaudeville comics in *The Sunshine Boys.* "I try to look as good as I can for my age," he says, eying my Cerruti suit with envy. "I love clothes and I always know where my handkerchiefs are. I get my hair cut every week and a fresh manicure. But it's my attitude that keeps me young more than anything else. I had a serious operation nine months ago. They by-passed the arteries in my heart and gave me new ones by taking a vein out of my leg. I asked the doctor what happens if I refuse and he said, 'George, you'll die.' I said, 'Then, let's do it.'

"If there's nothing you can do about it, put your life in the hands of fate. Now I take blood thinners and vitamins and do the Canadian Air Force exercises. And I play bridge. I used to play golf every day, but I was miserable to play with because every time I won, I'd sing on the golf course. It drove everyone crazy. Harpo Marx used to blame me for every hole he was under par. That's when I smoked twenty cigars a day. Now I only smoke five."

The deaths of Gracie Allen and Jack Benny were the two biggest blows in his life, but he's surged on. The team of Burns and Allen was a magic combination in show business history. He was a tough little Jewish kid from the Lower East Side; she, a dainty lady from a strict Irish Catholic family who ate fish every Friday.

"I met her in 1922. I was a lousy comic making forty dollars a week playing cheap vaudeville shows in Union Hill, New

Jersey. I always did lousy acts until I met Gracie. The only reason I stayed in vaudeville was the theaters I played were worse than I was.

"Anyway, Gracie came to see the show one night and said, 'You know, the fellow with the gold tooth isn't bad.' That was me. My tooth was okay, but my brother was a dentist. So we went to work as an act. I had wide pants and a red bow tie and stole all of my jokes from *Captain Billy's Whiz Bang*. Gracie was to be the straight woman. The first night, we had forty people out front and they didn't laugh at one of my jokes but every time Gracie asked me a question they fell out of their seats. So I made her the comic and the act was a hit from that minute on. That was the beginning of Burns and Allen."

They married in 1926. It lasted thirty-eight years. They were the hottest thing on radio for seventeen years and in 1950 made TV history for eight years until Gracie decided to retire in 1958. She died of a heart attack in 1964, but George went on without her. "She wasn't well and she never told me. But she was also never very interested in working. She was a helluva dramatic actress and sometimes she got tired of being considered a dumbbell. She did a dramatic sketch once on TV with James Cagney, and she was wonderful. But she went along with the act. Don't forget, she was never dressed up funny like Baby Snooks. She wore beautiful clothes and no matter how zany her lines were, the audience always believed her. That was her power.

"Lucille Ball is a great comic, but you could throw a pie in her face and the audience would love it. You couldn't touch Gracie. If I blew smoke in her face the audience hated my guts. She was like a piece of china. She would much rather stay home and listen to soap operas than go to work. When our own radio show was extended fifty-two weeks for the second year, I ran home with the good news, and she said, 'Wait, not now—Ma Perkins is in trouble,' and I had to wait fifteen minutes until she finished listening to *Ma Perkins.*

"Anyway, she finally retired. Hell, I was too young to retire. When I was sixty-five, I had pimples. So I played Vegas with a line of girls and found out I could do an act by myself. And here I am starting another career by myself in the movies. I'll never retire. Why should I? Isn't this nice? I call down, they bring up the food, I'm smoking a cigar, and it's all a tax write-off. I've paid writers all my life; now I've got Neil Simon writing for me, and I'm getting paid for it. It would be impossible for me to be bad. And I love the work.

"I knew the whole script of *Sunshine Boys*—not only my part but everybody's part—before we ever started shooting. All those years of memorizing radio and TV scripts helped. I've always believed in writers. First you gotta have the man to raise the curtain, then you gotta have the words to say. I used to sit around at four A.M. with an army of writers trying to think up jokes, and Gracie would walk in and say, 'Isn't that nice?' and everyone would fall on the floor. She was the genius, not me."

George's influences were the other "originals"—Cantor, Chaplin, Al Jolson. "Jolson's genius was he never sang with the music. The band would play 'dah-dah-dum,' and Jolson would sing 'When April showers.' Then the band would play 'da-da-da-dee,' and Jolson would sing 'come your way' . . . he sang in the cracks.

"I also loved W.C. Fields. When he was twenty-two, he played England with his young wife, who was twenty. His trick was juggling cigar boxes. The star of the show was an old geezer who had a funny voice. The wife fell in love with the old man. Fields stole his accent and delivery, and the old guy stole Fields's wife. I think Fields got the best of the deal."

And, of course, there was Jack Benny. "It was a great shock to me when he passed away. Three months before he died he was going to play the London Palladium. We always played practical jokes on each other. If you gave Jack a normal answer, he'd resent it. Thirty years earlier when Gracie and I played the Palladium, he surprised us and came for a visit. So I said, 'Jack, this time I have a surprise for you.' So he goes to London, plays six days, and he's got one show left to do and he calls me up in Hollywood to say, 'I thought you were going to surprise me.' I said, 'I am—I'm not coming!' He loved that. When he got back he said something to me which I thought was funny at the time, but now that he's gone I don't think so.

"Sinatra gave him a party when he was eighty years old and it embarrassed him. He didn't mind being seventy-nine, but it bothered him to be eighty. So six weeks before he died, we were sitting at the Hillcrest Country Club, and he said, 'I don't like being eighty. It's an unlucky number.' And I said, 'Jack, you want to be sixty-two again? You got a great agent, Irving Fine. Call him up and he'll fix it.'

"But Jack didn't laugh. It was an age that made him uneasy. He had a great life ahead. He had a TV special, four concerts, and the movie of *Sunshine Boys* coming up. So he was doing great for eighty, but he insisted it was an unlucky year and I guess he was right. He didn't make it to eighty-one. Now I'm replacing my best friend. That's irony. But I think he would approve. A lotta great people died—Caruso, Jolson, Barrymore—but none of them got the newspaper space Jack Benny got. And the reason was not because he was the world's greatest comedian but because he was the world's nicest man."

George still sees Mary Benny. They've spent many a lonely evening since Gracie and Jack died. George's voice grows soft when he talks about the loss. "When Gracie died, I was very upset and couldn't sleep. We had twin beds the last few years she was alive because she had a bad heart. So finally I decided to change over and sleep in her bed and it worked. There was something warm about that. So Mary called me one day and said she couldn't get to sleep at night thinking about Jack. I said, 'Sleep in Jack's room—all his trophies are there, all of his things. It'll work.' I don't know if she took my advice or not.

"Gracie didn't marry me because I was a sex symbol. We were in show business and we made each other laugh. That's why it lasted thirty-eight years. We slept together, ate together, dressed together, and worked together, and never had a fight. It was a partnership and a friendship, too. And she knew everything. The only thing I ever felt guilty about was a telegram we got in vaudeville. It was from Flo Ziegfeld and he was out front and that was one of the nights I blew smoke in Gracie's face and he hated my guts. So he sends a cable saying, 'I'll pay two hundred dollars for the dame, a hundred for the act.' I never read it to her. I told her it was from some of the boys at the Friars Club. Before she died, I said, 'Gracie, I got a confession to make. Remember that cable we got that time in vaudeville?' and she said, 'You mean the one from Ziegfeld?' "

He still watches some of the old TV shows he did with Gracie and sees the movies on the Late Show, but George Burns does not live in the past. "That's the way it goes. They're back to wearing wide lapels and spats. But I live for right now.

"So I'll be eighty in January, so what? There comes a time when they knock on your door and give you back your pictures and you leave. I'll take my music with me because I don't know where the hell I'm going and I want it in my key. Meanwhile, I'm having a nice martini, I live in a nice house and the soup is hot. I go out with young girls and some of their youth rubs off on me, but I'm no Jessel. I don't go to dark restaurants. What the hell? I got nothing to hide. I go to my office an hour a day, and I'm writing a book about how to be eighty years old and enjoy it."

And one more thing, he adds before closing: "If I had my whole life to live over again, I'd do everything the same way." George Burns grins. The grin is wise, but the spring in the step is pure sixteen. "The only difference is I'd do everything twice."

Melina Mercouri

ATHENS, GREECE—The eyes of Melina Mercouri, frosted with tears, catch the reflection of candles. It is her first Greek Easter since her return to Athens after eight years of exile. They were agonizing years, filled with terror and bitterness and longing, and the free world read about them in newspapers, heard about them on radio and television, and watched with interest while she struggled to free her country from a Fascist dictatorship of military colonels and return it once again to the cradle of Democracy it used to be. Now the junta is gone and Melina Mercouri is home—"not for the holidays, but forever."

She is not alone. The telephone rings incessantly. Gifts of chocolate eggs and flowering gardenias arrive hourly. And she is surrounded by friends: the entourage that followed her to Hollywood and Broadway and her home in Paris during the exile, her husband Jules Dassin (the Connecticut-born director who, in the nineteen years he's been with Melina, has learned how to use worry beads), and a flotilla of friends who keep her afloat when everything seems to be sinking. Margaret Papandreou, the stylish, intelligent

American who looks like Alexis Smith. Her husband is the opposition party leader in Parliament and one of the prime political forces in Greece today. Theoni Aldredge, the Greek costume designer who won an Oscar this year for *The Great Gatsby,* calls to say hello. Irene Papas, another great Greek star, who is making a film with Anthony Quinn. Set designers drop by. Michael Cacoyannis phones. His documentary on Cyprus is a huge success in the Athens cinemas. The censorship that held Greece in chains during the junta's reign of terror has been lifted. *Emmanuelle* is a big hit here. The Greek tragedies are once more being performed. *Time* and *Newsweek* are back on the stands. People are once more breaking plates in the tavernas and dancing to bouzouki music. The air is perfumed with the spring aromas of jasmine and roses. It's a good time to be in Greece. And it's Easter.

Greek Easter is like Christmas in America. It comes a month later, in May, and culminates in a weekend of rejoicing. For Melina, it begins on Friday night, when she leads a candlelight procession through the streets that wind crazily up to the Acropolis. At the cemetery where the Greek heroes are buried, she points to the spot where her grandfather, who was mayor of Athens for thirty years, commands a special memorial outpost. "When the junta was in power, they tore down my grandfather's statue and now I am insisting that it be returned," she says defiantly. "If it isn't, I will make such a scandal . . . " The eyes of Aphrodite turn to marble and you know she can.

From every window the old and the young wave lighted candles and blow kisses. The candles, like the Easter eggs resting in silver trays in every Greek home, are red, symbolizing the blood of Christ. On the following night, the resurrection celebration commences and the candles are white, symbolizing the spirit of purity. After the parade, the streets are filled with people. From Melina's rooftop gardens, I can see thousands of them marching like pagans through a zigzag path to the Acropolis, singing hymns. At midnight, every light in Athens goes out, like a wartime blitz, and the entire city is lit only by candles. Then the bells begin to toll, the fireworks explode into a galaxy of red and purple stars, and everyone kisses everyone else like New Year's Eve in Times Square. There is something emotionally contagious about it all—not only the extraordinary physical beauty of a great city lit by candles but the *esprit de corps* of so many people with their hearts beating in the same tempo. For one magical Easter night, everyone—old peasant women in black shawls, children with eyes like ripe olives, teenagers in their blue jeans, American tourists clutching their traveler's checks, and diplomats in square, boxy suits—knows what it means to be Greek and free.

Then they eat. For forty days they fast without meat. Now they begin the end of the fast with a rich soup called *magiritsa*, prepared with herbs and chopped liver to pave their stomachs' way for the sacrificial lamb. Melina has three bowls and is too full to eat anything else. "For eight years I roamed the world, but every year in May my heart would be in Greece. I dreamed about this soup. I would wake up in the middle of the night in Beverly Hills and taste it the way my mother prepared it all my life. I found nobody in the rest of the world who could prepare it like the traditional Greek cooks. It is one of the best things about being back in the country I love."

After dinner there is Mozart and wine and she is radiant in red with strings of gold coins around her neck. "This is why I wanted so desperately to come home—to have some peace in my life. It's more than just loving your country. It's in the blood." She talks of many things—childhood memories, the career her American friends fear she's abandoned, and hope for the future. It is her first exclusive interview since her return. Everybody knows she's back, but what is she doing there? "Listen, darling, the junta took everything from me—my passport, my citizenship, my sanity. Now it has all been returned and I don't want to let it go. They offered me twenty thousand dollars a week to do a revival of Cole Porter's *Can-Can* at the Los Angeles Music Center. I turned it down. I was probably a fool to do that, but I don't want to work right now. They offered me a tour of *Ilya Darling* in America. I said no. They wanted me to appear on the Academy Awards show. For what? I must stay here where I belong now. Every day the reporters and television programs call me from all over the world to do interviews, but I have nothing to publicize. I have a new film, *Once Is Not Enough*, opening in New York, but who cares? I have been cut out of it so much my part is nothing. I did it for my friend Jacqueline Susann, who was one of the most courageous women I have known in my life. When the right time comes, I will work again. Right now, let me have some peace. I've earned it."

And so she passes the days with friends, getting acquainted once again with the country she will die for. After nineteen years of chaos with Melina and an ever-constant Greek chorus of her followers, Jules Dassin is finally taking Greek lessons and is settling comfortably into the language. He is planning the first stage production of *Threepenny Opera,* which he will direct, in Greek. Melina led the women's march in Cyprus and is now mulling over a TV offer which would make her the Barbara Walters of Athens. All of her films, banned for eight years under the junta, are enjoying huge successes in the Greek cinemas and she draws big crowds of admirers and fans every time she takes her afternoon coffee in Kolonaki Square. It's enough for now.

On Sunday, we are to drive to the suburbs where one of her oldest friends is barbecuing a lamb for Easter in her honor. She is nostalgic. The taxi driver is instructed to take a tour of Piraeus, the jewel-like Greek port where *Never on Sunday* was filmed and where, upon her return eight months ago, Melina ran for Parliament. (She lost by ninety-two votes.) The U.S. Navy ships are gone now. The port is empty except for the fishermen eating ice cream in the square. People come out of their houses to offer her roses. The men make sweeping bows. In Piraeus, she is more royally welcomed than Constantine. "Here I smell the sea and touch the earth. You cannot imagine how much I missed that." It's true. In her autobiography, *I Was Born Greek,* she wrote: "It is infuriating to know how little the world knows about Greek history. Most people think Pericles died yesterday and Aeschylus is still writing plays." How little we know about the fantastic history here. Now Melina is part of that history.

Not that everything is perfect now. Everywhere she turns

there are poignant reminders of better days that make her melancholy. A block from her elegant apartment stands the house of her mother, Irene, whom she has tried to imitate all of her life. When Irene died, Melina gave up her half of the house to her brother Spiro, who lives in London. In his absence it has been turned into a boutique and now a neon sign lights up the balcony outside what was once their mother's bedroom window. Melina is furious about that. "What the hell," she shrugs. "There is nothing I can do about it. I hope my mother will give Spiro nightmares in his sleep." There is also nothing she can do about the ugly modern hotels and corporate structures now obscuring the quaint port of Piraeus. "The buildings where we filmed *Never on Sunday* and *Phaedra* are almost all gone now," she says sadly.

On the way to the barbecue, we detour to see the secret headquarters of the military police. "That is where so many patriotic Greeks were tortured by the junta," she says glumly. "And to think it is right next door to the American Embassy and just across the street from the Hilton. Didn't they ever hear the screams? The anti-Americanism has calmed down now, but a lot of Greeks still hate Kissinger." And how do they feel about Mercouri? "I think they have a mixture of pride and resentment. They were proud because I spread the fame of Greece throughout the world, but at the same time a few felt I might be doing it for my own personal gain. When the junta fell and I came home, the cynics thought I would stay a few days, make a few speeches, take the publicity, and go away again. I surprised them. I did not go away. It was not what they expected."

The taxi cuts through a quiet residential street and Melina points out the house of Papadopoulas, the dictator who ruled the junta. She is so disturbed by the memory that she loses her way to the barbecue and we drive around for almost two hours while she is on the verge of hysterics. Calmed by the sight of friends in the middle of the street who have been sent to search for her, and later by the lavish spread of salads and pies and roast lamb gaily offered on picnic tables under the grapevines, she once again becomes herself. "Greeks are, you see, passionate about everything," she laughs. "We eat with the same passion and fight with the same passion. And we must always be prepared for a fight. The Fascist colonels are in prison, but the jail is on a beautiful island and it is like a hotel. They have television and caviar. Many of their deputies still occupy positions of power, and now there is new talk of another coup. There is always the possibility of a terrifying tomorrow waiting around the corner. There are enemies everywhere waiting to destroy our new peace and freedom. But there are friends, too—Americans, Greeks, Europeans—who care about life and truth and peace. They are wiser and more courageous than I am, and they are not for sale. So I am optimistic about the future. Whatever happens, I must stay here to be part of it. Right now I am happy, but I also want to stay that way."

And so Easter ends, with a toast to freedom. Melina laughs that throaty sunlit laugh that made her a lusty, liberated star, and the Greeks raise their glasses in salute. They lost their most celebrated martyr when Melina Mercouri came home to Greece, but they reclaimed their most dedicated patriot. Salut, and amen.

ᙏarᴛin Ritt

Martin Ritt is a gruff Pooh Bear who speaks softly and carries a big stick. Right now he's directing a movie about horse-racing called *Casey's Shadow* in the dust of New Mexico, but even when he takes a break and wipes the grime and sweat from his shaggy brow it's clear that what interests and excites him most is not the film he's directing now, but the one he just finished—a blockbuster about the McCarthy witch hunts and what they did to destroy the talented people in television. It's called *The Front* and it's Marty Ritt's baby from start to finish.

The Front is a heartbreakingly true account of what happened in the early Fifties, told by the people who survived it. Ritt, along with screenwriter Walter Bernstein and many of the actors in the film, including Zero Mostel and Herschel Bernardi, were actually blacklisted in one of the most shameful and cowardly chapters in American history, and *The Front* is the courageous story they've been saving up inside themselves for twenty-five years.

This is the movie that tells how it was with the moral cowards who crucified and destroyed others, the victims who spied on their friends for government agencies to keep butter in their larders, and the brave arrogants who fought the injustice because they live in the world and believe in human rights. "Everything in it," says Ritt, "is true. I've been trying to get this movie made for twenty-five years, but I always met with the typical Hollywood resistance. I just never hit on the right way to do it until Woody Allen came along. Now I think it's entertaining, like an old Capra film, yet still says what I want to say. Audiences are proving that all those stupid bastards who run the studios were wrong. When Woody tells the investigating committee to go fuck themselves at the end, the audiences stand up and cheer. Then when they see the blacklist credits at the end, they cheer again. It's one of the few films I've made that came out at the right time."

A lot of people still don't know who McCarthy was. They think he had something to do with the navy. So you tell them what *The Front* is about, and they say, "Oh, yeah? What else is playing?" I hope it won't happen everywhere. "I don't think it will," says Ritt, shining with optimism. "It's easy to understand. It doesn't require a high degree of sophistication. Audiences go in expecting a Woody Allen comedy, and come out shattered. This is what happened in our country and you all better know what happened and what the ramifications were and how close the Constitution of the United States came to being stolen. It's because of what happened that the enormous amount of resistance came to Nixon twenty years later.

"This is a film that says, 'This is what I am, this is what I believe, screw you! I have a right to my beliefs and if I commit a crime, put me in jail, but to have an idea is not a crime!' That's why it's the first genuinely political film ever made in this country that questions the status quo. Now I liked *All the President's Men,* thought it was a damn good picture, but it was a movie about journalism. It never walloped me. Even the CBS show on John Henry Faulk made it implicit that he was falsely accused so as to ease the guilt of the same network that fired him.

"We don't do that in *The Front.* We are saying it was not against the law to be a Communist. The blacklisted guys took a very ethical position; it was the networks who were venal. I'm still angry about what happened. I'm a political animal. So *The Front* has been festering inside me for twenty-some-odd years. I'll always be grateful to David Begelman at Columbia for letting me make it. I hope it makes a fortune, but even if it doesn't, it's the movie I'll always be proudest of."

Ironically, through the shifting sands of time and the fickle finger of fate, it is now considered chic to have been blacklisted. With Lillian Hellman's memoirs, a dozen other books already published or promised later this year, and both *The Front* and *Hollywood on Trial* attracting the attention of filmgoers, it's a big year for saluting the folks everyone once threw rocks at. But according to Marty Ritt, it had curious, funny repercussions even at the time. "The blacklisted writers in the film are based on Walter Bernstein, Abe Polonsky and the late Arnie Manhoff, who was married to Lee Grant. They got credit for all the good things that came out of TV, whether they wrote them or not. Walter was on Fifth Avenue one day and some guy comes up and says, 'That was a helluva script you wrote last night, but what kind of a front name is that to use—Paddy Chayefsky?' I said, 'Fellas, stay blacklisted another ten years, and you'll end up Eugene O'Neill.' "

In the books on the period, Ritt's involvement is only mentioned as peripheral. "I was never named or subpoenaed, but I could have been. I was a member of the Communist Party when I was a kid. By the time I came out of World War II I had quit. But I joined under the impulse of all young intellectuals. I didn't think it was any more sinful than joining the priesthood or being any other kind of evangelist. It had to do with beliefs for what could save the world. When I no longer believed that, I dropped out.

"So I was never an important part of the McCarthy era, but I *was* blacklisted. I was fired from CBS in 1951 because they accused me of giving money to Communist China. Now everybody's trying to get to Communist China and it's a status symbol if you go there. I only got one job after that, directing a lipstick commercial for Revlon."

Paddy Chayefsky had written the role of "Marty" for Ritt

to play as an actor. He never got the job. So he turned to theater, where nobody cared if you were a Communist or not, acted in Clifford Odets's *The Flowering Peach* for a season and eventually directed Arthur Miller's *A View From the Bridge*, which got his directing career soaring in the right direction. At one point, he supported his family at the race track. (He still has quite a reputation as a lucky gambler and everybody on the *Casey's Shadow* location plagues him for tips on the long shots.)

"It was a rough time, but I was lucky. I also had a wife who had a lot of guts. She helped out by selling space for the telephone book. It was harder for others. How do you face a fourteen-year-old kid who comes home from a fight at school and says, 'Why are you a Communist who wants to throw bombs at America?' Nothing was ever proved about anybody. It was all guilt by association. It's a period of history many young idealists today only read about and relate to from a distance, but it did happen and it wasn't long ago."

Could it happen again? "Yes. But it's less likely to happen because of the position guys like myself took. And because we were fighters, it has made fighters out of others. Remember, the cold war had already started before World War II ended. The Soviet Union was already an enemy. When I went to make *The Spy Who Came in From the Cold*, I couldn't get into either East or West Berlin. I had to shoot it in Dublin.

"So I think there was already a world plan. They were already preparing for Korea in the Pentagon. One of the important weapons was thought control. If you held an unpopular opinion they didn't want articulated in Washington, they could make your life miserable. I myself was accosted three times by FBI men just like it happens in *The Front*. They'd come to your house, one would play a tough guy, the other a nice guy. The tough guy would say, 'You're in big trouble, you better confess,' and the nice guy would say, 'Take it easy, Jack, this is a decent citizen.' I just slammed the door in their faces. But I was harassed continually."

Show business makes strange bedfellows. How do artists who were blacklisted face their accusers at cocktail parties? "It's hard. Friends and lovers and colleagues and even husbands and wives stabbed each other in the back with knives to save their own necks. I have sympathy for the victims, but not the ones who cracked. Lee J. Cobb was one of the so-called friendly witnesses. For years, he'd say, 'Why doesn't Marty ever hire me for a picture?' It wasn't because he was a ratfink. But if I had a part he was right for and it was a toss between him and a friend, I'd hire the friend.

"Elia Kazan was the saddest personal disappointment to me. He was one of my closest friends when I was young. I admired and respected him enormously and he was a great help to my career. I've seen him on and off in the twenty years since he named names. Obviously, our relationship is impaired. We say hello, but the interesting thing is not what we say, but what we don't say. I think he made a terrible mistake in his life and I think he's paid for it. I don't feel any bitterness. Still, what he did makes it impossible for us to be friends.

"I knew other witnesses, like Larry Parks, but they were not in Kazan's league. Kazan was the greatest director in the theater. He didn't have to do it. His career wasn't threatened because he could name his play in the theater. He was a safe, secure idol of thousands of people. He ruined himself. None of the friendly witnesses came out of it heroes. All of the men who behaved on a human level have come out of it decently."

Now that *The Front* is out of his system, he's exorcised the old ghosts that haunted him, and other jobs are calling, Martin Ritt is settling down to making other people's ideas into movies again. Ray Stark, producer of *Casey's Shadow,* says his film and *The Front* represent two dreams coming true for Ritt in the same year. The director, growling, raises an eyebrow. "I don't know what that means. I like horses and Walter Matthau and this will be a popular, commercial film. But it's just a job. *The Front* is my life."

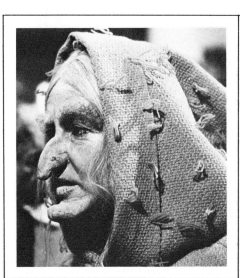

ELIZABETH TAYLOR *(with director George Cukor, lower right)*
"I've been through it all, baby. I'm Mother Courage."
(PHOTOS ABOVE AND LOWER LEFT COURTESY OF TWENTIETH CENTURY-FOX
The Blue Bird © 1976 WENLES FILMS LTD. ALL RIGHTS RESERVED,
LOWER RIGHT AUTHOR'S COLLECTION)

CICELY TYSON
"I have a white stand-in."

JIMMY COCO
"The first indication I had that things were going wrong
was when I saw my costume." (AUTHOR'S COLLECTION)

SOPHIA LOREN
"Everything I am I owe to Carlo Ponti and my children."

AUDREY HEPBURN
"There's never been
any question of
my not being me."
(WIDE WORLD PHOTOS)

SYLVIA SYMS
"I've paid my dues."
(PHOTO BY ROY BLAKEY)

HILDEGARD KNEF (*with the author*)
"I have been so close to death that now just
growing old would be a luxury." (PHOTO BY OLIVIER REBBOT)

LOUISE FLETCHER
"I'm American clear through, and I know about winning."
(UPI)

PEARL BAILEY
"I've cared about other people all my life, and I won't stop, but now I'm gonna start carin' about me."
(WIDE WORLD PHOTOS)

GEORGE BURNS (*with Gracie Allen*)
"She was the genius, not me."
(PHOTO COURTESY OF THE NATIONAL BROADCASTING COMPANY, INC.)

MELINA MERCOURI (*with Jules Dassin, right*)
"It's more than just loving your country. It's in the blood."
(UPI)

LILLIAN HELLMAN
"I've never seen any of the people who testified against me. I even
try not to speak to them, but that gets embarrassing at parties."
(PHOTO BY RICHARD DE COMBRAY)

MARTIN RITT (*with Woody Allen*)
"I'm a political animal."
(REPRINTED WITH PERMISSION OF COLUMBIA PICTURES)

JACQUELINE SUSANN
(*with the author*)
When she was there, she was
really *there*.
(PHOTO BY L. ARNOLD
WEISSBERGER)

BETTE DAVIS
"I'm the nicest goddam dame
who ever lived."
GLENDA JACKSON
"I've long since outgrown the
crushes I had on film stars as a child,
but Davis is still impressive."

MABEL MERCER
(*with Mrs. Roy Wilkins, Ellis Amburn, and Roy Wilkins, right*)
At 75 . . . a night to remember.
(PHOTO BY PAUL HOSEFROS/NYT PICTURES)

CAROL CHANNING (*with the author*)
"I don't mind critics who want to be controversial, but I
hate dishonesty." (PHOTO BY L. ARNOLD WEISSBERGER)

Lillian Hellman

Mark Twain used to say honor was something you get after you're dead. But tonight on Broadway, the lights will go on at the Circle in the Square, honoring Lillian Hellman at the height of her life and craft "for her contribution to the theater, to literature and to the protection of civil liberties." No tribute has ever been or will be more deserved. Lillian Hellman is an oak among saplings.

Warren Beatty, Jane Fonda, Ellen Burstyn, Jason Robards, Maureen Stapleton, Irene Worth and Mike Nichols are some of the people who will be reading and performing excerpts and songs from her plays *(The Children's Hour, The Little Foxes, The Lark, Another Part of the Forest, The Autumn Garden, Watch on the Rhine, The Searching Wind, Toys in the Attic, Regina* and *Candide)* and books *(An Unfinished Woman* and *Pentimento).* The applause will all be for a great American writer, but the money will go to the Committee for Public Justice, an organization she founded five years ago to support the Bill of Rights and protect private citizens against threats to their constitutional rights and liberties.

"Times are getting dangerously close to McCarthyism again," she was saying a few days ago over coffee in her book-lined eagle's aerie above Park Avenue, "and some group had to be formed to wake people up. We've existed on peanuts, but we've done good work. We held a conference on the FBI that so disturbed J. Edgar Hoover he wrote a seven-page letter to us. We did others on the grand jury, Watergate, the CIA, invasions of privacy and the Justice Department, and we hope to expand to cover everything that menaces the public of this nation. We're even investigating fish toxins. We've had a few grants, but foundation money is scarce now, and we're not always the most attractive group to ask for aid. But it is my belief that we need every protection we can get, and this group carries more than its own weight. McCarthyism was resurfacing under Nixon, but thank God some of us saw the handwriting on the wall."

When trouble surfaces, so does Lillian. From the Spanish Civil War to the McCarthy witch hunts, she has always been on the front lines. She herself was blacklisted from 1948 to 1956. She worked in the theater but was wiped out in Hollywood. "I was very broke by that time, and the scars of that period still show today. Some people have a forgive-and-forget attitude, but I feel very sharply about it. I've never seen any of the people who testified against me. I even try not to speak to them, but that gets embarrassing at parties. Too many lives got mangled for the wrong reasons. It was a very cruel time, and if it ever happens again, it will make McCarthy look like a runt. Everyone you know who ever signed any bill on civil rights will be in big trouble. We have to fight to make sure that never happens. The tribute is really to the work the committee has done. I was worried and embarrassed at first, but I've worked very hard for this cause and if we can raise some money, it's worth it."

These are dog days for Hellman. She's just returned to the city from her pastoral home in Martha's Vineyard to put the finishing touches on a new book about the McCarthy period, and her life is at sixes and sevens. "It's very short, about thirty thousand words. I call it *Scoundrel Time.* It's mostly about me. I've tried to write about that ghastly period be-

fore, but this time I've forgotten about historical back-
grounds and stuck to personal feelings, and I think it's
worked out better."

She rises at dawn, markets at eight, works from nine to
one and knocks it off for the rest of the day. "The older I get,
the more tired at night I am. I don't go out much anymore.
I don't enjoy small talk, and people bore me. I go to parties
and find myself walking out of the room in the middle of a
conversation."

Those hard-drinking years with Dashiell Hammett are
long ago. She has a scotch before dinner or maybe a martini,
but "I haven't been good and drunk in eight years. It's very
funny. One night in Martha's Vineyard, I said to myself,
'Who says you have to go bed?' So I got good and drunk and
woke up the next morning on the staircase. I thought my
neck was broken, and I couldn't move my arms and I had
a cold and the hangover of the universe, and that's when I
knew I wasn't young anymore."

But despite her formidable reputation for being tough
and tyrannical, there's another side to Lillian Hellman that
is not often publicized. She is very emotional and feminine
and easily moved by the plight of others. In many ways, she's
younger than the first thrush of spring. "I am sixty-nine
years old, and *Who's Who* is always getting it wrong. I hate
being sixty-nine. I'd like to be young again, and I pay heavy
penalties for that. I am my own toughest critic. I look back
on the body of my work and see so many, many things I'd
redo. I've grown rather frightened of rereading myself. It
makes me inhibited. Sometimes I can remember what emotion was going through my mind at the time I wrote certain
scenes and passages. Other lines and chapters seem to have
been written by someone I've never met.

"Two years ago I did a TV interview with Bill Moyers,
based on an agreement that I would read parts of *Pentimento* aloud. He had selected passages from the 'Julia'
chapter. Now, I had written 'Julia' with enormous difficulty
for too many reasons to go into here or anywhere else. But
when I started to read, I started to cry, and we had to stop
the program. I had to take an hour off and rest. It was the
most shocking thing that ever happened to me in public.

Verbalizing your own words—something triggers emotions you can hide when you're at the typewriter. A psychiatrist once told me something very revealing about myself. I was too young to understand what he meant at the time, but now I see the insight. He said I look at myself as though I'm a total stranger."

She always had her own mind, her own wits and instincts, and has never been easily influenced by the fads and fashions of the day. She can be very temperamental and stubborn, as many former colleagues in the theater can testify, but she doesn't suffer fools easily. "It's really hard to see yourself as others see you. If you're not a fool, you don't see yourself as famous or great or a genius or any of those tags. I've been told I accept praise ungraciously, but the truth is I simply don't know how to say thank you in an interesting way. I want to be praised and flattered desperately, but when it happens, I feel embarrassed. I've been loathed and dismissed by so many people through the years that I tend to be suspicious. It might not last, I tell myself, and it usually doesn't. I've had too many failures to get a big head this late in life. My problem is I always took the successes for granted and worried too much about the failures."

She's a woman of great wisdom, a strength that shines through in her work. But she's suffered for what she's learned. "I pick up a newspaper and read about the two or three greatest American playwrights, and I'm not listed as one of them. That's painful. But the theater is a place of fashion and whim. I think I knew that from the beginning, but it's hard to recognize the weaknesses in something when you love it so much."

Lately, she's getting the kind of praise usually reserved for funeral orations, though a friend recently visited her mother's home town, Demopolis, Alabama, and looked up an elderly aunt at Lillian's request.

"I'm a friend of your niece's," he said when the old woman came to the door.

"Which niece?" she asked suspiciously.

"Lillian Hellman," he said.

"We don't like her," said the aunt, slamming the door in his face.

Neither did Tallulah Bankhead, who feuded with Lillian from the opening night of *The Little Foxes* until the day she died. "That hatred was mutual," admits Hellman, "but we did have a brief reconciliation at Truman Capote's famous party. I was sorry about the reunion later because it had been so boring." She has always spoken her mind.

She tries to hide it, but a bitterness creeps through when she talks about the theater. "I was an instant success with *The Children's Hour*, and it was hard to duplicate success after that. There was a long period of my life when I was totally ignored and then forgotten. I kept picking myself up and trying again. The sad truth is that now I've had enough and I never want to go near the theater again. The disillusionment set in with *Candide*. I was forced to work fast, which is against my nature, and told how to work in a form I didn't care for. The show was a spectacular failure, even with Dorothy Parker, John Latouche and Leonard Bernstein all working together with me. It certainly did not feel like we were creating a cult show at the time. It was a very upsetting experience. I have seen the Harold Prince revival, and it is not the way I ever saw *Candide*. It's too gimmicky and cute for my taste. But very pleasant."

The final nail in the coffin came with her last play, *My Mother, My Father and Me*, which flopped in 1963. "It was a black comedy that was ahead of its time. Gower Champion was replaced by Arthur Penn, so we had two different styles of direction; the casting was wrong; we opened during a newspaper strike. I began to see that timing is everything in theater, and I have to work at my own pace. I'm not one of those people who can sit in a hotel room in Boston and bang out a new scene in one night. I began to see myself in relation to the theater as a stranger in a hard, alien world. I didn't see life the way other people did; I didn't laugh at the same jokes others found amusing. When you're young, you tend to blame other people for these things, but now I blame only myself. With books, I stand as the lone creator of my work, and the result is much more rewarding."

She prefers movies to plays now and rarely goes to the theater. "The past eight or nine years have produced very few things on the stage I've wanted to see. I get bored and irritable and walk out impatiently after the first act. It breaks my heart. The theater has got to improve in some country, somewhere. It can't go on being dull and irrelevant, in this sad decline forever. But I don't think the change will occur on Broadway. I used to think I was the only one who felt this way, but last spring I had a pair of tickets to something, and I couldn't find anyone to take me. Everyone I called said, 'Thank you, but I can't bear the thought of being trapped in a theater all evening.' The theater requires a formal commitment I am no longer prepared to make."

Born in New Orleans, she's one of that special breed of southern Jews with dignity "and none of that junk about proving yourself. Dashiell Hammett always said I was the only Jew he knew who was also a Puritan." Last year, she was sitting in the Pontchartrain Hotel staring from her window, when suddenly she exclaimed: "I'm looking right down on the house I was born in. I had diphtheria when I was three years old and spent an entire year on that porch!"

It's the constant rediscovery in herself that charges her work with distinction. She has pruned away the clutter. Tallulah Bankhead used to nastily say Lillian Hellman looked like George Washington. Tallulah was wrong. She only lives like him—with humility, courage, truthfulness and, after tonight, the honor that is justly hers whether she wants it or not.

Jacqueline Susann

I sit in the lemon yellow library, twenty-three stories above
Central Park, staring at the bookcase. Stuffed between *The
Brothers Karamazov* and *The History of Dirty Words* is a
peculiar volume of unusual size, simply bound in copper.
The words on its spine say: JACQUELINE SUSANN (1921–1974)
I pick it up. It is cold and heavy, and when I turn it upside
down, I can feel the hermetically sealed ashes and splinters
of bone inside, moving softly around like bread crumbs.
That is all there is left of the most famous fiction writer in
the history of the world. The finality sets in hard, and it is
a long time before I can swallow.

I look around the room. In an atmosphere where the celebrated and the rich and powerful people soared through her
parties the way her books about them soared to the top of
the best-seller lists, an unnatural calm has asserted itself
upon the once-gay ambiance like bad breath in a crowded
elevator. The kitchen fridge that always gushed forth caviar
and champagne is almost empty, except for a can of Tab and
the limp plastic bag of ice from a local delicatessen. In a
corner where I once watched Barbara Walters move in for

the kill with Clifford Irving, only a framed best-seller list from *The New York Times* remains as a memory of the good old days.

Then I see Irving. It was never just Jackie. It was always Jackie and Irving. Now Irving Mansfield, whose marriage to a flaming success lasted thirty years, sits unshaven, quietly feeding the poodle and fingering through the stacks of hospital bills and telegrams from people like the Duchess of Windsor and Princess Grace of Monaco. It was Irving who gave up his own career as a television producer and made Jackie five million dollars and a household name overnight. And it is Irving who will carry on the legacy she left behind. He can do it.

It makes me feel good, knowing that. Because Jackie Susann is dead, but not gone. "It's a pity nobody ever erects a monument to businessmen and housewives," she used to say. "Songwriters live on every time you put a quarter in a juke box. Actors' movies are run forever on the Late Show. Painters hang in museums as reminders to future generations of art lovers. And writers live on bookshelves. I'm lucky, because even after I'm gone, I'll still be around. But what about the ordinary people?"

There was never anything ordinary about Jackie Susann. She had a comfortable childhood near Philadelphia's Rittenhouse Square, where her father, a portrait painter named Robert Susann, got $5,000 a commission from society matrons, merchant princes, and Booth Tarkington. Her mother, Rose, was a retired public-school teacher. When Jackie was in the fifth grade, her teacher tested her I.Q. at 140 and told her mother, "Jackie should be a writer. She breaks all the rules, but it works." An only child, she was always obsessed with carrying on the family name and decided the best way to be famous was to become an actress. When she was sixteen, her parents gave her a train ticket to New York and some good advice. "Be a people-watcher," said her father. "And always give people a second chance." Her first major role was with Eddie Cantor in *Banjo Eyes*, which opened Christmas night, 1941, at the Mark Hellinger Theatre. Jackie played Cantor's secretary. A week before the show opened, Cantor took her to Lindy's and informed her: "There are several revisions being made in the show. We're cutting one of your two scenes." Jackie started to cry. "But, Mr. Cantor, this is my big moment in the show." "Sorry," said the star, "but it's out." Then Jackie got mad. She threw a plate of scrambled eggs in his face. "Gee," said Cantor, wiping the yolks off his eyebrows, "I didn't know you didn't like scrambled eggs." They both fell apart with laughter, and Jackie kept both of her two scenes. From the beginning, she wasn't afraid of anything.

The acting career didn't work out. She tried to follow her father's advice and be a people-watcher, but she was too pretty and too glamorous, so she always ended up playing rich divorcées who got murdered in the first act. She didn't care. She was having lunch with Walter Winchell, dinner with Billy Rose, and keeping the Susann name alive. She married Irving when he was making $250 a week producing Fred Allen's radio show and they made all the columns. But Jackie wasn't satisfied. She wasn't famous enough. One day she flew into a temper because George Abbott turned her down for a part, and Eddie Cantor told her, "Kid, if you'd throw all that energy into something that would make you a success, they'd all say, 'We could've had her and we blew it!' " Jackie made that her personal philosophy and started writing.

She always refused to admit her age. One day she'd be forty-two, the next day forty-five. "Just say I was born in November 1963 because that's when my first book, *Every Night Josephine*, came out," she'd say. Write what you know, Irving told her, and all she knew was her poodle. Josephine was no ordinary poodle. She was a social-climbing canine Cassandra who breakfasted with Laurence Harvey, took tea with the Duke and Duchess of Windsor, dined with Greta Garbo, and slept in Richard Burton's bed. Jackie spent nine years writing 240 pages about her that sold 35,000 copies and 1,700,000 paperbacks. It was her favorite book and when she died she was hard at work on a sequel, to be called *Good Night, Sweet Princess*, about "Irving and me and the further adventures of the dog who owned us." Josephine died in 1970, at the age of sixteen, and her ashes, like her Mom's, remain in a book. The difference is that Josephine's book is no bigger than a paperback and it rests on the kitchen cabinet next to the new poodle's doggie biscuits. Jackie's book is the size of an encyclopedia and rests in the center of a wall covered with best-selling editions of her own four works translated into thirty-nine foreign languages. Jackie always believed in the natural order of things.

If the literary saga of Jacqueline Susann began with *Every Night Josephine,* so did her tragic medical history. When she finished the book, she took her mother, Rose, on a trip around the world. On Christmas Eve, 1962, she was in Hong Kong. Sitting in the bathtub, she felt a lump in her right breast. She called her mother to come in and feel it. Mrs. Susann, without blinking an eye, summoned all those years of strength as a schoolteacher and calmly said, "Jackie, you've got to see a doctor." Jackie hated doctors, but she was worried. She called Irving from Honolulu. First, the good news: *Every Night Josephine* had been bought by Doubleday. Then, the bad news: Irving had made an appointment for a biopsy with a New York doctor upon her return.

Jackie put up a fight. Secretly, she was afraid Irving would stop loving her if she had a mastectomy. It was the fear many women face daily, and when the chips were down Jackie was no different from any other mortal. Irving said, "Jackie, I don't care if you have one breast, two breasts, or none. I love you and they have terrific bras, and who cares? Don't do it for yourself, do it for *me.*" It was malignant. The doctor recommended psychoanalysis, which he described as "customary in cancer cases." Jackie said, "What's a shrink gonna do—teach me how to get my breast back?" For the first time, they all laughed. The ice was broken. Six days later, she was home. Two months later, she was driving a car and playing nine holes of golf with an 18 handicap. By summer, she had won the Class C golf championship at the Alpine Country Club in New Jersey and was back at the typewriter working on the first draft of *Valley of the Dolls.* (None of her readers, not even her closest friends, ever suspected that when she was describing the mastectomy in *Valley of the Dolls,* she was writing about her own breast surgery.)

Valley of the Dolls made instant history, as did all of her books. It sold 25 million copies, stayed on the best-seller list for sixty-five weeks, and is now in its fifty-fifth paperback printing. *The Love Machine,* issued in 1969, on the list for thirty-seven weeks, sold 10 million copies, and *Once Is Not Enough,* which was to be her final book, had a guaranteed first printing of 150,000 copies before it even hit the book-stores. It went on to sell almost 4 million paperbacks in the United States alone, and is still going strong in its fourteenth printing. Jacqueline Susann became the Wonder Woman of the publishing industry.

For ten years, she went without cobalt treatments and chemotherapy, thinking the cancer cells had been arrested, and lived an absolutely normal life. Two years ago, on a yacht in Palm Beach owned by Walter Annenberg's sister Harriet Ames, she developed a strange cough. She thought she had bronchitis. She went to Mt. Sinai to cure the cough. I'll never forget the day I arrived at the hospital unexpect-edly to bring Jackie some cheer-up balloons. The nurse said I could go right in, as though the patient inside was suffering from nothing more serious than a hangnail. Jackie was in an oxygen tent. Irving was white as Banquo's ghost. The jig was up. They had removed a piece of her lung and the prognosis was negative. Cancer of the lungs and bronchii.

Every day for six weeks she endured the cobalt and chem-otherapy treatments, and for a while they really did think they had arrested the malignancy. Through it all, Jackie remained moot. Those of us who knew, respected her need for secrecy, her fierce pride and her gnawing terror of being treated like a sick and wounded animal. She had a consum-ing pride, and whatever her critics thought of her (some-times they were brutal) she never wanted sympathy. She kept her cancer a secret, just as she had kept the existence of her autistic twenty-one-year-old son, Guy, a secret from the prying press and curious outsiders. She was determined to live out whatever days were left with no sad songs on her phonograph, no tears in her beer.

For years, Jackie had been making secret bargains with God. Everyone thought writing was easy for her; some of her angriest critics accused her of turning out novels like cheese omelets. But there were many nights in the pent-house above Central Park when she stalked the living room alone, unable to sleep, the blood pounding in her temples from the pain-killers she took—moments in the early morning hours full of anguish and desperation, when nothing worked. She would watch the sunrise over the park, talk to the sculpture of her father that dominated the living room ("Don't go away, I'm getting a fresh drink, and I'll be right back," she'd say) and make her bargains with God. She had an autistic child. She had eye infections, double pneumonia, bronchial asthma, and now cancer. But she never complained. She stopped smoking in January, 1968, paying off one debt. Once she gave up drinking for Lent. One year she gave up hashed brown potatoes for twelve whole months. She promised God if she made the best-seller list with *Valley of the Dolls,* she'd give up smoking. Then she got so nervous going on the talk shows she had a cigarette in both hands. So she amended the promise. She'd give God a month for every week she stayed on the list. Well, who would have thought she'd been on it for sixty-five weeks? Then Irving had a polyp removed from his intestines and she promised God if it wasn't malignant she'd give up smoking for good. She finally made it, unaware that cancer was already spreading throughout her body. Irving used to kid her about those bargains, gingerly chiding: "You're treating God like he was the William Morris office."

But Jackie plunged on, more determined than ever to immortalize her father's name. When *Once Is Not Enough* was published, the dedication read "To Robert Susann, who would understand." She left the hospital on the day of publication, drove straight to the *Today* show at 7 A.M., and chatted gaily with Gene Shalit as though nothing had happened. Instead of taking to her bed and playing Camille, she launched a nationwide publicity tour. In every city, she had the name of a chemotherapist who performed painful treatments between lunches and interviews with the press, many of them hostile. They attacked her for riding around on her book-promotion tours in a chauffeured limousine, and she never said a word. Secretly, she felt like a snob. But Irving kept the car in twenty-four-hour service for protective purposes. You never could tell what might happen at two or four in the morning if she had to be rushed to the hospital.

When Jackie arrived in London for the British publication of *Once Is Not Enough,* the headlines screamed: "D-Day Has Arrived!" Little did anyone know that Jackie's own D-Day was approaching. The day for her chemotherapy treatment at Hammersmith Hospital came and Jackie didn't want to be recognized or asked any embarrassing questions by the press, so she took a taxi, wearing a black wig and sunglasses. At the hospital, the nurse excused herself for a moment and while the doctor was applying a Band-Aid to the anonymous cancer patient, the nurse returned with a tiny package and asked quietly, "Miss Susann, would you autograph my copy of *Once Is Not Enough*?" Jackie laughed that dark purple laugh of hers. That's how famous she had become. Disguises and phony registrations meant nothing. She was recognized everywhere. It was her sense of humor that got her through everything, plus the most indomitable will power I have ever witnessed. Even in her agony, she didn't want to miss anything. One night in London she loaded herself with Demerol and went to dinner with Doris Day and Melina Mercouri because although she felt lousy, she knew the press would be there and she didn't want the reporters to start rumors if she didn't show up. She stayed up all night talking to her close friend Doris Day and told her the truth. Doris was one of the few who knew and she kept the secret. A few weeks before Jackie died, Doris flew to New York to see her. Jackie was already in a coma. Irving warned the perky star that she would have to give her brightest performance since *Pillow Talk* and she did. It wasn't until she left the room that the girl who has often been called a walking daisy broke down and sobbed all alone in the hospital corridor.

It was like that with all of us who knew her. Jackie was loyal beyond description to her friends. She once said to me: "All I care about is my husband, my friends and my work—in that order. I like pretty clothes, but I hate shopping. I once had a lot of jewelry and everything was stolen. I never replaced it. I had a watch from Eddie Cantor that was inscribed 'To my sixth daughter, Jackie!' and I was so upset about losing it that I developed a philosophy right then that I would never care that much about material possessions again. If I die, my royalties will take care of Irving and my son for the rest of their lives. That's all money means."

She never threw money around recklessly. She developed a crush on Emilio Pucci and wore his banana-split nightmares long after they ceased to be fashionable. "Well, they're all paid for," she'd explain. "I can't just throw them all out." She had four mink coats and gave them all away. She never learned to cook, but preferred room service and sending out for Chinese. She never gave lavish dinner parties, and if she entertained a publisher or visiting bookstore manager, she always went to "21" or Danny's Hideaway in New York, or Chasen's and Matteo's in Los Angeles. She never met anyone for lunch. "You can't be a writer and go to lunch," she'd scold when I'd ask her to meet me somewhere in the middle of the day. "It takes an hour to take a bath, then fifteen minutes to get there, then two hours talking gossip, then you see the same faces and come home at four drunk and exhausted, and have to take a two-hour nap. The whole day is shot and you've got nothing but blank pages in the typewriter."

Whether the critics liked her work or not, Jackie took her writing very seriously. She could be quite vain ("Maybe *Gone With the Wind* sold more copies than I have, but they didn't keep records in those days") and developed some lasting hatreds for critics she didn't respect. She once demolished John Simon on a talk show, threw a drink in Johnny Carson's face at a party (they later became friends), and openly attacked Dick Cavett for insulting her on camera. "With a little help, he could grow up to be Mason Reese," she sniffed. But even when she was bitchy, she did it with ladylike aplomb. The famous feud with Truman Capote, which began when he called her "a truckdriver in drag" on the Carson show, ended when she killed him off with charm. Appearing on the same show a few weeks later, Carson asked her what she thought of Truman. "I think he was one of our finest Presidents," she smiled sweetly, later adding that Capote was too fragile and vulnerable for her to openly cudgel. "Besides," she beamed, "an eagle never chases a butterfly."

What pained most critics was not what she wrote but how

much money she made doing it. They didn't review her novels; they reviewed her. Always quick with a wise retort, Jackie once turned to a TV interviewer who had insinuated she was no Tolstoy and chirped: "There is a distinct differ-ence—*my* books are interesting!" Millions of readers thought so. A new Jacqueline Susann novel meant seductive prose and succulent dialogue, lived and spoken by dying fashion models, ruthless television executives, horny as-tronauts, lonely millionaires, drug-crazed stars of nude rock musicals, suicidal Palm Beach hostesses, sex-starved secre-taries, incestuous Mike Todd legends, reclusive lesbian movie stars, macho-drenched Ernest Hemingway writers, and speed-injecting Dr. Feelgoods. The inside cover of *The Love Machine* pants: "In this hidden world . . . Robin Stone is driven from those who love him to a series of harrowing experiences, a brutal confrontation with a prostitute, a gro-tesque encounter with a beautiful transvestite in Hamburg's red-light district . . ." Never a dull moment, although not perhaps the kind of literature that wins honorary degrees or Pulitzer Prizes.

Jackie cried all the way to the bank. When anyone asked if she thought her writing was important, she had her an-swer already memorized. "I don't write for artsy-craftsy crit-ics. I write in order to communicate. A good writer is one who produces books that people read—someone who com-municates. So if I'm selling millions, I must be good." Se-cretly, she was furious about her critics. But the fact that she communicated with more readers than any other fiction writer in the history of publishing (a fact now substantiated by the *Guinness Book of World Records*) will be the final test of her importance. Her books were better than most people credited them with being. They had warmth, humor, wit, sharply defined characters, complex relationships, star-tling plot twists, hypnotic story lines, and enough thinly disguised public figures to keep cocktail parties guessing and every movie star in Hollywood fighting duels to get into the movie versions for months after casting had already been completed. If there were no simple folks in her novels, it was because Jackie didn't know any simple folks. Her father had taught her how to listen, and many of the most lurid passages in her work came out of actual events in her own living room because of her powers of concentration, her total recall, her ear for dialogue, and her ability to get it all down on paper.

It's possible that time will be kinder to Jacqueline Susann than her contemporary critics have been. She was, in a sense, like Guy de Maupassant, Victor Hugo, even F. Scott Fitzgerald—none of whom were ever respected in their own time for the rich stories they told. In one day, Jackie outsold Solzhenitsyn, Graham Greene, Mary Stewart, and the Bible. Not exactly a way to win friends among the critics. But Jackie earned her success. She worked hard for it and fought like a tiger to maintain it. She began all of her books with yellow scratch paper in her typewriter, sitting on an orange leather chair covered with a white towel because the upholstery made her fanny perspire. Then she'd type on the backs of press releases (with her millions, she was paranoid about saving paper). Thousands of pages came out of her typewriter without the aid of a secretary. She never hired a professional typist. Every word in her books was typed with two fingers, using the old hunt-and-peck system. Then she would correct the yellow pages by hand. As the books progressed, they traveled through various drafts on blue, pink, and, finally, white paper. Then Irving would read the finished first draft and Jackie would Xerox it herself for the publisher. She was a natural-born editor. She always knew instinctively when something was wrong. Everything she ever wrote after *Josephine* was bought sight unseen. She never auditioned. She wrote by herself, nobody saw it until she was ready, then she'd sit down and tell Irving "Welcome to the Monday night fights" and he'd read it and they'd talk about it. She was the talent, he was the businessman. He negotiated the deals and brought in the most colossal contracts ever drawn up in the history of publishing, but he never signed anything until Jackie had given him final approval. No contract was ever drawn in which she didn't find a flaw that could be improved—and she was always right!

After a book was finished, Jackie logged more air miles promoting it than Henry Kissinger on peace missions. She stormed off talk shows if she got on at the wrong time and opened up a whole new tradition for writers who used to get the last ten minutes to sell their books. It was a block of time, when the talk show hosts thought everyone was asleep, Jackie called "the writer's ghetto." She changed all that. She not only wrote books, but taught sleepy publishers and timid authors how to sell them as well. More writers than you will ever know learned valuable lessons from her techniques. Her loyalties to other writers were fierce. For friends or authors she admired, she purchased twenty-five copies of their books at all of the bookstores that reported to the best-seller lists. She phoned columnists and store managers to prepare for a new author's arrival on promotion tours. Nobody asked for these favors. She just did them.

She advised me from the publication date of my first book until the day she died. I never signed a contract without consulting Jackie and Irving. She took Elia Kazan and Barbara Walters by the hand and introduced them to bookstore personnel. She helped James Kirkwood, Kurt Vonnegut, and Mario Puzo. She defended Irving Wallace and Harold Robbins every time they got a bad review, and never dissipated her energy feuding with other best-selling authors. Once, at a Richard Rodgers concert, she was approached by James Michener, who bluntly announced: "I've hated you since May 8, 1966." Jackie was stunned. "What happened May 8, 1966?" she asked. "That," laughed Michener, "is the date you knocked me out of first place on the best-seller list." They became instant friends.

It made her furious when major storytellers were relegated to capsule reviews in the back of *The New York Times Book Review* and Joyce Carol Oates got the front page. "She writes a new novel every three days," Jackie complained. "Anything that takes less than three years has got to be a bore." She was right, of course. She was no towering intellectual (the only time she was ever floored for a comeback, George S. Kaufman called her "apocryphal" on TV and she didn't know what the word meant) but she was well read. She was an expert on art, medicine, and psychology, but she never played games. When she read novels, she wanted them to be as juicy as her own. "Life is too short to waste time being bored," she always told me. Once, on a plane to

Los Angeles, she was determined to tackle *The Gulag Archipelago.* She read studiously for about an hour, closed the book, turned to Irving, and sighed: "How soon are you gonna be finished with *Playboy?*"

A Jackie Susann quote often meant millions of dollars in revenue to other authors. Publishers sent her everything before publication, figuring a Susann blurb in a newspaper ad was worth more than a good review. One day her friend and publisher, Oscar Dystel, president of Bantam Books, sent her an advance copy of *Portnoy's Complaint.* Irving was on one side of the bed reading the *Times;* Jackie was on the other side reading her new book. "Oh, my God!" she exclaimed. Then, "I don't believe this!" Irving put down the paper and asked her what was wrong. "Every time you turn the page," said Jackie, "this guy is masturbating!" A few weeks later, she was asked for a quote. "Well," said Jackie, "I think Philip Roth is a good writer, but I wouldn't want to shake hands with him." It became part of the language in twenty-four hours, and everybody was repeating it. She brought the same snap to publishing that she brought to the parties she attended. When she was there, she was really *there.*

She was tough. But she was a marshmallow inside. She worked hard, she played hard, and she hurt hard. She never forgave Gloria Steinem, whom she admired, for attacking her unsympathetic attitudes toward Women's Lib. And she never recovered from the hatchet jobs she got from two reporters. Irma Kurtz misquoted her in the British magazine *Nova.* Sara Davidson came to interview her for *Harper's,* used her phone to call her mother long distance, told her all of her own personal problems, said, "Jackie, I can't begin to tell you how nice you've been to me," then murdered her in print. Jackie did a slow burn, then got even in her own way. When *Once Is Not Enough* came out, it featured a neurotic female character described as "ugly as Tiny Tim." Jackie called her Sara Kurtz.

These are the little things about the private life of Jacqueline Susann nobody knew. From 1959 to the very end, her second home was the lush Beverly Hills Hotel. The first thing she did each time she checked into her permanent suite (135–136, and they always kept it ready) was call the operators and catch up on their domestic problems. Swen at the pool kissed her hello. The bellboys grinned, "Hi, Jackie!" The midget phone call announcer in the Polo Lounge gave her stock market tips. The hairdressers in the beauty parlor knocked the biggest stars out of their appointments with, "Jackie's coming!" Jackie watched the price of her suite gradually increase from $65 to $106 a day. On her last trip, she urged Irving to go ahead of her to the dining room. "Why one at a time?" asked Irving, ready for anything. "Because," came the reply, "if we go out together, they'll change the price of the room while we're gone."

One of my most vivid memories of Jackie occurred during one of her visits there. She had developed a fondness for Sharon Tate during the filming of *Valley of the Dolls*, even appeared in her funeral scene in a cameo role. Sometime later, on August 8, 1969, Jackie was sitting by the pool at the Beverly Hills Hotel when Sharon called and invited her to the house for a late drink. She was dressing when I arrived unexpectedly. She phoned Sharon, told her I was in town, and Sharon said by all means drop by together. We decided on an early dinner instead, and retired early. The next morning, August 9, it was a bright and glorious Sunday. We met at the swimming pool for lunch and Johnny Carson called us both with the news. Sharon had been murdered the night before. Jackie turned white. With the horror of what had happened came the dawning realization that if we had gone to Sharon Tate's that night we might have been part of the headlines. It was one of the ironies that ran through her life.

Jackie had no regrets. "If I die tomorrow," she said, "I've had it all." She faced death the way she faced her critics. And nobody knew about the good things she had done to pave the way for a peaceful passing. She turned over all of her money on British talk shows to the surviving families of men killed in a coal-mining disaster. She gave away huge percentages of her royalties to autistic children, afflicted in the same way as her son, Guy. She canceled vacations when she needed rest because the actors needed her presence on their movie sets and appeared on panels because her being

there meant brownie points for the program chairmen. She
was a sucker for anything involving animals. When Doris
Day staged her charity bazaar for animal shelters on the
backlot of the CBS-TV studios, it was Jackie who phoned
Joan Crawford and talked her into donating eighteen thousand Pepsi-Colas, then stood in the hot sun for three and a
half hours after one of her torturous chemotherapy treatments, autographing five hundred copies of *Every Night
Josephine* which she herself had donated free.

Mike Frankovich once took her to the Palm Beach Casino
in London, where she won $1,100 at the crap table. There
was a honeymoon couple at the same table. They had lost
$10. "Here's a wedding present," said Jackie, handing them
$200 in chips. Then she tipped the stick man $100 and dis-
tributed the rest of the wealth among the hotel staff at the
Dorchester. Another time, she gave a friend in trouble (now
a famous jet-set name) $1,000 for an abortion, no questions
asked. "If anybody asks me for money," she always said, "I
never ask why. If they've got the guts to go through the
humiliation of asking for it, I owe them the courtesy not to
embarrass them further by asking what they need it for."

Jackie had nothing to be ashamed of. And it was the little
people who let her know it. On one of her last tours, she
talked to the book truck drivers at Chicago's Charles Levy
Circulating Company. It was an annual ritual. "The TV
shows are glamorous," she said, "but it's the little people
who get the books into the stores. They deserve a personal
visit, too." One of the drivers asked her when she'd have a
new book ready. She told him it would be about a year, and
he smiled. It was good to know, he told her, that in case of
a depression they could rely on her to keep their families
from starving. She'll be missed not only by her fans and
friends, but by a lot of people who don't even know their
debt to her.

The last book was never finished. Seven weeks before she
died, she developed a fever of 105 degrees. Irving called an
ambulance to rush her to the hospital. It's an uncanny tribute to Jackie's never-flagging sense of humor that on the way
to the antiseptic room from which she would never emerge,

she rallied long enough to look out of the window. "Look, Irving," she said groggily, "there's a car stopped at that red light that has a license plate JSM-5, just like ours." Irving yelled, "My God, you know something else—it's our car!" Somebody had stolen it from the garage.

It's a final irony that Jackie, even in death, was looking for a story. Hers had been a life of adventure and she had done it all. Two years earlier, her friend Anna Sosenko asked her pointedly: "If you had a choice—twenty more years of health or the past ten years of success—which would you take?" Jackie never flinched. "The last ten years of my life. I have lived it to the hilt."

She didn't really want to die. Toward the end, she got scared, which wasn't like her. She started playing solitaire, seeing how it would come out each time, dealing and redealing the cards, gambling with herself about how long she had to live. There were so many stories left unwritten, but all she had the strength for were the diaries, meticulously detailed, about the cancer and what she was going through. Publishers are offering Irving a king's ransom for the publication rights to those last pages from the typewriter of Jacqueline Susann, but it will be a long time before he has the courage to read them himself.

Jackie was in a coma for seven weeks. The last time she spoke to Irving, she opened her eyes long enough to say, "Hi, doll. Let's get the hell outta here." It's just the sort of thing one of her characters would say. Jackie was the best character she ever invented anyway. The day after she died, Harold Robbins appeared on the *Today* show to plug his new novel, and startled everybody by saying, "I don't want to discuss my new book—I want to talk about Jacqueline Susann." A week after she was gone, Irving paid $900 in secretarial fees (not counting postage) just acknowledging personal condolences, with ten 50-pound canvas bags from the post office still unopened. A lot of people miss her already.

Once, at a party, Jackie and I watched together as someone helped the late Noel Coward into an elevator, feeble and ill, a pallid forgery of his once-dapper self. Jackie turned to me with tears in her eyes and said, "Gosh, Rex, I hope I die before I grow old." Jacqueline Susann died at 8:01 P.M., Saturday, October 21, 1974, at Doctor's Hospital in New York City. She was fifty-three years old. She always got everything in life she wanted, but this is one wish she got too soon.

THE
SURVIVORS

Bette Davis

SAN FRANCISCO—They come and go in their sarongs and skates and sapphire sunglasses, but there is only one queen of the silver screen. She always was, still is, and always will be. She clawed her way to the top, and the nails are still sharp. "I was never, repeat *never,* a movie star on a level with Joan Crawford," seethes Bette Davis. "I was more like Katharine Hepburn and others who came from the theater because we could act."

Nostrils flare, eyes dilate like targets on a rifle range, and each word and gesture is emphasized by a blast of cigarette smoke that makes her look like she's walking in a cumulus cloud. It is 4:00 on a cool, sunny afternoon in San Francisco, and Bette Davis has a day off from shooting her eighty-fifth film, *Burnt Offerings.* It's one of those Gothic horrors about a family being driven to insanity and death by a spooky old house. Karen Black and Oliver Reed are the young couple, and Bette is the aunt. It is being directed entirely on location by a newcomer from TV, Dan Curtis.

The legendary Mother Goddam who brought Warner

Brothers to both its zenith and its knees paces the living room of her Victorian hotel suite like a caged jaguar.

"I feel like I've spent the past six weeks in jail. I brought my own coffee pot and my own picture frames from Connecticut to remind me of home, but I can't *wait* to get out of here! I love San Francisco because all the theater scenes in *All About Eve* were shot here, and it has always brought me luck. It's the great city of the future, even if it is right in the middle of a fault and they're expecting another earthquake any minute.

"But I hate locations. You work six days a week from 6 A.M. till 6 P.M., and it costs a fortune in food, hotel rooms, and transportation bills. The conditions are horrible, the money is tight and everything is total chaos. This film has been amateur night in Dixie. I said I'd never make another horror film after *Baby Jane,* and here I am in the biggest horror of them *all!*

"They've got a new way of making movies today, and it *stinks!* I've been in this business for forty-five years, and in all that time they haven't learned a goddam thing. They still make all the same mistakes—it's waste, waste, waste. This is a penny-wise, pound-foolish industry. My curse is that I've always been a perfectionist, and that doesn't exist anymore.

"The director's daughter on this film committed suicide and we had to shut down a week. Then the cameraman was fired because we couldn't see one thing on the screen, the rushes were so dark. That cost us two weeks of retakes. Karen Black showed up six months pregnant, so they had to remake her clothes because they didn't fit. She changes her makeup in the middle of a scene so nothing matches on the screen, she sleeps all day, never goes to rushes to see what she looks like, and you can't hear one bloody thing she says on the set. When I made movies, you could hear me in a tunnel! Oliver Reed comes piling into the hotel at 5 A.M., and he's on the set at six with the hangover of the world. He fell down a mountainside the other night playing bagpipes!

"He lives right across the hall. I called up the hotel manager and had six locks installed on my door. I never had a drink on a set in my life, and I never will—I'd drop dead before I did that to a company with money this tight.

"I just spent the last two days writhing and dying and looking like the wrath of God, and I planned the hair, the aging, the lines under the eyes, the falls on the floor—I spent weeks working out the movements for my death scene. They all think I'm crazy to work so hard. At six o'clock last night after dying all day I was so exhausted I couldn't move, and my makeup man wasn't even there to take my makeup off. He was out in the front yard playing cricket! I tell you, my kind of professionalism is *dead!*"

She pours coffee, she raises a window, she brushes off her hand, she lowers the window, she drops cigarette ashes all over her starched white denim hostess gown, she adjusts the solitaire game on the card table, she takes the phone off the receiver, she spots a bald man down by the swimming pool who looks like her third husband and lets out a roar, she slashes lipstick across her mouth like iodine, she empties ten ashtrays overflowing with butts—she is like a locomotive, puffing and smoldering through the room. It is clear to see why the small black-and-white movie screen was too small to hold her energy. She overpowers the room the way she spilled out from the edges of the screen. She is bigger than life.

"I argue with audiences on this point," she snarls. "The greatest thrill for me today is not movies, but traveling around the world with my one-woman evening of film clips and conversation. At the end, I invite questions from the audience, and somebody always says, 'You were better than the movies you made,' and somebody else says, 'The thing I remember most is that you smoked in every movie—long after the film is forgotten, we still remember you smoking,' and I say, 'You forget about all the heroines I played. I did not smoke in every movie. I played schoolteachers and housewives, too.'

"But something I have had to face is they did not want to see me as a middle-aged schoolteacher. Their image of me was a *bitch!* So if I played bitches, or certain types of women who were nervous or angry or full of energy, I worked with cigarettes as props. If you're a woman who smokes, you can't just smoke one in the first scene and never be seen smoking again in the whole movie! You've gotta *stream* it out of your mouth and blow it all over the *screen!*"

One doesn't exactly interview Bette Davis. One just sits back, coughs while the smoke screen builds into a tornado and lets her do all the talking. She's been through all the wars, carried all the flags, and earned the right to say anything she bloody well pleases. She is strong and tough; she is coy and flirtatious; she is crisp as lettuce and warm as cocoa. She is a million things to a million people, but she is not now and never has been a phony or a bore.

"I'm like a cat," she grins. "Throw me up in the air, and I'll always land on my feet. I spent my whole goddam life saying, 'Why should I apologize for being bright?' and I'm not stopping now. Bogart and I walked out of Warner Brothers sixteen times, but we survived. When horror movies came in, I did them instead of staying home like the other broads. When talk shows came in, I hated them, but I did them. When Warner Brothers sold its first batch of movies to TV twenty something years ago, sixty-five of them were *mine,* and I didn't get one penny in residuals. But I can't beef because millions of people today have seen those movies and I kept my whole career alive.

"I started in 1930 and made eighty-five movies, and now I've had it. I have no drive anymore. I'll never be poor, but I'll never be rich, either. Still, I wouldn't go to Switzerland and rob this country blind like the Burtons did. I couldn't sleep for the guilt. If we'd had the same lobby the gun-control lobby has, we'd be running the country, but actors are the most lily-hearted people who ever drew breath.

"So I am up to my ears in taxes and debts, and that's why I come out of my house in Connecticut every few years and work. I can hole up just so long, then I gotta get out and stir things up again. It's half for income, and half for *me.*"

Last year, she shattered her fans by closing in Philadelphia in a musical version of her film hit *The Corn Is Green.* The musical, which was bound for Broadway with millions of advance tickets already sold in anticipation of her return to the stage, was called *Miss Moffitt.* She becomes enraged when she talks about it.

"It was a mistake. The audiences stood up cheering and

screaming every night, but I knew it wasn't what they wanted. They wanted me to be a bitch, not a middle-aged schoolteacher. The songs were wonderful, I sang them and I was good at it, but it was nothing but hell. I had to carry the burden of the rewrites, and I spent three weeks in a hospital in traction from the nerves and tension. The monkey on your back when you're carrying a show is wicked.

"Joshua Logan finished me off in two weeks. He was terrified of the critics and started changing things on opening night in Philly. I had one year on the road to do those changes, but I couldn't work twelve hours a day and play a different show at night. They wanted me to learn forty pages in four days! I had to get my health back before I could concentrate on that kind of work. So we closed it down. I will never go near the stage again as long as I live!"

Now she's concentrating on her one-woman show, which has toured America and is now heading for four weeks of sold-out one-nighters in England, Wales, Scotland, Ireland, and the London Palladium. "When I started, I was scared, but now I love it. Nobody will ever know what that love and applause mean to me. Move on, never get repetitious, learn how to handle the audience—those are the things I believe in. I always walk out and say 'What a dump!' and that brings down the house. Then they know it's not going to be a pompous evening; it's going to be a ball!

"They've asked me everything. One woman asked me which of my four husbands was my favorite, and I said without blinking an eye, 'Obviously I had no favorite since I dumped them all!' The worst question was: 'What would you do if President Nixon came to your house for dinner?' I thought for a second and said, 'I'd do just like Baby Jane, and serve him a dead *rat!*'"

It's sad to see a woman with history for a middle name reduced to making movies with wall-eyed Karen Black, but on the day of her big death scene forty journalists showed up on the set. Bette roared at the publicity girl: "I won't see them. Tell them to interview Karen Black. She's the star!" Not one journalist wanted to interview anyone but Bette Davis.

"I rest my case," she sighs. "I'm the nicest goddam dame

who ever lived, but they made me the monster of the earth. They tried to blackmail me, they tried to run me out of Hollywood, they tried to ruin me, but I outfoxed them all. I made money and earned respect from the public and that's what makes a star. These kids today haven't got a chance.

"When I made *Dark Victory,* Jack Warner said, 'Who wants to see some dame go blind and die?' But they let me do it because I wanted it so much. They paid for three sound stages with that one. Now actors have become inconsequential. Directors are the stars, and that to me is sad. There are no roles, no stars, and no excitement left on the screen."

The last of a dying breed, she's already got her funeral plot bought and paid for at Forest Lawn. "It's the final irony," she shrieks. "From where I'll be buried, you can look right down and *spit* on Warner Brothers!" Don't hold your breath. She's sixty-seven, but I'm taking bets. Bette Davis will bury us all.

Mabel Mercer

Mabel Mercer, the grande dame of popular song who has influenced more singers than anyone in the history of music, was seventy-five years old last week. For three-quarters of a century, she's been the best thing that ever happened to the art of song, and four hundred of her friends and fans showed their appreciation by wearing their best diamonds and top hats to a birthday celebration high on top of the roof of the St. Regis Hotel. It was a night to remember.

It was sad that some of the biggest names who claim to have learned all they know from Mabel Mercer didn't show up. Frank Sinatra, Peggy Lee, and Leontyne Price sent telegrams. Sarah Vaughan, who was scheduled to sing a birthday song for Mabel, was missing. The Duchess of Windsor was too ill, Joe DiMaggio was too busy, and Cole Porter, George Gershwin, Jerome Kern, and Dorothy Parker were dead.

But there was enough glamour and music for all. The mayor's office gave her the key to the city. She deserved it. And while Alexis Smith, Teddi King, Arlene Francis, Julius Monk, Harold Arlen, Helen Merrill, Tom Tryon and Margaret Whiting feasted on diced cream chicken Truman Capote

and Cole Porter's personal recipe for strawberry mousse,
the world of show business sang and read their tributes like
the farewell scene in *Good-bye, Mr. Chips.* Leonard Bernstein said, "She is the eternal guardian of elegance in the
world of popular song." Warren Beatty said, "When you
hear her sing, you know, she becomes your wife, mother,
sister, mistress and accountant." High praise, indeed, for a
seventy-five-year-old woman, but Warren should know.

Sylvia Syms and Cy Coleman sang "The Best Is Yet to
Come," Thelma Carpenter did an old Twenties medley
from *Blackbirds* to signal the year she first met Mabel,
Bobby Short deserted his own piano bench to sing Cole
Porter standing up, and Mary Lou Williams played an ener-
getic version of my least favorite song, "My Funny Valentine," proving that in the hands of artists even banality can
seem sublime. With grace and warmth, the extraordinary
actress Marian Seldes read, with that melted chocolate voice
of hers, tributes from Alec Wilder, Bart Howard and Frank
Sinatra, who said, "Everything I know I learned from Mabel
Mercer." It was that kind of night.

But the best part of the evening happened around one,
when Mabel herself descended to the stage, sat on her Louis
Quinze throne, and paid everybody back by singing. She
would have sung all night, but the musicians' union wanted
to go home. It was enough. When she sang, the intelligence
and imagination brought tears to the eyes of grown men.
She knows everything worth knowing about the interpretation of lyrics, her selection of material is faultless, the sound
is that of a lonely cello behind a vocal line drawn with an
emotional artistry unmatched by any other singer. The
once-fine soprano has grown parched with the years, but the
impact is the same. While that favored four hundred stood
and cheered her birthday, I thought back to the beginnings
of my own association with the legendary Mabel and I realized that there has scarcely been a time in my life that I
haven't been aware of her greatness.

Years ago, in that pre-Beatles era before sweat was fashionable, when the Beautiful People read *Vanity Fair,* the
smart women wore gardenia corsages to Preston Sturges
movies, and nobody had ever heard of LSD, people were a

lot younger and the world was a sweeter place to be. Music was still something you could fall in love listening to, and Mabel was already a legend.

She was an elegant British lady from Burton-on-Trent, Staffordshire, who, shortly after she was out of her knickers, had already sung her way into the rich and fashionable bistro society of London and Paris, ending up at the equally legendary Bricktop's, where she became the darling of the roving geniuses of the restless Twenties. Hemingway, Sartre, F. Scott Fitzgerald, Edith Piaf, Gertrude Stein—they came every night and sat at her feet, listening to her polish off the sadly fading art of the popular song with the regal aplomb of a dispossessed duchess. Opera composer Gian-Carlo Menotti fell so in love with her voice that he wrote it into the libretto of *The Consul.* No matter where it is performed in the world, you will always hear the voice of Mabel Mercer on record as the Act One curtain rises.

Mabel's world was swanky. To outsiders like me, growing up in the claustrophobic atmosphere of small country towns, it was a world to read about on the newsstands of Greyhound bus depots in the pages of *Town and Country.* Everyone I knew was listening to Glenn Miller; I knew there was something else out there if someone would just show me where. In high school, when the others were off bopping to Fats Domino records at sock dances in the gym, I was home listening to Mabel Mercer, daydreaming about going to New York, where I figured sophisticated people sat up all night in gilt-edged cellars like the Blue Angel and "knew" things. I was young, but my beanstalk was halfway there.

Years later, when I finally got to New York, it was all over. Harlem was a slum. The Cotton Club was only a memory. No trees grew in Brooklyn, the Dodgers had moved to Los Angeles, Winchell was gone, and the "posh watering holes" in the East Fifties I had read about in the *New Yorker* had all either burned down or been turned into Italian restaurants. Mabel Mercer had moved to a farm in upstate New York to water her zinnias. The era I had come to see had passed away and I hadn't been around for the funeral.

The Seventies are bringing it all back and New York is once again a swinging place to be. Everything has changed, yet when Mabel Mercer sings, nothing has changed at all. Listening to her lush, round tones hold hands with the greatest lyrics of our age, observing her love for what she is doing, watching her subtle mastery of how to turn a difficult phrase with wit, discipline, craftsmanship, and supernatural class, the reasons why she is studied like a textbook by all serious practitioners of popular music (but never equaled by any of them) come through. She has survived the fads and the fetishes with an aura of clockless grace.

The night of her seventy-fifth birthday party, there were roses and tears and bravos so loud they could be heard over on Times Square, and it all came back, that whole lost musical age, when the crowds at El Morocco punished the parquet and the Stork Club was a great deal more than just the title of a Betty Hutton movie.

It would be patronizing to appraise Mabel Mercer in her own time, but examine this: night after night, while the pop society watusis in the here-today-gone-tomorrow discotheques, the cultured and wise sit catatonically in ecstasy, listening to Mabel's songs like kids in school. In these baffling, bitter times of androgynous monsters in glitter bras, bizarre rock vulgarities, and screeching, dissonant nightmares passing themselves off with a jerk and a groan as musicians while they pass off their reckless, cacophonous fantasies as music, Mabel Mercer is still reminding us of the beauty and value of popular music. She sings about love, the one item on the Top 40 charts that will never be a camp. I feel lucky to have lived in her time, but after I'm dead and gone, it is comforting to know that the enduring brilliance of her art will still be around, teaching newer generations yet to come what heights popular music can attain when it stays out of juke boxes.

Mabel rejected the path to commercial success years ago and set her sights on loftier goals. The big money and easy fame eluded her because she refused to compromise her integrity by singing trash. She was a light. She opened doors. And that is why, years from now, what she contributed to the world of popular music will still mean something. Her voice will always be up there somewhere lifted in song, stubbornly united in the battle against the mundane and the obvious, relentlessly pursuing "do" when everybody else says "don't." She has dedicated her life to art and made history happen.

Now Atlantic Records has re-issued three of her finest albums in a special package called "A Tribute to Mabel Mercer on the Occasion of Her 75th Birthday," Rod McKuen's Stanyan Records has rereleased her only Decca album, wisely retitled *Mabel Mercer for Always,* and *Stereo Review* has devoted a special issue to Mabel Mercer and the special art of the cabaret singer that is flourishing once again. Wait long enough with patience, and the good things in life return.

So happy birthday, Mabel.

Carol Channing

Carol Channing flies through her suite at the Waldorf like the aurora borealis. Her eyes, targets held together by imported mink eyelashes long as shish kebabs, are Timex alarm clocks. Her real hair, which nobody has ever seen and which she describes as "the color of a dead mouse," is imprisoned under one of her yellow cotton-candy wigs. Her mouth is wide and red as a strawberry pie, her face is pure Cinemascope, and someone has sewn a huge valentine heart upside down on the seat of her pants. Half Aubrey Beardsley and half Donald Duck, this Technicolor rag doll who proved twenty-five years ago, once and for always, that *Gentlemen Prefer Blondes* is back on Broadway doing it again in the brassy new musical *Lorelei*. Other Loreleis have come and gone, but Channing is still the original. If history doesn't repeat itself when *Lorelei* opens tonight after an eleven-month tour, it won't be because they couldn't find the right girl.

"This is the longest pre-Broadway tour in theatrical history and we're still in a panic," she says in her cider-cellar subway-level baritone, plopping her pogo stick legs out on the sofa and sipping organically bottled water from a silver watering can that once fed the carburetor of a Pierce Arrow motor car. "I've never done a show that was easy. On the opening night of *Hello, Dolly!* we tried out the second half of the first act for the first time in front of the critics and some of the costumes hadn't even arrived. I said I would never go through that again as long as I live and here I am going through it all over again."

Lorelei has been plagued by chaos from the start. The original choice for director was Robert *(Boys in the Band)* Moore, who had other commitments, so Carol hired Joe Layton, who had done her dance numbers in *Thoroughly Modern Millie.* He opened the show last February in Oklahoma City, fell ill, and was sent to Acapulco under doctor's orders. Betty Comden and Adolph Green, who were the original choices for book and lyrics, were busy opening *Applause* in London and could only do the lyrics to songs by Jule Styne. The first draft of the book was done by Gail Parent and Kenny Solms, who used to write sketches for *The Carol Burnett Show.* "They write Sheila Levine beautifully, but Lorelei is not Sheila Levine," says Carol dryly. Comden and Green came back, rewrote the book in Detroit and doctored the show until the patient was ready for Robert Moore to take it over in Philadelphia. Then he got sick with a mysterious disease and directed the show from a hospital bed in Boston. "They wheeled him into the theater in a wheelchair and he went back to the hospital and blocked the show on the telephone.

"Then his assistant would come in and say, 'Robert said to take two steps back, keep your eyes on the audience, think mischievous thoughts, give a wink, walk up the gangplank, and then smile,' and I'd do it and it worked and then he would go back and report how it looked and Robert would say, 'Go back and tell them to take a slower curtain there,' and he saw the whole show through his assistant's eyes, as he ran back and forth from the theater to the hospital. It's the darnedest thing!"

The catastrophes don't show. Like a well-oiled cuckoo clock, it's the humor that shines through in Carol Channing when all else breaks down. In Oklahoma, she was made an

honorary Oto Indian, and the Cherokee Nation, not wanting
to be upstaged, made her a Cherokee, too. Her name in Oto
is Princess Blazing Star. She has another name in Cherokee,
but can't remember what it is at the moment. "We exchanged blood and I have this father named Chief Running
Foot and everyone was so excited it turned into a civic
event. The governor came, the mayor came, and all the
Indians came, and everyone was so proud we chose them for
the world premiere of a Broadway musical that they completely overlooked the fact that the show needed a complete
overhaul. I knew the show was a mess, but the Indians didn't
care. They were supporting a blood relative, you see. I broke
records there in *Dolly* because it was the world's largest
indoor theater, with seventy-five hundred seats, and David
Merrick booked me because he wanted to read the headline
in *Variety*. The man who owns the newspaper was a hundred and one years old and we also celebrated his birthday.

"The local critic never even bothered to mention whether
the show was good or bad. He simply said everybody came
and it was a wonderful civic event and the whole company
looked friendly and the Indians gave everyone moccasins
and he never mentioned the show. Wasn't that dear?

"The next big city was Detroit. My eyelashes were stolen.
I don't smoke, but I keep all of my eyelashes, which are
handmade in Hong Kong, in a silver cigarette case and it was
stolen along with my wedding ring and my watch. All they
wanted was the silver case. They didn't need the eyelashes.
I thought, 'My gosh, nobody will recognize me without my
eyelashes, my own mother wouldn't know me!' You can't
stand on the stage with no eyes. They're like a carpenter's
tools. And I can't wear those cheap things you buy at the
drug store. They are Lorelei's eyes! If I don't have them, I
look like Anna Magnani. So I ran to the nearest TV station
and told all of Detroit whoever stole my case could keep it
—they could even keep my wedding ring—but please return the eyelashes. I could do a show without my arms, but
not without my eyelashes! Then the Detroit paper ran a
headline on the front page: 'Please Return Carol's
Eyelashes!' Then on Easter Sunday morning, outside my
hotel room there was the silver case with the Hong Kong

eyelashes in it. They kept the ring and the watch, but what do I care about material things? It's those eyelashes I wanted back. Wasn't that the sweetest thing? I thought Mary Baker Eddy heard me and it was a Christian Science demonstration.

"Then we went to Chicago and a fire swept through the orchestra pit and burned up the grand piano at eight o'clock in the morning. Thank goodness it didn't happen during a show because it would have burned up the drummer and Milt Rosenstock, the best conductor I've ever had. It also burned the scenery to a crisp. We still don't have all of the scenery. It's six weeks late. Then I got out of place in the fight scene between the button king and the zipper king and broke my arm and I had to play the whole show with my arm in a sling. We had to cut the right sleeves out of all of the costumes.

"In Washington, there was something called 'Luncheon with the First Lady,' given by the congressmen's wives, and they asked me to entertain Mrs. Nixon. Well, Watergate had just broken wide open and I gave her one of my diamonds after I sang to make her feel better and she said, 'Oh what a sweet diamond!' I tried to explain that the quality that gives a diamond its value is the amount of sentiment attached to it. She put it on and smiled sweetly and I thought, 'What a dear lady.'

"A week later, in Cincinnati, the Nixon Enemies List came out and it was alphabetical so I was at the top of the hate list under C. All of these profound political minds— Arthur Schlesinger and Barbra Streisand and all—were under me and I don't know how I got the honor. All I can figure is the President had the diamond I gave Mrs. Nixon appraised and put me on the Enemies List when he found out it was only a rhinestone! It was a week later in Cincinnati and it was the middle of the summer and all of a sudden we went from ninety thousand to one hundred twenty thousand dollars a week when the hate list came out. When Nixon backed Debbie Reynolds, he helped *Irene,* but when he puts you on his hate list he helps you even more! I guess it's better to have him against you!"

In Los Angeles, she had the worst audience on the tour

when she opened for a Jewish benefit on the night the Arabs bombed Israel in the worst battle of the war. The best audience was in Chicago the night Alfred Lunt and Lynn Fontanne came to see the show. When the Lunts applauded, the audience cheered. When the Lunts stood up to give Carol a standing ovation, the audience climbed on their seats to clap louder. And all along the way, the critics kept frowning and the crowds kept coming. "Most of the critics have been constructive forces throughout the country and have guided us to correct our mistakes. The worst place is Los Angeles, where they feel shows should not be tried out on their way to New York. All they want is tried-and-true, known hits that have already been approved by the New York critics. I will never try a show out in Los Angeles again. I think theater should mushroom everywhere in America, but they have the attitude, 'Don't try your show out on us,' so I won't.

"One TV critic pulled me off the stage before all of my final curtain calls, while the audience was still cheering, and told his cameras, 'Even Carol Channing couldn't save this show!' and I said, 'Well you must have been in some other theater!' He was trying to whisper this to his TV audience without my hearing it and that's what I didn't like. If you don't like it, say so and say it to the person's face. Don't insult the person and then hope you'll still be friends. So I don't think much of Los Angeles and its critics. I don't mind critics who want to be controversial, but I hate dishonesty."

Lorelei has already made $5 million before it even opens on Broadway. Real diamonds will still be this girl's best friend, whether the show runs or not. And she can use the bread. Her food bill alone would pay off the national debt. She carries her own cuisine into Sardi's in Mason jars and hires a full-time staff to ship organic foods to her all over the world because she thinks she's been poisoned by the bleach in her hair. "If I eat anything with chemicals or pesticides in it I get laryngitis. I have a farm in Porterville, California, that I share with twenty other families and it provides all pork, lamb, meat, fruit, vegetables—everything I consume. It is sent in dry ice and the only thing that wilts is the lettuce. The chemicals from peroxide went through my scalp into my bloodstream thirteen years ago, and I can't allow any preservatives into my body or I lose my voice. It's very expensive, but it keeps me alive."

It's a crazy way to live, but eccentric or not, it makes her a cheap date. "Except," she adds, "for the toothpicks and the tip." She even carries her own food and water with her in airplane seats and keeps four times the amount on hand in case the plane is late, snowed in, or grounded. "It's better than showing people my real hair. It's an ish-ash-nothing. My son, Chan, and my husband, Charles, put paper bags over my head when the doorbell rings. Without my Lorelei wigs, I look like Anne Morrow Lindbergh."

Broadway needs laughs. If her wig doesn't blow away and her Hong Kong eyelashes don't disappear, Lorelei Lee will be back tonight to give us some. Candy makes her sick, telegrams make her fingers itch, flowers make her sneeze, and she's already got enough talent, but if anyone wants to send organic good luck, the name is Carol Channing.

The Andrews Sisters

1.

Quote of the Year: Japanese emperor Hirohito, just interviewed on his fiftieth wedding anniversary, was asked, "Looking back among all the moments of happiness, what do you regard as your greatest mistake?"

His answer: "World War Two."

The Andrews Sisters laughed when they heard that, but there was irony in the sound, because without the war they might not have become the American institution they are today and always will be. Looking back nostalgically at the war years, three memories come immediately to mind: eagles, flags, and the Andrews Sisters. La Verne sang low, Maxene sang high, and Patty was the bouncy blonde in the middle, singing and swaying the melody.

La Verne died of cancer in 1967, but Patty and Maxene are still as imperishably durable as "Don't Sit Under the Apple Tree," and next week the Andrews Sisters will be bringing it all back to Broadway in a new musical called *Over Here!* It's a show that brings along with it words like Bataan and Guadalcanal, ankle-strap espadrilles and colored nylons, stage-door canteens and GI Joe cartoons, victory bonds and Veronica Lake, bobby sox and "Jukebox Saturday Night."

"You want the Forties?" asks Maxene. "Well, we got it for you. You tell it like it is? Well, we sang it like it was."

"This is an audience show," says Patty, "and at the end we come out and do the old hits. That's the frosting on the cake."

When they step out of character and blaze their way through the old gold records, the audience goes wild, like they've never been away. It's been a long trip from bandstands to Broadway, but the Andrews Sisters have never changed. Talking to them both in Maxene's hotel suite last week was like being in a cage with two jitter-bugging magpies. Everything they do is punctuated with rhythm and sometimes it's hard to tell where one begins and the other ends. "We made ten movies, recorded a thousand songs, double that for flip sides, and out of that we got nineteen gold records in twenty years," quacked Maxene. "And let me put it to you this way—we only got about fifty good songs out of it all. The rest were dogs. We hated the movies."

"Yeah," said Patty. "Everybody else got Alice Faye and Betty Grable in Technicolor. We got Carmen Miranda and Abbott and Costello. We were the queens of the B's. But we were unique."

"Let's face it," added Maxene, bouncing on the sofa. "The reason all this stuff is coming back is because of Bette Midler's record of 'Boogie-Woogie Bugle Boy.' "

"Yeah," said Patty. "That word 'camp' doesn't bother us. We think it's very funny."

"I hate the word 'nostalgia,' though," said Maxene. "They don't call Rembrandt's paintings nostalgic. Anything good is gonna last, honey. I don't care if they say I'm eighty-six years old."

"Well," quipped Patty, "aren't you, boobie?"

"No, I'm ninety-two."

It only seems that way. They've been part of the public heartbeat since they were kids in Minneapolis. Three little Greek-Norwegian girls who sang in kiddie revues at the Orpheum and hit the road before the age of sixteen. "We got a dollar a day and even if there were three people in the audience we performed as though it was a full house. We learned discipline, timing, and respect at an early age. We copied the Boswell Sisters so much, and they were from New Orleans, that we developed southern accents. If you listen to our first record, 'Bei Mir Bist Du Schoen,' we sound like shrimp trawlers."

"Well, there are southern Jews, too, Patty."

"We didn't read music, we sang what we heard. La Verne also played great piano by ear. She sang the lead and played the third part. The harmonies just came natural."

"After the first year on the road," said Patty, "we didn't want to go home. We called Mama from New York and she got on a bus and came to New York and Papa gave us three months to make the big time or we all had to go home. We got a job with a band at the Hotel Edison and we got fifteen dollars for the three of us to do a radio broadcast. It was during this broadcast that the top A and R man at Decca, Dave Kapp, was riding in a cab and the driver had the radio tuned to this station. We did a chorus of 'Sleepy Time Down South,' and he asked the cab driver, 'Where's that broadcast coming from?' and the man announced it was coming from the Hotel Edison and Maxene and I were sitting out in the lobby talking to the musicians when this man comes up and says, 'Excuse me, but can you tell me where I can find the Andrews Sisters?' and we said, 'Well, you're lookin' at two of them,' and he asked us to come up to Decca the next morning and sing for the president of the company. I was sixteen, Maxene was eighteen, and La Verne was twenty, and the three months were up the next morning so Papa unpacked the bags and we got a record contract and that was the beginning of the Andrews Sisters."

"We sang 'Bei Mir Bist Du Schoen' in Yiddish and the president of Decca went right off his cork and said, 'You'll either be the biggest hit or the biggest flop.' We lived in a tiny apartment between Seventh and Eighth avenues and the three of us slept in the same bed with Mama and Papa in the next bed and about eight o'clock in the morning Papa woke us up on Christmas morning, 1937, and said, 'Get up and come down to Times Square, they're playing your record!'

We went down to Broadway and the crowds were lined up all over the street with police keeping them back and over this loudspeaker they were playing our song and hundreds of people kept shouting 'Play it again!' and we were telling everybody 'That's us!' We didn't have a dime, but we were an overnight sensation, so we borrowed ten dollars and bought our father a box of White Owl cigars and a box of Elizabeth Arden for Mom and four cans of dog food for our English setter and that was the best Christmas of our lives."

"Today," says Maxene, "you make a hit record and you're a millionaire. We still couldn't pay the rent. So we got a job in Boston but we couldn't afford to get there. An accountant for Sunshine Biscuits who made twenty-two dollars a week introduced us to a dress designer who made black metallic dresses and Mama, who was practically blind, sewed our initials on with magenta chiffon and for three dollars and a half we got some shoes from A.S. Beck on credit and we borrowed forty dollars to buy bus tickets and we were on our way."

"We only knew three songs," said Patty, "so we sang 'Bei Mir Bist Du Schoen' ten times and they were screaming for more. All we did was sing that song and we got five hundred dollars a week. Then we have seven smash hits in a row for fifty dollars a record. We were the first artists outside of Bing Crosby to get five cents a record. We were singing in Chicago on the *Wrigley Show* and it took seven hours to get to New York by plane and by the time we got to our recording sessions we were so hoarse that the records came out flat and we started to cry. But the records were hits and we learned then and there that the public does not want perfection.

"The only things in our minds then and now is pleasing the people. We don't want to educate the public. We just want to entertain them."

Not everybody loved the Andrews Sisters. "Stan Kenton followed us into the New York Paramount once, so we went backstage and Stan says to Maxene, 'It's nice to know you but I can't stand your singing.' Maxene says to him, 'It's nice to know you, but I can't stand your music!'

"We took Gene Krupa on the road for the first time. We hired Harry James. But the musicians all wanted to be stars and they didn't really dig the kind of harmony we sang. It was the public that made the Andrews Sisters."

Their first film was *Argentine Nights* with the Ritz Brothers. "We went to the premiere at the Fordham Theatre in the Bronx," said Patty, "and we looked like the Ritz Brothers in drag. Our makeup was done by the man at Universal who did the makeup for Frankenstein. We were so ugly that Maxene walked all the way back to Manhattan from the Bronx in tears."

They never looked like Carole Lombard, but as a trio they couldn't be topped. Considering all the other vocal groups on the scene—many more musically complex and prettier to listen to—what was it that made them unique? "We loved to sing," said Patty, "and we were honest." They discovered Judy Garland when she was still Baby Frances Gumm and got her sister act its first job with Georgie Jessel. They turned out pictures in ten days. Their records went to war with the aircraft carriers. Once, when Patty broke her ankle during a polka number, Universal kept the cameras going and all three sisters finished the "Beer Barrel Polka" hopping on one leg. The Midas touch lasted for thirty years (one year they sold 5 million records in twelve months). Are they millionaires?

Maxene: "My sister Patty might be, but not me."

Patty: "Oh, the crying towel! She's always broke. She goes out and buys a new Mercedes, then says 'I can't pay the taxes on my ten acres in Malibu.' You know the type."

After La Verne died, it was never the same. The joy went out of the act. Maxene became the dean of women at Tahoe Paradise College in 1969, teaching speech and drama. Patty has been married for twenty-two years to Walter Weschler, the act's pianist-conductor. Maxene has two children. Patty has dogs. The act broke up for two years in 1954. Mama and Papa died, Maxene divorced the act's manager, Lou Levy, they disbanded their corporation, and everybody needed freedom.

"We had worked so hard we never had time for our personal lives," says Patty. "We even spoke like a trio. So we broke up for two years and when we started the act again it was like being reborn. Even when La Verne died, we were still working. We were a group image and also a family, so it wasn't easy to break up. Now Maxene and I have privacy we never had before, but we enjoy our work more than ever."

"Now," says Maxene, "we respect each other's privacy. We've learned to compromise. We think the same way musically, but our taste in clothes, friends—our life-styles—are completely different. We had to learn to respect this. We've been together eight weeks rehearsing this show. Offstage, we've never seen each other socially. Onstage, it's as though we've never been apart. We survived because we had a sense of humor. Without that, you ain't gonna get through this life."

Their first review said, "The Andrews Sisters sound like a Chinese jigsaw puzzle set to off-key music." The pieces still fit. The only thing the Andrews Sisters haven't done is a Broadway show. Now they're on Broadway, and it's happening all over again.

2.

Like Kate Smith, apple pie, and the national anthem, the legendary Andrews Sisters have always been unknockable American institutions. The tradition has now been interrupted. Somebody is knocking them, and the noise is being heard all over Broadway.

On March 6, 1974, the two remaining Andrews Sisters, Patty and Maxene, opened in a splashy Broadway musical called *Over Here!* The show was awful, but it was an instant hit. Last night, January 5, 1975, it closed suddenly, in the middle of threats, controversy, and possible lawsuits. The producers blamed the Andrews Sisters, claiming a "massive feud," and immediately canceled the national tour, which had scores of eager ticket-buyers throughout America already lining up with checkbooks in their hands. The Andrews Sisters blamed the producers, claiming they had mismanaged the show from the very beginning and were now using the stars as scapegoats to hide from their investors the true financial reasons for canceling the tour, reasons which remain a secret to everybody.

In the middle of the confusion, the producers (Kenneth Waissman and Maxine Fox) circulated a rather nasty press release further blackening the professional reputations of their stars, and rumors were even circulating through Sardi's that the act was breaking up. Pistols at dawn under the dueling oaks is pretty corny in 1975, but it was obviously time somebody started defending the Andrews Sisters' reputation. Patty refused to talk on advice from her attorney, but Maxene, the firebrand of the family, was, as always, scarcely at a loss for words. She held forth in her backstage dressing room in a state of anger and bewilderment, doing her level best to explain a situation that remains clouded in mystery.

"I do not know why a smash hit like *Over Here!* is not going on tour," said Maxene. "I am heartbroken. But whatever the reason, it has nothing to do with the Andrews Sisters. This show has a golden opportunity to make millions and the producers are throwing it away. They have a tiger by the tail and it's slipped right through their fingers because they are amateurs. They are too young and inexperienced to control a show this big. None of this would have happened under a David Merrick or a Harold Prince. There has never been anybody in control. I came to Broadway expecting the epitome of discipline and class. What I discovered was that vaudeville was classier.

"I'll give you a perfect example. Just today, the actor who plays the black porter on the train was out with laryngitis and we discovered the producers had not hired an understudy. The white stage manager had to go on in his place, playing a black part. Equity rules state there has to be an understudy to cover all roles. These producers have been getting away with pulling things like that since the show began. Let me give you the biggest laugh of all. For the first seven months, the understudy for Patty and me couldn't even sing."

In the producers' press release of complaints against the Andrews Sisters, they claim the stars are "signed to a two-year contract which provides the producers with the right to send them on a national tour within that two-year period. However, in spite of this contract, both Patty and Maxene have been demanding more money. Maxene sent the producers a doctor's note saying that she is too sick to perform on the tour. However, according to management, a follow-up call made by her attorney stated that in spite of the letter, Maxene Andrews would be healthy enough to perform if she were given additional monies by the producers." Maxene claims this is "an outrageous lie," and produces a handful of letters from doctors, lawyers and the producers to prove it. "My sister gets thirty-five hundred dollars a week and seven percent of the show; and I get twenty-five hundred dollars a week and three percent of the show after the show makes $60,000. That was a stupid contract on the producers' part, but if I hadn't agreed to work for less money there wouldn't have been a show in the first place. I did agree, because that's how badly I wanted to do it.

"This is the first time we have ever worked under an unequal salary, but Patty's husband negotiated her deal. They asked me to take a cut in my percentages to get the show on the road, and I agreed to start my percentage at eighty thousand dollars instead of sixty thousand dollars, giving them twenty thousand a week more to spend on production costs. All I asked was that they make it up to me by helping to pay for my medical expenses on the road. What it amounted to was four hundred dollars a week toward my doctor bills. I agreed to a cut in percentage, and I agreed to take no raise in salary, and all I wanted was some financial aid to pay the doctors in every city who would have no medical history of my case. All through the show I have spent a fortune in therapeutic, medical, and analytical expenses because of my legs and high blood pressure. For the past six months I've been working in leg braces. I've been through cortisone shots in my legs, acupuncture, and therapy at paraplegic hospitals, and every time the doctor ordered me to leave the show, I refused. It was only right that I ask for some medical compensation on the road since I was going to get less money anyway, and the crazy fact is, the producers' lawyers agreed. In twenty-five minutes, they had worked out my road deal. In the meantime, I learned they had gone over to see Patty and her husband to play one sister against the other. At the same time, I learned they had financial troubles with the stage designers' union and the rumor was that the scenery was too expensive to take on the road. So they used the sisters as excuses for the blame. Now, they have a two-year contract with us. Even if we have been difficult and asked for more money, as they claim, why didn't they just take us into Equity arbitration and force us to go on the road? They were holding all the cards. They simply are not telling the truth.

"Now let's look at the producers' accusations in their press release. They allude to 'a massive feud.' I don't know what they're talking about, because they are so rude that I haven't even seen them in over two months. All negotiations have been conducted by lawyers. At the end of October, they announced to the cast that we were under a two-year contract, told us what theaters we would be playing on the road, and advised everyone to start negotiating for the tour by November 8. The twenty-eighth of November came and went, and not one person in the cast had been contacted. They kept saying 'We're not ready yet.' On December 9 we met with the lawyers and the deal was solidified. Everything was fine until Monday, December 16, when they delivered a letter backstage demanding that we retract all doctors' claims, agree to do all publicity, make the third act at the end of the show where we do our old hit songs a definite part of each performance, and sign our consent before curtain time, or the tour would be canceled. This made all negotiations invalid. We had one hour to decide. It was seven o'clock at night, we couldn't reach our lawyers, and naturally we didn't sign. So they made an announcement over the loudspeakers that the cast must meet in costume after the show and the Andrews Sisters were not invited. I went to the meeting anyway and Ken Waissman said, 'Get out, you're not wanted here!' The cast was stunned. So I got up and said fine, but first I want to talk to the cast. I explained that we loved them all and were very sorry the show was not going on the road, but it had nothing to do with us. The entire cast applauded and I left.

"It was like a kangaroo court. Every member of the cast has come to me since and personally apologized for the rudeness of the producers. That shows what a wonderful cast this is. They are just innocent kids who have been caught in the middle of the producers' inexperience. They are playing games and I don't want to be any part of it. The backers aren't losing money on my account, and it's time they start asking questions."

The controversial "third act" the producers insisted upon has never been part of their contract. They performed it whenever physically able out of the kindness of their hearts, and on the nights when it was impossible, the audience came close to a riot. "That," adds Maxene, "is why we didn't want it in the program. We did that medley of hits because we wanted to. We're too hammy to give up that applause after thirty years in show business. There was never any threat from us that we wouldn't do it, but we didn't want to guarantee it, because if one of us got sick there wouldn't be any Andrews Sisters. We don't read music and you can't teach those arrangements to other singers. So we didn't want to make promises we might not keep every night. That also gives the producers the right to dock your salary. As far as refusing to do publicity, that's dishonest. Patty refused, but I didn't. I even did high school interviews between shows, some days I didn't even get a chance to eat dinner. I did interviews on Sundays, after the final curtain at night.

"I've been in show business all my life and nobody knows the value of publicity more than I do. For seven weeks, the producers very stupidly pulled all of the ads out of the newspapers and they did two TV commercials in which they didn't even ask the Andrews Sisters to appear! If anyone did a lousy job of publicity, it was the producers. They violated our contracts by changing the ads so that our names appeared in smaller print than the ad copy, so Patty got mad and refused to cooperate with doing publicity. We called Equity into it, and they made them change the ads, but what it finally boiled down to was little kids playing games. Even after they changed the ads back to the proper size, they advertised it as a dancing show. Now we all know people have been coming to see the Andrews Sisters for thirty years because of their dancing! Everything has been done to annoy us instead of making the show the hit audiences wanted."

The producers now state "even if the sisters capitulate completely, agree to live up to their contract, perform the third act and do all reasonable requests for publicity, we will remain unmoved. The tour is definitely off!" That doesn't sound like rational behavior to me on behalf of any producer sitting on a golden egg. And the turmoil is now threatening the Andrews Sisters as an act.

"The biggest mistake is that we were both represented separately, not as an act," says Maxene, "and it cannot go on this way. Maybe the time has come to go our separate ways. But it was immoral for Waissman and Fox to pit one sister against the other. They created the problem by negotiating separately at the beginning, and we never got together to iron it out. So now there is friction. We've always had different life-styles, different friends, different tastes offstage. The only thing we've ever had in common is our work.

"We've survived. We overcame seventeen rotten pictures at Universal, World War Two, all the bad pressings Decca turned out that turned into gold records anyway, husbands and ex-husbands, bad publicity, and amateur Broadway producers. The only people who love us are the people. They just keep on coming."

It would be a shame to see the Andrews Sisters go the way of Martin and Lewis and the Beatles. Only one Andrews Sister would be like Tarzan without Jane. Right now emotions are frayed, avenues of communication are closed, and only time will tell. I think they'll make it. Kate Smith, apple pie, and the national anthem did.

Ginger Rogers

Get ready, America, Ginger Rogers is on her way. She's already blazed through New York like a four-alarm fire, and now she's taking her brassy, bouncy new nightclub act to San Francisco, Dallas, and Las Vegas. She brings on the boys. She cooks on four burners. And for sixty-four, she looks like a kid.

"I have no secrets," she says, "and I have no diets. I use lanolin on my elbows and knees, wash with soap, take off my makeup with cold cream you buy for two ninety-five a jar and drink ice cream sodas. It's all the power of positive thinking. God does the rest."

It was midnight, she had just finished her second show at the Waldorf-Astoria, and now she was sipping sassafras tea and putting her feet up to cool off after a night of soft shoe, waltz, and Carioca. Everyone is amazed to see her looking so young, with the body of a girl. But when you get to know Ginger Rogers, she's pretty amazing in all she does.

There's a whole museum dedicated to her great-great grandfather, a doctor who discovered the quinine cure for malaria. She comes from pioneer stock and is American as blueberry pie. Her family tree includes lots of governors and soldiers in the American Revolution. She's a member of the DAR. "As soon as I have time, I wanna see if any of them were horse thieves," she winks. But the only thing she's stolen are a few million hearts.

She once played a movie queen named Irene Malverne in a movie called *Weekend at the Waldorf.* During her stay this time at the Waldorf, the dancers in her show called her "Miss Malverne." Friends flew in from everywhere to see her. Fans brought her pantyhose and orchids. Every night brought a standing ovation. And she did about a million interviews. "Honey, I don't fake this energy. It's just there. But the one thing I have not adjusted to after forty years in show business is interviews. They all want to know about Fred Astaire. Then they use the same old cliché in their headlines: 'Ginger Snaps!' Or, 'Ginger Still Snappy!' It drives me right up the wall."

Even Fred Astaire's sister, Adele, insists there was never a feud between Fred and Ginger in the days when they made Hollywood history dancing across waxed floors in a heavenly embrace while half the world broke legs trying to imitate them. Some people say it was Ginger's mother who caused trouble by being the kind of show business mother that would make Mama Rose in *Gypsy* look like an amateur. "Not true!" says Ginger. "My mother had her own apartment, her own friends, and was only on the set when I called and yelled, 'Help, we gotta problem!' She wasn't hanging around on my doorstep. And she didn't live a career through me. She already had her own career."

Lela Rogers was entertainment editor of *The Fort Worth Record* when teenage Ginger won that now-famous Charleston contest that catapulted her to stardom. The prize was four weeks on the Texas circuit for the little girl from Independence, Missouri, which led to *Girl Crazy* on Broadway and then Hollywood movies.

"The legendary feud was the work of the studio publicity department to get space in the papers. Fred and Ginger weren't having a romance, so they had to invent something. Those fights never happened. Fred even did a twenty-minute discourse on the Cavett show. He said, 'I would like to squash this whole thing once and for all.' We are both so tired of defending ourselves over these boring rumors about a feud that never existed. I love Fred and he loves me."

She does not like to talk about her mother or her five marriages. She simply says, "The performing part of my life has been happier than my private life. Because it's an unselfish giving. I was pushed into show business when I was a kid. I had no ambitions. I have never been hard-driving or ambitious for stardom. It deprived me of a normal childhood. But it's the thing I love most.

"During some of my marriages, I stopped working, but in my entire career I've only had two years when I did zero. And even then, I knew it was only a hiatus. I got tired of sitting on a leaf. I've gotta be in the traffic, with the horns tooting. When I was a kid, I played hard. Then I grew up and worked hard. But I still call it 'play.' The joy I get out of dancing has been a great source of energy for me. Even when I'm not working, I paint. I've got thirty canvases ready now for a show. I play eight sets of tennis a day. If I wasn't performing, I'd be painting, sculpting or using a potter's wheel. I'm not the rocking-chair type."

It's kept her young. "Christian Science has taught me that our decisions master us. I decided a long time ago to do the things that would make me a better person. In this school we're in—because that's what life is—it's the learning that pays off. I've learned to pay more attention to the positive things in life, not the negative things. If you take the despondent path, you make your own unhappiness. But either way, it's your own decision, and you can't blame anyone else for your decisions. I've made thousands of mistakes, but they've all been stepping stones toward a better concept of life."

Somehow, she's managed to save herself from the disappointment and bitterness that wreck so many show business ladies her age who are no longer in demand on the silver screen. "I enjoy this business I'm in, and I'm unafraid to work. The trouble with the world today is that people are afraid of hard work. When Jiminy Cricket sang that song in *Pinocchio* about how the world owed him a living, he foresaw the problem of this world we're in now. Everybody wants something for nothing. And that's where we are, in a welfare state. Take away a person's incentive, and you demoralize him mentally."

Not that she's a Goody Two Shoes about her life. "I look at my old movies like old cars. Sometimes you get a lemon. But I knew the ones like *The Groom Wore Spurs* with Jack Carson, *The First Traveling Saleslady* with Carol Channing and *Forever Female* with William Holden were dogs when I made them. Success is three-fourths hard work, and the rest is whatever ingredient you need to complete the requirement.

"Today it would be impossible for a Ginger Rogers to happen. There's no Hollywood left. Hollywood is like an empty wastebasket. It made me sad to watch the movie business change, but there was nothing I could do about it. The joy has gone out of picture-making. That little box over there"—she points to the TV set, crooking her finger like a gun barrel—"that's the handsome villain. It keeps millions of people entertained for nothing. You pay three hundred dollars for a big ticket, and you never have to buy another one. All you need are instructions on how to fix it.

"I knew it was over for me when they stopped making musicals. Then they stopped writing movies for women. I'm not one of those stars who are full of regrets, though. Those ladies could do stage plays. No, darling. When you're an actress, nobody can keep you from doing what you want to do if you really want to do it. You just have to find another way to do it. I made seventy-three movies. I won an Oscar. Suddenly I was out of work. I got tired of waiting around to see what kind of script someone would hand me.

"And you should see the stuff I turned down! I could hold them in my hands, and I knew they were terrible scripts. All those horror films and that's spelled 'H-O-R-R-O-R-R-R-R!' I enjoyed a happy image in films. Why should I become a destructive force in the minds of the young people in this country who grew to love the Fred and Ginger musicals on the Late Show? No thank you. I can do creative things elsewhere. I don't have to stoop to horror films."

So she packed up her Mary Baker Eddy books, hit the stage in *Hello, Dolly!* and *Mame,* and broke records everywhere. Now she's bringing back the old spirit and the old songs and the old graciousness in her dazzling new act. She's back in the dancing shoes, and they still fit. Even though Fred Astaire is not onstage with her, he shares the spotlight. In her tie and tails and top hat, she ends the night by saying, "Goodnight, Fred," and throwing a kiss to an empty spotlight.

"Today's dances are horrible! Everybody looks like a spastic scarecrow. Dance floors look like they opened a box of worms. Whatever happened to the fun of touching? It's neat, it's sweet. Exercise? You can get the same result from doing push-ups. I'm turned off."

Every day she meets young people who tell her they love Cole Porter and ballroom dancing and pretty clothes. They all tell her they're living in the wrong era. "If enough people feel that way, maybe good taste will come back. I never had enough men in my life who liked to dance. Either they were afraid because it was Ginger Rogers they were dancing with, or they just weren't any good."

She has a ranch on the Rogue River in Oregon and a house in Palm Springs full of boxes she's never had time to unpack. "I spend all of my time in hotel rooms," she sighs. She doesn't own any of the costumes she wore in musicals, but she does have the films. "I paid for every print, and now even the studios are asking to borrow them. I've got the only copy of *Roberta* that hasn't been chopped to shreds. My uncut version of *Lady in the Dark* is very valuable. Anyway, I couldn't take care of them, so I gave them all to Southern Methodist University in Dallas. I had no idea they would end up in museums when I made them. Fred and I were just doing our work.

"We were never in any sense married, but the teamwork was a kind of marriage. I guess I had an individuality, and he had a sense of rhythm and cadence that made it all work. I don't live in the past, but class is class. It never dies. That's why I resent it when reporters get it all wrong. They make too much out of the past instead of looking at what we did as part of a beautiful gift.

"Recently some reporter asked me if I learned things from the famous men I worked with, and I said, 'Yes, I observed things they did.' Cary Grant, for example, always made me laugh. So the article comes out, and it says 'Cary Grant Taught Ginger Rogers How to Play Comedy!' Now that's not terrible, but it's not true. Can you imagine Cary sitting down and giving me instructions? I know Cary, and Cary's gonna wonder what happened to my head."

She finished her tea, yawned, and it was a cue for bedtime. "Listen, honey," she said, scratching her golden Ginger Rogers curls, "I just do what makes me happy. I did an act before, but it was all pretty clothes and no dancing. The critics hammered me right into the floor. They said, 'How dare you think you can just stand there and look pretty and sing Gershwin songs without dancing?' This time I'm dancing and people ask me why I don't do readings from my dramatic films. You cannot, in this life, do everything. You can't please 'em all."

But she tries, succeeds better than most, and if she'll pardon the pun she hates, Ginger still does it snappily.

Dody Goodman

When *Mary Hartman, Mary Hartman* returns this fall, there just might be a new Dody Goodman, Dody Goodman. "I spend my life on that show stirring cake batters and watering plants. We have a suggestion box on the set and if we get an idea, we drop it in the box, and some of our best shows have come out of that. Louise Lasser got so tired at one point, she wrote a note saying she felt like she was having a nervous breakdown. So on the next show they let her have a nervous breakdown. I handed in a suggestion that I was sick of washing and ironing and cooking and I yearned to go to night classes at the Fernwood High School. So I think this fall I'll finally get out of the kitchen. In my house on the show, I only have one room. I've never been in a bedroom except when I go over to Mary's to get her out of bed. When I go back, I'm going to ask them for a bedroom to go with my kitchen."

The real Dody Goodman can't even cook. She lives in a small furnished apartment in Culver City with a cat named Sophia, she loves junk food ("especially all kinds of crappy cookies"), and she never goes near the stove. She's just signed for another thirty-six weeks of the phenomenally popular sick soap opera. Now everyone stops her and asks what's going to happen in the fall. She doesn't know. The scripts haven't been written yet. Meanwhile, she's spending the summer touring America in a smash revival of *George Washington Slept Here,* blasting a hole in the old Dody Goodman image by turning in a performance of great skill, depth, and warmth. As the wife of Jimmy Coco who buys a dilapidated farm inhabited by plagues of problems, Dody is expanding her horizons as an actress and surprising everyone who thinks she's a cross between Billie Burke and Zasu Pitts. She is genuinely touching.

Offstage, she's no dumb broad, either. Her delivery is laced with "Lemme see . . . one day . . . I can't remember . . . oh, yes, I know what it was," etc. But that's just part of being Dody. She always sounds like she's got a mouth full of sealing wax. She is sweet and gentle but her daffy style and delivery made her famous. She started out with a minimal ability and parlayed it into a healthy, productive career. "I never thought of being an actress," she says honestly. "All I ever wanted to be was a ballerina. I started dancing when I was eight years old, and after I graduated from high school, I went to New York with a girlfriend whose brother had danced in Broadway shows. It was a very scary thing for a girl who had never left Columbus, Ohio. We went on a Greyhound bus.

"The first thing I did was walk into Radio City Music Hall and audition for a job in the ballet. They hired me to dance on point in a dress shaped like a mushroom. My legs were the stems. I did four or five shows a day and rehearsed the next show in between. There was no time left over for classes or auditions.

"Then I did a season at the Met and finally landed in *High Button Shoes,* where I danced for Jerome Robbins. Then he hired me for *Miss Liberty,* and Irving Berlin always called me Red. I'm always telling interviewers about my ballet career, but they don't ever believe me."

Betty Garrett sent Dody to her vocal coach, who taught her how to sing comedy songs. Everyone in the ballet was always breaking up over her voice, but the comedy career was an accident. The funny voice wasn't. You could work all your life and never develop a voice that funny. It sounds like a Tweety Pie cartoon bird strangling on peanut butter. "People think I put that voice on for laughs. After the Jack Paar show they used to come up to me and say, 'Oh, my God, you really do sound like that!' I'm used to it now. When I did *Born Yesterday* in summer stock, I didn't even have to develop a voice. I just opened my mouth and people laughed."

Jack Paar made her a household name. His writers had seen her in the off-Broadway *Shoestring Revue,* and he called her in for a meeting. "I wasn't nervous," she says, wide-eyed. "I didn't even know who Jack Paar was. And he never told me what to say on the air. The show wasn't that well planned. He just wanted someone to sit and talk to. I didn't think anyone would want to hear anything I had to say. I wasn't very interested in the show because at that point I still wanted to be a dancer. But I went on and people started laughing every time I opened my mouth. It was all a big accident."

She was on every night, with no preparation, ad-libbing her way through whatever oddball subject Paar threw at her. "Today, people have techniques they use on talk shows, but not then. The show was live, and there was no way I could watch it later and improve my mistakes. Sometimes I'd start scratching myself because I was nervous, and people would roar. The dumb blonde reputation didn't bother me then because it was a good job. But later it was hurtful. I learned to rely on laughter so much that when I left the Paar show, I was afraid to branch out and try serious acting. I had no self-confidence."

She never sees Jack Paar anymore, and one gets the impression that their professional parting was not exactly rosy. "At first, he couldn't do enough for me," she reminisces. "Then I started getting too popular. We were asked to make personal appearances together, and he refused. And I guess I was overexposed. So he cut me down to two or three nights a week. I was already enough of a caricature when I started, but I finally became a caricature of a caricature. When he started phasing me out, I questioned his motive, but now I know it was the best thing for me." They never correspond.

After Paar's last TV comeback disaster, he vanished into the woodwork. Dody's career zoomed. She's worked ever since.

She's the darling of dinner theaters, regional theaters, summer stock, you name it. She played the tipsy mother of an Olympic athlete with Carol Channing in *Lorelei* on Broadway and most recently appeared as Bette Davis's side-kick in the ill-fated musical *Miss Moffitt.* Her most consistent review has been: "She didn't have enough to do." She never made a TV pilot until *Mary Hartman,* and even then she never thought it would sell.

"Everything I've ever done has been unexpected," she grins. "I could never have visualized anything like *Mary Hartman* taking off. Years ago I did some sketches on the old Martha Raye show. Norman Lear was the director. They had auditioned everybody in Hollywood for the mother on *Mary Hartman,* and it was Norman who remembered me and hired me. It all proves that you can't plan a career in this business. I used to have big dreams of fame and money. But as I got older, my values changed. Now I'm content with my life. Look at Liz Taylor. She has pans of jewels, but she has a terrible amount of trouble. She lost all of her husbands, poor thing. And she's always having operations. I guess money isn't everything."

Mary Hartman, Mary Hartman has now taken over her life. "The one thing I said I'd never do is a soap opera. Now here I am in one. The hours are killing me. We were getting up at 5 A.M., and with a completely memorized script we'd be in full makeup and costumes by 8 A.M. Then we'd have a camera rehearsal and shoot all day. Then at night, we'd block the next day's show and go home dead tired to memo-rize the next day's script. Now we go in at eight thirty, rehearse each scene on the set and shoot one scene at a time. We do the whole thing without cue cards. Sometimes I'm so tired and confused I forget the lines and start making up my own dialogue, which is often better than the words they give me to say. I get out about five thirty and go home and watch myself every night.

"I get a whole week of scripts in advance and we just beat it out until we have them learned. Sometimes they throw out a scene on the set and write a new one before you even learned the old one. It's the hardest work there is. You give up your life to a show like this, and I find myself being grumpy all the time and living on doughnuts because there's no time for lunch. I also like to sleep ten hours a night, but I haven't been getting much sleep since I started the show."

I offer the suggestion that maybe that's why Louise Lasser always looks so sleepy on the show. "Oh," she says, her eyes innocent and big as pancakes, "she doesn't get much sleep at all!"

The show has brought in some crazy mail, she says, but "I get worse mail just from being myself." Regular viewers worry about Mary and her friends and even take on their problems. "They have more to agonize over on this show than most soap operas because we deal with more problems. A lot of viewers get the Norman Lear shows mixed up, and I get mail addressed to *Maude* and *All in the Family.* But I think the show is healthy because at least it does bring out in the open a lot of subjects that have been hush-hush. It doesn't solve them, but at least it shows it's not disgraceful to talk about homosexuality, adultery, impotence, and V.D. A lot of young people wrote that they had gone to their doctors for checkups after Mary got V.D. I think the show might have a value because of that."

Dody has never been married, but she's not a prude. "One thing does make me mad, though," she interjects. "That Wayne Hays scandal. I don't care what anybody does, but it shouldn't cost the taxpayers five million dollars. I'd rather give that money to stray cats than to Elizabeth Ray."

She has no regrets that she's never had time for marriage or children. "You have to feed them, and I can't even eat what I cook for myself. Sometimes I think wouldn't it be nice to have a mate or a companion—you know, all those safe words. But every time I ever got close to marriage it was never with anyone like that. Also, I have never been any good at disciplining children. I have a lot of nieces and nephews, and none of them ever do what I tell them to do. I just couldn't stand the pressure of worrying if they were taking the Pill or out robbing a bank. I have enough trouble with my cat."

If she ever gets tired of acting, Dody can fall back on

another little-known side of her talent. She's a fine writer. Two seasons ago she turned out a fine comedy, *Mourning in a Funny Hat,* about how her Ohio mother coped with her father's death. Shirley Booth was the star, and if you still don't think there's more to Dody Goodman than the bubble-brain image she projects, ask the insiders who are still rolling in the aisles over their clash in rehearsal. Miss Booth, who is something of a prude, refused to say the word "crap" in the script. Dody mounted the stage, stared down the nose of her star, and said: "Honey, I'm not asking you to hold it in your hand—I'm just asking you to *say* it!" She's dumb, all right. Dumb as a mink-dyed fox.

Carroll Baker

Andy Warhol is up to something. Except for painting Willy Brandt and running barefoot on the beach with Elizabeth Taylor, he's been frightfully quiet lately. Now I know what it is. The silver-haired, exotic king of pop art is making a dramatic plunge into big-budget big-time movies. As usual, Andy will be the Big Daddy, or overseer. Somebody else will direct. In the past, all of the Warhol movies have been put together with enthusiasm, spit, and chewing gum. This one is called *BAD*, a brave title that is already giving a lot of critics a lot of ammunition. But good or bad, it will be different. Even Warhol's *Frankenstein* epic cost only $450,000. *BAD* is costing $1.5 million, complete with big Hollywood names, first-rate union technicians, and up-to-the-minute cinematography.

The *BAD* set is in a converted warehouse on West Nineteenth Street near the Hudson River docks. The sound stage is usually used as a set for toilet paper commercials, but today it has been turned into a middle-class house in Queens, which may or may not be the same thing. Andy Warhol is nowhere in sight, but on the third floor, behind a

"Keep Out" sign, the producer of *BAD* is fending off *Time*, *Newsweek*, and *People* magazines on an office phone.

"Everybody wants to get on this set," says Jeff Tornberg, a twenty-four-year-old ex-executive of the Robert Stigwood Organization (the group that made *Tommy*). "But we're keeping everybody out until the picture comes out. We're doing this one the right way." Tornberg, who looks like Huck Finn playing a Madison Avenue account executive, raised the million and a half by traveling across the world and meeting with movie distributors in Japan, England, Germany, and Italy. "I sold them on the basis of how much money Warhol's movies bring in internationally—like you'd sell encyclopedias. The rest of the money came from private investors. A lot of people gave money because—well—Andy is Andy."

And what are they buying? Well, there isn't an available synopsis of *BAD* because nobody ever got around to typing one up, but basically it's about a Queens housewife who runs an electrolysis business as a front for a crime ring of hit girls. Among other things, they throw a live baby from a window and burn down a movie house with seventy-three people inside because the film is dubbed. At one point, they even push a man under a subway train, cut off his finger, and put it in a ketchup bottle. "It will probably get a hard R rating," shrugs Jeff.

The stars are Carroll Baker, Susan Tyrrell, and Perry King. An assortment of Andy's friends are playing the hit girls, including debutantes, reporters for the Warhol magazine *Interview*, some of the Beautiful People, Peter Beard's girl friend Barbara Allen and Lenny Bruce's daughter, Kitty. The girl who plays a nude scene with Perry King left the next day to work on a Communist work farm in Cuba. One thing is certain. Nobody looks like Central Casting.

Down on the set, the cast is assembling for a scene in which Carroll Baker, as the gangster queen, takes an order for a grisly wipeout so big it would baffle the Godfather, then locks up her kitchen phone so her hit girls can't make personal calls and cost her toll units on her phone bill. The role was originally offered to Shelley Winters, who read the script and screamed. "I already played Ma Barker," quipped

Shelley, before saying no. "This one is bloodier than *Bloody Mama*. If they really do all the stuff in that script, they're going to have a lot to answer for." So they got Carroll Baker, who always had a lot to answer for in the old *Harlow* days. "This is not a return to American films," says Carroll, surveying the clutter of cigarette butts, coleslaw forks and "Eat Me" T-shirts around her. "Is this America? I thought I was on the moon."

Nobody seems to mind that she looks twenty years younger than Susan Tyrrell, who plays her semiretarded daughter-in-law. That's because Susan, a great actress who was nominated for an Oscar for *Fat City*, has been made up to look like one of the zombies in *The Night of the Living Dead*.

"I know everybody thinks we're all crazy doing a Warhol picture," says Susan. "But I've done so much crap the right way that I figure I've got nothing to lose. Most of the big Hollywood films I've done are nothing but crap. This one at least will be different. I've got three new films that have not been released—*The Killer Inside Me* with Stacy Keach, *Islands in the Stream* with George C. Scott, and *To Kill a King*, in which I play the wife of a president who gets assassinated. This Warhol picture is more fun than any of them. At least it's not just a part written as added spice to jazz up a man's picture. Practically the whole cast is women."

She's wearing her costume for *BAD*—a creation she calls a "Thorazine special": flowered duster, mustard socks, plastic "in the clouds" mules, wet stringy hair, dime-store beret. "It's like the smocks people wear in insane asylums. I'm the only one in the film who isn't a gangster. I call my character a 'worm woman.' I sit around being terrified of the whole world with a baby in my lap.

"You should see the baby they got. It's bald and it throws up all over me. I didn't read the script beyond the third page. I couldn't understand it. So I gave it to my army of friends, and they all said 'Do it!' so here I am. They know what my career is all about, even if I don't. I never read scripts anyway. I just underline the part to see how many lines I have, then I get the smell of it, take a deep breath, and plunge in."

Perry King plays L.T., a "character totally unexplained as yet," originally written for drag queen Jackie Curtis. "After all those slick Hollywood films like *Mandingo* and *Lipstick,* I wanted to do something wild," he says, and this is apparently it. Carroll Baker shuffles onto the set wearing plastic rope wedgies, a pink hairnet, and a pink beautician's smock, with her luscious blonde curls tied up in pink and blue curlers from Woolworth.

"Nobody has been able to explain this script to me yet, but I think it's antipeople," she grins. "It's about the premise that normal, middle-class people have no morals and they'll do anything for money. I guess you could call it a social comment. I order murders like most housewives order a loaf of bread. My character commissions crimes with no more guilt than if she were ripping off her neighbors at a Tupperware party. Everyone in the film lives on relief, injury pay, social security, food stamps and welfare. I play a housewife who runs an electrolysis business in her living room in Queens. When the movie opens, I'm taking hairs out of my husband's back. I do six hundred and fifty hairs an hour."

For the past few years, Carroll has been making movies in Rome. She says one reason she decided to do the Warhol flick was to get an expense-paid trip home. "The first thing I did was order two kosher hot dogs, a corned beef and mustard on rye, and a gallon of ice cream. Then I plopped myself down in front of a TV set and watched everything that came on the screen.

"The two things I miss most living abroad are junk food and American TV. So when Andy called me and asked me to do this film, I thought, Why not? I have pages and pages of monologues and ten thousand bits of business. And I don't mind playing an older woman. I was so terrified of the lighting on a Warhol film I asked to play the oldest part."

She giggles that *Baby Doll* laugh that made her famous. It begins in the cleavage and works its way up in a series of gurgles that end up in a hee-haw. "I'll tell you one thing. Working in Italy, where everything is total chaos and none of the scripts ever make sense, prepared me for this kind of unconventional film. I would never have been able to do it fifteen years ago. Why, I even did one film where they dyed three hundred extras' pubic hair."

She couldn't have made a comeback for more willing movie buffs than Andy and his gang. They've seen every Carroll Baker movie ten times. "They're so darling," she whispers confidentially. "At one point, they wanted Tab Hunter and me to play the parents, and Sandra Dee for the daughter. Then they wanted me to play the daughter and Peggy Cass as the mother. Now they're billing it as Carroll *Baby Doll* Baker Meets Perry *Mandingo* King! The director is Andy's friend Jed Johnson, who is only twenty-seven. It's his first film. The other day, he turned to me and said: 'Did I direct that scene right?' I haven't been bored for a second. And frankly, I think the film has a chance of being very successful."

"It doesn't fit into any logical mold," says Perry King. "That's why it's such an adventure."

They're ready for the cast in the Queens kitchen. Airplanes fly over the stove on their way to LaGuardia. The table is littered with potato chips, Cokes, coffee cups, movie fan magazines, and baby bottles. Nobody seems to know what they're supposed to say or do in the scene. The writer hasn't finished writing it yet. Somebody sends for the fresh pages. Carroll licks her lipstick. Susan goes into her Thorazine trance. The bald baby screams its head off. Perry King whispers: "We had one day of rehearsal and the main direction to the entire cast was 'Remember—think *low!*' I went out and bought *Helter Skelter* for character study."

BAD will be ready for Christmas release. Just in time for suicide under the mistletoe.

Geraldine Fitzgerald

Steaming porridge. Frosty moors. Crisp Irish linen. Plain talk, no nonsense, and nourishing barley soup. These are the images one conjures from Geraldine Fitzgerald. She's too old to be called a colleen, but she's still a handsome, hearty broth of a woman with the same radish-cheeked complexion, sensible carriage and blarney-kissed humor of her native Ireland that made her an instant commodity back in the Forties on the Warner Brothers backlot. She still shows up on the Late Show in classics like *Dark Victory* and *Wuthering Heights,* but the winter of her years has now evolved into a new career—first as a character actress lighting up New York stages in recent hit revivals of *Ah, Wilderness!* and *Long Day's Journey Into Night,* and at this moment, as the rage of a new nightclub act that is packing them in at a tiny, smoke-filled cabaret called Brothers and Sisters. From the Brothers Warner to the Brothers and Sisters, she's come full circle.

It's impossible to describe what Geraldine Fitzgerald does to mesmerize an audience. Playwright Arthur Laurents says, "She can't sing a note, but she destroys you!" Go figure that one out. Geraldine says, "I've only got about four tones, but it's not what you've got, it's what you do with it that counts." She does plenty. She takes the ambition every man on the street has to sing, adds a fantastic acting technique and makes what she calls "street songs" personal and moving.

"These are the songs I used to sing as a young girl in the streets of Dublin and in the Irish countryside. I have done a lot of research and I find audiences enjoy learning where these songs came from. 'Greensleeves' was really written by Henry the Eighth. 'Danny Boy' is about the potato famine. 'The White Cliffs of Dover' was a World War II song sung by mothers in air-raid shelters under the subways to put their children to sleep while the bombs fell on London. I call them street songs because they can be performed anywhere, without microphones or stages or props. It's the most basic kind of popular art."

To aid her, she's got a pianist who plays for Benny Goodman and Gerry Mulligan, and a percussionist who fills in on everything from saxophones and wind instruments to an exotic Irish drum called a "bodhran," which looks like the pans miners used when panning for gold.

From such bizarre remnants, she has assembled an unusual act that leaves audiences screaming with applause. "It's all been quite an accident, really. It all started when I went to audition for the role of Joanne Woodward's mother in Paul Newman's film *Rachel, Rachel*. I wore a gray wig, and they thought I was the new nanny. Joanne was terrifically pleased to see me and said, 'Thank goodness you're here.' I said, 'Don't you want to know what I've been doing lately?' and she said, 'Oh no, we don't care about your references, just go right into the children's room.'

"It took her a few minutes before she roared with laughter and said, 'Oh, my God, it's Geraldine!' Well, what happened was they rewrote one of the men's parts and made me a crazy revival tent preacher, and I had to sing in the scene. There was a vocal teacher named Andy Anselmo on the set that day, and he said he could teach me to organize the sounds so they wouldn't fly all over the place, and I'd be able to express myself musically the way Rex Harrison does! That's really how it all began."

Most people wonder why a mature woman, whose aunt was the woman Sean O'Casey wrote all of his great plays for, with a rich husband (Stuart Scheftel, former publisher of *The New York Post*) and a comfortable life would want to toil for a living in a shoebox-sized nightclub. "Because," she says, wide-eyed with surprise at the insouciance of such a question, "I really, really love to sing. My family hated the idea. At first, Andy took me out to these remote clubs in the slag heaps of New Jersey, and I'd get up and sing 'More,' and they weren't very polite. My family would tag along loyally and say, 'Don't do this to yourself!' But I have always wanted to sing.

"I'm probably the only mother alive whose lullabies were rejected by her own children in their nursery. But serious people in the theater like Julie Harris, Henry Fonda, Eileen Heckart and James Whitmore are all doing one-person shows. That's how this act started.

"I had to devise my own way of working because nobody is writing parts for actresses my age anymore. In this business, if you aren't thirty, you must at least give the impression of being thirty to be considered usable, especially if you're a woman. When a woman reaches that middle period, when she stops looking twenty but isn't old yet, she has a terrible time finding enough work to sustain her creative needs. If I had stayed in films, I'd be all washed up. That's why so many celebrated film actresses end up being so miserable and confused. They are expected to look the same forever. They're never allowed to develop into whatever they become. Audiences still want to see Bette Davis, but when they get into the movie they're disappointed because they aren't seeing the Bette Davis of thirty years ago."

Geraldine Fitzgerald's own Hollywood days were less than glorious. She was poisoned by George Sanders in *Uncle Harry*, terrorized by Peter Lorre and Sydney Greenstreet in *Three Strangers*, swindled by John Garfield in *Nobody Lives Forever* and gave up her life as a spy for Alan Ladd in *O.S.S.* They could never figure out what kind of slot to fit her

into. "I wasn't exactly this, I wasn't exactly that, and Jack
Warner was never very good at developing what a person
really was. Bette Davis was the only one who got to do
everything, and she had to fight like hell to do it." Geraldine
had beauty, brains, talent, and an unusual chocolate-syrup
voice. For a while, she was the "best friend." Then she was
an Ingrid Bergman type. She was never herself. "The place
where I could have broken through was *The Maltese Falcon*
because John Huston would have presented me as a siren,
but I was having a row with Jack Warner at the time. If I had
played that, then Warners would probably have said, 'Ah,
yes, that's what she is, at last we know!'

"What I should have done is what Humphrey Bogart told
me to do. He said, 'Do everything they throw at you and
maybe you'll click in one of them!' But I was always trying
to get back to the theater or worrying about whether what
I was doing was art. That's not the way to have a career. I
didn't have the vaguest idea how to survive in Hollywood.
Bette Davis fought all these violent battles, but she staged
her greatest fights at a period when she was big box office.
I didn't have any muscle, and I didn't have a big enough
body of work for the public to support me. I made awful
mistakes, but looking back on it, it was my own ignorance
that prevented me from becoming a star."

She had grown up in the intellectual Dublin theater—that
Irish equivalent to London's Bloomsbury group. O'Casey.
Yeats. Synge. James Joyce. They shook the world. Total integrity. Nothing vulgar like interviews in the press or (God
forbid!) money. The young Geraldine's pretty head was full
of arty plans. She played with Orson Welles's Mercury
Theatre in *Heartbreak House* and *Julius Caesar.* Then
Welles decided to combine all five of Shakespeare's Henry
kings into one play, and there was no role for her, so she
accepted an offer from Hal Wallis to travel to Hollywood for
a screen test.

While she was working with Bette Davis and Bogart in
Dark Victory, the Mercury went bankrupt and she was
stranded in Lotus Land in a state of frustration and terror.

"It was 1938, when all sorts of dazzling people were at
Warners—Ben Hecht, Aldous Huxley, William Faulkner.

Dorothy Parker used to sit in a tiny room while Joan Crawford slashed red lines through her dialogue. I used to think
these people were standing up to the system like I was, but
they weren't. They were giving in when they had to, which
was the right way. The answer to people like me is don't go
to Hollywood. Don't have the hubris to think you can make
it work with integrity when you are, in fact, dealing with an
industry.

"Movie-making is not too different from manufacturing
airplane motors, except it's people, instead of machinery,
being turned out on an assembly line. Igor Stravinsky was
there working for Walt Disney, and he didn't have anything
to do with anybody, but he wasn't in the position of having
to find parts or build a career. Now I read in the papers that
Miss Somebody is going into TV or the movies, and she's
determined to do only good things. I just laugh, because I
know these youngsters are going to suffer. By the time I
figured it all out, the war was on, I was separated from my
first husband with a child to support, and I couldn't stay on
suspension any longer. I had to earn a living. So I did everything I was offered, but by that time I had lost the momentum and the contacts, and my career was in a shambles."

So she left Hollywood, married Stuart Scheftel, whom she
met in 1943 when he was running for Congress on the Lower
East Side, and after a long struggle to keep a career alive,
she retired. Her daughter, Susie, was born and she stayed
home. "Then when I did start to pursue a career again, I was
able to do it as the person I had become. If anyone was
looking for the lady in *Wuthering Heights* they didn't find
her.

"One day when I was playing Gary Cooper's wife in *Ten
North Frederick*, Norma Shearer came to see me. I'll never
forget what she told me: 'I admire your courage, Geraldine,
starting all over again in character roles. It's something I will
never do, because time has passed me by.' That's the saddest
thing about Hollywood. It has no memory."

She's not a woman who lives in the past, but when she
thumbs through her old scrapbooks, funny memories come
back to prick her. "Here's a photo of Orson Welles and me.
We had a great flirtation that didn't come to much, but we

never had the great love affair we were rumored to have had at the time. The rumor is that Michael Lindsay-Hogg, my son, is really Orson's son. I've never discussed it for publication, but I can understand the rumor because there is a resemblance." Michael is now a successful director himself, having just completed a film of Muriel Spark's *The Abbess of Crewe* with Glenda Jackson, Melina Mercouri, Geraldine Page, Sandy Dennis, and Anne Jackson.

"It isn't true, but I can tell you how it got started. During the war, Michael's father, Eddie Lindsay-Hogg, was in New York raising money for the Red Cross, and I was out in Hollywood staying with Orson. We were just good friends. He was having a terrific love affair with Dolores Del Rio, and they kept an apartment in town. One night he came to the house he owned where I was staying to pick up some things, the servants were away, and I was in bed with a terrible case of career depression, in an advanced state of pregnancy. So Orson came in and said, 'Get up, get dressed, and I'll take you out to a smashing supper at Chasen's and tell you about what I'm going to direct for my first movie.'

"So here I am living in Orson's house, and the two of us showed up at Chasen's with me terrifically pregnant, and that's where the rumor started." The movie turned out to be *Citizen Kane,* the structure was an idea he got from his house guest, and she ended up with a scandal. "So at the bottom of this whole heap of people who gave birth to that classic film was your heavily pregnant old friend Geraldine." And that's how Hollywood autobiographies are born.

Walter Matthau and Alexis Smith

RUIDOSO, N.M.—From the air all you can see is a sea of Stetsons. For 364 days a year, this peaceful mountain village is the home of three thousand five hundred ranchers, a few sleepy Apaches and one stop sign. On the 365th day, it becomes a crowd scene from *The Day of the Locust* as thirty-five thousand brawling Texans invade the soft rural mesas draped in Indian turquoise jewelry, cowboy boots, peroxided beehive hairdos cemented with spray net, pot bellies hanging over their Roy Rogers belt buckles, and polyester double-knit suits.

They are here, with more money than taste, to watch the $1 million All-American Futurity—a tiny race on a tiny track in which two-year-old quarter horses run 440 yards and it's all over in twenty seconds. They fly in on their private planes, which they line up at the local airport, cruise around the track on a narrow course that leads from the Jockey Club to the horse barn in dust-covered custom-made Cadillac pickup trucks from Neiman-Marcus, and the townspeople line up when they leave town to applaud their exits. It's an annual circus that brings in enough Texas silver dollars to keep the town of Ruidoso in tacos for another year, and nobody complains about the five thousand tons of garbage that must be cleaned up when everybody leaves. Sort of a Mardi Gras with spurs. And when it's Texas garbage, there might be a diamond in it.

This year, there's more excitement than usual because in addition to the big race, Ray Stark and his Hollywood film factory have arrived to shoot a genuine, old-fashioned, G-rated horse-racing epic called *Casey's Shadow,* about a man, a horse, a villain, and a wealthy lady horse-owner. Martin Ritt is directing, and in addition to the Texas matrons who look like Jane Withers in *Giant,* the rich, battered ranchers who look like Gene Autry find themselves standing next to swell folks like Walter Matthau and Alexis Smith at the $5 daily-double window.

The horses are at the starting gate for the first of the day's thirteen races, and because I'm green as a loblolly pine, I'm depending on Walter Matthau to handicap the winner. "The most important thing about betting," says Matthau, studying his racing form, "is how you manage your money. You can pick a winner every race and leave the track broke." After Matthau balances the horses' weight, age, and winning record against their breeding background, he comes up with some fancy calculations. The result is a sure winner. I place $10 on You Rascal You, while Matthau explains the movie.

"I play a Louisiana Cajun who falls in love with a horse nobody has any faith in. Somehow I manage to drag that nag all the way to New Mexico and enter the Futurity. It's like *National Velvet.* I'm doing the Cajun accent in what I call Brooklyn Jewish Southern, with a bit of *Merci* thrown in. Marty Ritt said we'd need English subtitles. But I'm pretty good at accents. I did a hundred accents on the old *Mr. Eye-magination* TV show—six German, forty-two Jews, and I don't know how many others. I also do a serious French and a comedic French. The accent is the easiest part. The physical work is the hard part. I haven't done a Western for years. I thought it would be a good change of pace to get back into jeans and cowboy boots. As you know, I haven't been well. But I got tired of sitting around the house."

Matthau is recovering from open-heart surgery. He's suffered and survived several heart attacks. He also has, at this very moment, walking hepatitis. Marty Ritt, who directed him in *Pete and Tillie* and loves the guy, says he's holding down the rough stuff, changing some of the fight scenes, and preserving the star's energy as much as possible. "He's usually good for two takes, then when I see he's getting winded, I shut it down." Matthau looks pallid and exhausted, but he's full of the old moxie. He says, "The high altitude is killing me. I did two takes yesterday, called my doctor, and said I was dying. He said, 'What were you doing all day?' I said, 'Rooting for horses at the top of my lungs!' He said, 'Schmuck, you're just hyperventilating!'" He stuffs Vicks Vap-o-rub in his nose to breathe, and before each shot he chews three packs of sodium saccharine sugarless Carefree bubblegum. "I mix it with chocolate syrup in my mouth, then spit it all out, and on the screen it looks like I'm spitting tobacco juice." And that's how you win Oscars.

Mrs. Matthau, the exotic ex-wife of William Saroyan, sits in a corner with a handful of $10 bills, smoking violently when Walter's back is turned because he disapproves of cigarettes since his surgery, watching the race on a TV monitor with binoculars while a sassy black lady named Rae-Rae keeps a ledger of all the money she's losing. "Does Rae-Rae work for you?" I ask. "No," Walter interrupts, "she just hangs around with us on salary. I don't really know what she does."

Matthau has a $500 bet on You Rascal You to show. The horse comes in fifth. "This is not makeup you see—it's my arteries collapsing."

There are two private clubs atop the Ruidoso Downs track. The Turf Club is where rich Texas cowboys pay as much as $17,000 apiece to sit in plastic chairs to watch the races on TV and drink Coors beer. The Jockey Club is where they pay even more to sit in suede chairs and eat tamale pie. The Jockey Club is where the sophisticated highrollers hang out. That means they wear one turquoise ring instead of five. Alexis Smith is sitting in a reserved seat for the third race marked P.J. Higginbottom. "Oh, I've been P.J. Higginbottom for three days," she grins. She tells me to bet twenty dollars on Phone the Baby. It's a hot tip from the ladies' room attendant. "How are you doing?" I ask, still recovering from the French jeans and bandana she's wearing. It's a far cry from the sequins and feathers she wore on Broadway in *Follies.* "Oh, I've lost a fortune," she smiles cheerily.

Alexis plays a wealthy owner-trainer who tries to buy Matthau's horse. "I'm always playing a wealthy something. I don't think I've ever been seen washing kitchen pots, except at home. I'm having a ball, though. All I know about quarter-horse racing is that they're called quarter horses because they only run a quarter of a mile. They always said in Hollywood that I was the well-bred horsey set type. Well, I used to resent that but now I'm glad they still think that way because I finally got a job. Actually, I do look good on a horse, but I never stay on very long. People talk about the good old days but I prefer the way films are made today. As opposed to sets and sound stages, we're shooting this whole movie on location with hand-held cameras, new fast film, very little light—in a straightforward, direct, almost documentary style. It's a tougher industry, but much more exciting. In the old days when I was making Westerns with Errol Flynn at Warner Brothers, we'd be riding into an ambush while they ran the scenery by us on a rear-screen projector. Errol Flynn and I would be sitting in a rocking chair with a tail on it."

Phone the Baby gets lost in the backstretch. We tear up our bets and amble over to the auction barn, where dirt-soaked critters who look like Yosemite Sam are bidding $150,000 on foals, mares, and nags who look like plow horses. Real people who sound exactly like the TV auctioneers in Philip Morris commercials yell jabberwocky while the millions light up on the sale board. The only difference is they're selling horses, not tobacco.

It's the real thing, but it looks like a movie set. Producer Ray Stark has set up extra cameras for the movie-within-a-movie he's making about the four-legged star of *Casey's Shadow.* "I've fallen in love with a horse," he says, red-nosed and beaming. "So I'm doing a comic documentary on him. This movie has been a blast. I own horses, so it's right down my alley. We could never get this footage anywhere else in the world. We stop workouts in the morning to shoot real horses, real jockeys, real trainers. We've put our cameras everywhere. My own little movie starts with Casey's Shadow living in Burbank, looking through a kitchen window at a TV soap opera, and ending up in the movies. He gets bored with the life of a star, and a voice-over which represents the horse thinking aloud says, 'This is a crummy life, up at 6 A.M., meeting journalists, signing autographs!' But it comes out okay in the end. I've got a great cameraman lining him up for a shot and he says, 'If he can make Barbra Streisand look good, think what he can do for me!' " Stark, who brought Streisand to the films, roars at the comparison. The real horse in the movie is lovable, but a lousy runner. He uses five other horses as stand-ins in the action scenes. When I ask Stark how old the star is, he sneers: "Would I ask you how old you are?" There's one major difference, he adds, between Casey's Shadow and Streisand—this one gets paid in oats and hay.

Back at the Turf Club, my wallet is several pounds lighter. Martin Ritt, who used to make his living at the track during the days when he was blacklisted, has lost me $20 on Baron Frankenstein, cameraman John Alonzo has lost me $50 on Pinball Wizard, and Alexis Smith has cleaned me out of another $50 with another of her hot tips from the ladies' room on Mystic Moon Dust. Alexis orders a bowl of Texas three-alarm chili. The waitress says, "It's so dang hot it'd give a mule harelip!"

An ancient crone in blue jeans and diamond earrings stops the glamorous star on her way out. "You in the movie?" "Yes, I'm Alexis Smith." "Smith? I know some Smiths up by Big Springs. I'm Cole. Cole Ranch. I'm sure you heard of us?" She had never heard of Alexis Smith.

The last face I see, in the debris of day's end, is Walter Matthau, alone and dejected, staring at a table full of torn betting tickets. It hasn't been a bad day. He only lost $10,000. "My gambling is a sickness. I went to a psychiatrist to get cured, but after the second appointment I became so depressed I went straight to the track and lost a thousand dollars and that cured me forever."

"Of gambling?"

"No, of the psychiatrist."

And the next morning, when the loudspeaker announced "The horses are at the starting gate," Walter Matthau was the first Stetson in line at the $2 window.

William Holden

William Holden is an enigma. He's been a movie star for thirty-seven years, yet the idea of an acting career still embarrasses him. He's appeared in more than sixty motion pictures, yet he takes so little interest in them he can't even remember their names.

He won an Academy Award, but calls himself a "limited talent." Now, at fifty-eight, the golden, open-faced beauty of his youth is gone, replaced by lines and bags and life-battered fatigue. He's made a fortune and lost most of it. Married for thirty-two years to Brenda Marshall, he's now divorced and a grandfather many times over. Once the extroverted darling of Hollywood, he now spends little time in America, preferring instead to roam the exotic outposts of the world in search of headier pursuits with his new soulmate and traveling companion, actress Stefanie Powers. The man is world-weary.

And yet . . . Holden may have given up interest in movies, but the movies still care about him. Since 1960, his appearances have been rare. Since *The Bridge on the River Kwai*, his films have been bombs; his performances tired, listless, and mechanical. Now there's *Network,* the brilliant, provocative new Sidney Lumet film, and once again, like a rocket, William Holden is soaring to attention. This one he likes—so much so that it is obvious from his touching, deeply felt portrayal of a TV executive from the old Ed Murrow days replaced by the industry's new breed of piranha fish that he cared enough to do his very best. "I'm at the age of male menopause," he says with a grin, "so why shouldn't I play it?" He even came out of the woodwork to publicize *Network,* yet just in case anyone gets the idea that William Holden is going back for good, he's going right back into his hole again. "Acting is just a vocation that pays for my avocations."

He spent all of his time in New York between interviews trying to get into the Egyptian exhibition at the Metropolitan Museum and the Alexander Calder exhibit at the Whitney. The most unassuming of actors, he shunned the glamorous hotels for a remote pension without a lobby or a doorman. And when he does settle down for a chat, he glazes over with boredom on the subject of movies, but he brightens like a kid on his birthday when he discusses archaeology, botany, and animal conservation. When he's in California, he spends his spare time cross-indexing the history of every *National Geographic* he's collected since childhood.

"Life," he says, "becomes so undimensional when it revolves around that sole endeavor of just being an actor."

He met Stefanie Powers at a celebrity tennis match. They were both going through divorce pains. Hollywood insiders credit her with curing Holden's drinking problem and him with providing a focus for her travel lust. Together, they've brought back a treasure of New Guinea art that is selling out at Bloomingdale's. "When we got to know each other," he confides, "we realized we had this great opportunity to use movie locations to study the culture of people in remote places instead of just the amount of celluloid that has to be accomplished. Some people spend their time on location looking for good restaurants; we spend our time studying the heritage, the art, the rituals, ceremonies and mores. I've never had a relationship with any woman so fulfilling."

He can discuss the funeral objects buried with the emperor of the Huang Dynasty in 210 B.C. the way most actors discuss their percentage of the gross, and he country-drops the way most people name-drop. "My parents always subscribed to the *National Geographic.* It was my greatest escape as a kid, reading about the flora, fauna, and tribal life of Africa. That was always a dream of mine, to see the world, so, finally, when things could be coordinated with a film project, I took advantage of it. Sometimes I had already been to a place before I made the movie. I was in Hong Kong in 1951, three or four years before I did *Love Is a Many-Splendored Thing.*

"One of the reasons my marriage ended was because my wife was not simpatico with my wanderlust. She went with me sometimes, but most places were too dangerous to take a woman. I was exploring the northern frontier of Kenya on safari before it was safe. We grew apart in our interests. That's fine. To each his own. Now I come back from the Gobi Desert or the Southwest Pacific and people say, 'Do you play golf?' or, 'There's marvelous skiing in Aspen this winter,' and I say, 'Sorry, but Stefanie and I are going to the Galapagos Islands on a Darwin Explorer, then we'll follow the headwaters of the Amazon.' After I finish promoting *Network,* we're going to north East Africa, then I have an assignment to capture two more Somali wild ass in Ethiopia for the Basel Zoo in Switzerland. So we're leaving for Venice, then we'll ship over to Egypt through the Valley of the Kings and Aswan, boat down to Khartoum and the source of the Blue Nile, which I've never seen, then to Addis Ababa, then drive back home to Mount Kenya."

"Home" is the famous Mount Kenya Safari Club, a Shangri-la right out of a Hemingway setting, with sixty acres, fruit and vegetable gardens, tennis courts, swimming pools, trout streams, a hundred and twenty employees, a complete African village and a prize rose garden. In recent years this "avocation" has expanded to the Mount Kenya Game Ranch, where Holden develops nucleus breeding herds among endangered species like bongos, gazelles, and white zebra. He also conducts tours for African children ignorant of their own country's magnificent animals, experiments on red fever epidemics, trains teams to ship and accompany animals for export, and has even helped established game preserves as far away as Iraq and Japan.

"I try to explain to people what I do, and they just look at me blankly. They can't comprehend what it's like to work twelve hours a day on the equator, dehorning and castrating wild eland or spending four and a half months trying to capture a Somali wild ass. It's about as tough a thing as you can do, physically. I do the roping and my partner does the driving. It's a very active life, especially when you're holding on to the ass end of a wild animal that weighs a few tons when he doesn't want to go into the crate. It's a labor of love. There's no money in it."

So where does that leave acting? "I make movies to pay for it. I've established my priorities. After a certain age, acting is just no longer a very manly profession. Actors have to put on wigs and beards and wear togas and God knows what to express themselves. I was never the toga type. Somebody said to me, 'Charlton Heston is getting all the parts you should play,' and I said, 'Have you ever seen my legs?' My corridor is narrower. I'm not a great actor, I'm a competent contemporary reporter. I can get across, at certain times, a quality of humanizing a character so that some garage mechanic in Des Moines can say, 'Jeezus, look what that poor sonuvabitch is going through. He's just like me!'

"It's getting harder to find those parts to play. I usually get gun-slinging cops in trenchcoats. Then I just have to find a way to make the incredible characters credible. A picture like *Network* is a hot roll of the dice. I'm damned lucky to get it. Faye Dunaway and I were in *Towering Inferno* together, and on that one we were two cardboard characters making points of exposition about where the fire extinguishers should go. We were something to cut to while a burning building was the star. Compared to that, our work in *Network* is a piece of cake.

"We brought *Network* in eight days under schedule and seven hundred thousand dollars under budget, so you know we worked like sonuvabitches. I think it's a helluva movie, and now Hollywood is talking its usual Oscar talk, but awards mean nothing. Winning an Oscar has never been a consideration in choosing a role. I'm just proud of it, and that's more than I can usually say about my films. I've been up and I've been down. When I did *Golden Boy* in 1939, I didn't know anything about acting. Barbara Stanwyck coached me at night, even gave up her best takes to make me look good. I'll never forget her for that.

"Then I went into the army, and when I got out I was artistically and financially bankrupt, with three kids to support and back income tax to pay. I used to do a radio show at seven A.M. before I went to the studio, just to make extra money. I took all the jobs nobody else wanted just to make the ends meet. It was five years before *Sunset Boulevard* came along. That was the turning point. After that, I was under contract to two studios at the same time, and I was grinding out six pictures a year. I went on suspension eight times for refusing the junk they threw at me. I was in a ninety-nine percent tax bracket, so I had to work to pay the expenses. I finally just ran away to Hong Kong, Switzerland, and Africa to get out of the rat race."

When his face started to deteriorate, the wags said he was drinking heavily, a reputation that Holden says was "highly exaggerated."

"You're shaving in this racket while other people are having martinis. Your whole clock is turned around. It doesn't really matter what time of day you take a drink, because it's your night. I can't take the physical punishment any longer. I haven't had a drink in years."

If he writes his autobiography some day, this articulate, well-bred iconoclast says, he won't be ashamed or guilty about anything. "The word I feel is regret. I'm sorry I had to do so many damned silly things on film. I had to shave my chest every day on *Picnic* because the motion picture code said hairy chests were dirty. Do you think it's fun to stand in front of a mirror and start at your sideburns and sweep that razor all the way down to your navel every morning at six o'clock? I hated it. I hated anything that was phony. I hated makeup. I wouldn't wear stomach binders or chin lifts or hairpieces, either." One of the most moving things about his performance in *Network* is hearing so many old-fashioned virtues like dignity, pride, and love coming out of such an old, shopworn face.

Holden says he can now look into a mirror, and like what he sees. "What am I? A craggy-faced, middle-aged man. I can't grow younger. People seeing *Network* say, 'God! He's getting old.' Fortunately, they don't have reruns of their past on TV. They don't realize that when they see me playing the violin and trying to learn how to box on the Late Show, it was thirty-eight years ago and I was twenty years old. But at least I no longer have to sit on the edge of Gloria Swanson's bed with one foot on the floor and my overcoat on. The movies have grown up and so have I."

With that, he was off to catch a plane for home, 12,000 miles away, where the baobab trees don't come from studio props, and the life you save in the jungle may be your own.

THE
NEW BREED

Jimmy Coco

Jimmy Coco says he is one person who can accurately testify to having witnessed a genuine miracle. The miracle, he explains, is his career. "For a fat little kid from the Bronx whose father was a shoemaker, I've had some pretty terrific leading ladies—Liza Minnelli, Sophia Loren, Elizabeth Taylor, Raquel Welch, Dyan Cannon! I definitely believe in a hereafter. I cannot wait to join that repertory company in the sky and meet Jean Harlow."

Right now, he'd settle for Priscilla Lane. "I spent my childhood being madly in love with her. I saw every movie she ever made ten times, and I still have eight Priscilla Lane scrapbooks. I never met her, but once on a TV show they arranged for a phone call to her and she actually talked to me. I was a babbling idiot. For Priscilla Lane, I'd even drop a hundred pounds and give up Mars bars."

Maybe Priscilla wouldn't mind. Nobody else does. The old cliché about how everybody loves a fat man is certainly true where Jimmy Coco is concerned. His fans love him, his co-stars love him and the critics love him. Although his recent

TV series, *The Dumplings,* folded, he's the big hit in this summer's detective spoof, *Murder by Death,* and is now touring to standing ovations in a summer stock revival of the old George Kaufman–Moss Hart comedy *George Washington Slept Here.*

Priscilla Lane hasn't shown up in the audience yet, but Coco is praying. "I always pray. Before every opening night, I stand in the wings doing the sign of the cross. I'll promise anything to God if He'll just make it go right. 'Just do it this time, God, and I swear I'll never ask another favor!' " The way he figures it, at the present time, he owes God about 475 years of back payments.

Backstage at *George Washington Slept Here,* or for that matter any set where Jimmy Coco works, is always a funny, comfortable place to be. He exudes an epidemic of smiles. "The whole point is to be happy. As a kid I did summer stock with stars who cut all of my laughs, and I'd go away miserable, thinking, 'That's not what acting is all about.' Why can't we all have a piece of the limelight? Ever since then I've tried to gather around me a group of people I love and respect, and I always have a good time.

"When I read this play, I said, 'I can't do this—it's all wrong for me.' The husband was a ninny and the wife was a tough, wisecracking broad. Dody [Goodman] couldn't play that, either. So we reversed the roles the way they did in the movie with Jack Benny and Ann Sheridan, and it was much funnier.

"Then Kitty Carlisle and George Kaufman's daughter objected to that because they hated the movie, so I had to convince them to let us do it. They both came to Stockbridge to see the show and loved it. Now they're talking about bringing it to Broadway!"

Coco is truly dedicated to the business and that rubs off on his audience. "If I'm happy, I can't wait to get to the theater. It's like Judy Garland and Mickey Rooney saying, 'Let's put on a show in the barn!' That's the best part of making it. You can set your own pace and establish a tone for your co-workers to follow. Carol Burnett does that. You get on that set and everybody falls into the same happy mood she's in.

I have never done anything where I was miserable that was ever a success.

"The worst experience was making *The Bluebird* in Russia. Everyone was miserable. My room was the game room, and everybody gathered there and played cards all night. The last time I saw Ava Gardner, she was drinking vodka out of a milk bottle and yelling, 'Get me out of here!' I knew that movie would be a bomb." Coco ended up getting out of it by going under the knife to have his gall bladder removed. Now the critics are all saying he was the luckiest member of the cast.

It was a different story on *Murder by Death.* "There were ten major stars, and on the first day we all met to read the script aloud for Neil Simon, I thought I would have a coronary. The door opened, and people like Alec Guinness and Maggie Smith and Peter Sellers walked in, and Eileen Brennan grabbed my hand and said, 'Sit next to me, please, don't you feel tiny?' Well, Doc Simon is such a marvelous audience that he started laughing at his own lines, and after five minutes we were like a family. David Niven said, 'Is anybody here as nervous as I am?' and we were off.

"There were ten trailers with ten stars on the doors. All the same size, so nobody felt like a bigger star than anybody else. Everyone had a chair with a name on it on the set and a monogrammed script. There was no temperament. Even Truman Capote joined in. At first the word was, 'Don't say anything in front of him, or you'll end up in his book!' But we got over that. Maggie Smith spent her time in my trailer playing Scrabble. Peter Sellers kept breaking me up on camera. David Niven took everyone to lunch. Estelle Winwood was always smoking one cigarette after another and playing gin rummy in full makeup and high heels at age ninety-four, nobody helping her, always on time. It was terrific."

He went from that to *The Dumplings,* which was also fun but a ratings disaster. "I don't regret it. That's the difference between New York actors and Hollywood actors. The Hollywood actor in a flop sits around his pool in Beverly Hills getting a depressed ulcer. The New York actor goes home and says, 'Okay, I'm ready to do a play.' I've been in eight hundred flops that closed in New Haven. So thirteen weeks in a TV series is a long run, baby!"

Coco is like Sylvia Miles. He'll go anywhere and do anything if the role is good enough. "That's what acting is all about. I admire that lady. She's done two seven-minute scenes and been nominated for two Oscars for both of them. You've got to go where the work is and not be afraid of some phony status. I still live in a small apartment in Greenwich Village and study with Uta Hagen between jobs, and I'll go anywhere to check out a part. I'm always hanging out in off-off-Broadway lofts looking at new plays. I've been known to go to Pittsburgh to see a good horror film. I have no patience with actors who are snobs about acting. They price themselves right out of the business."

And it's the "business" that still awes him. "I went to see a play in Los Angeles, and this beautiful lady turned around in her seat, threw her arms around me and told me she was my biggest fan. It turned out to be Lana Turner. *Lana Turner!* I almost fainted."

It's always been like that. As a fat kid growing up in the Bronx, he spent every waking moment at the old Pilgrim Theatre staring at the movie screen in a hypnotic trance. "My father thought I was crazy. I was no Clark Gable. If you lived in the Bronx, you either had to open a grocery store or become a gangster. I got a job in a children's production of *Snow White and the Seven Dwarfs.* Later, I discovered Snow White was a hooker and the seven dwarfs were perverts. I played the wicked witch in drag. I didn't care. I was in the theater."

Timing was part of his success. It was a time when character actors were coming across in TV commercials, promoting the "common man" identity factor to sell products. "Suddenly you could sell Drano and not have to look like Tab Hunter," he grins owlishly. "But I still had to make my own opportunities. I was the one who begged my friend Terence McNally to write a play for me, and he came up with *Next,* about a fat man who gets drafted. Elaine May brought Neil Simon to see it, and he handed me one act of *Last of the Red Hot Lovers* and wrote the other two acts around my personality. How lucky can you get?" He was an instant star. It only took twenty-three years.

Now he calls his own shots, and some of the toughest people in show business hug him a lot. In Paris, Sophia Loren makes spaghetti for him when he's in town. In Russia, Elizabeth Taylor sat on the floor eating whatever he cooked on his hotplate and even helped him wash dishes in the bathtub. Otto Preminger calls him regularly and doesn't yell. And to his old friends in the Bronx, he's a hero.

"Whenever I'm in a flop on TV, everybody in the Bronx writes letters to the president of the network saying, 'We'll get you for this!' All the Bronx watched *The Dumplings*. Why don't they have Nielsen boxes in the Bronx?"

His biggest disappointment is still that lamented series, *Calucci's Dept.*, which, he says, "was truly ahead of its time. It now has a cult following, but at the time, they said nobody knew what an unemployment office was. Well, everybody knows now. Also, I was very disappointed in *Man of La Mancha*. I spent eight months in Rome on that one, and it was awful. But you can't brood about those things. I never worry about the next job."

He still worries about his weight. The irony is that although it's been a source of personal agony all his life, his roly-poly, dancing-hippo quality has been partially responsible for his career. "I once got up to three hundred pounds, and then I had to do something because it was beginning to interfere with my work. Now I take off thirty pounds at a clip, and I do feel better.

"But I get tons of mail from fat people who believe if I can make it, anybody can. It gives them hope. Mainly I just got tired of being offered plays about fat jokes. I didn't want to be a sight gag. And my pet peeve in life is skinny people who go around talking about how easy it is to be skinny. It isn't easy."

His pet hate at the moment is Cloris Leachman, who announced on a talk show that "fat people pollute the environment." He turns into a raging rhino at the thought. "She said there should be fatcatchers, just like dogcatchers, and fat people should have nets thrown over them. Well, there was an uproar. I got on the Dinah Shore show and said somebody should throw a net over Cloris Leachman!—and meant it! Who the hell does she think she is? Not exactly the happiest, most well-adjusted lady in the world, is she?"

So Jimmy Coco is quite content the way he is, thank you very much, skipping through fields of pasta with an occasional detour through Baskin-Robbins. He's clean, but not neat. "I might drop my clothes all over the house, but my Priscilla Lane scrapbooks are in perfect order."

He might not do another TV series ("My best show on *The Dumplings* was never seen because we were preempted by a Ronald Reagan speech!"), but he plans to die onstage. Today, it's rave reviews and playing onze and poker till 4 A.M. Who knows? At 175 pounds, with a lettuce diet and a Cardin bikini, tomorrow it might be the world.

THE ANDREWS SISTERS
"We don't want to educate the public. We just want to
entertain them." (UPI)

GINGER ROGERS
"There's no Hollywood left."

(PHOTO BY JOHN ENGSTEAD)

DODY GOODMAN
You could work all
your life and never
develop a voice
that funny.
(PHOTO BY CRIS ALEXANDER)

CARROLL BAKER
"The two things I miss
most living abroad are
junk food
and American TV."
(PHOTO BY ZOË DOMINIC,
COURTESY OF CARROLL BAKER)

GERALDINE FITZGERALD
"Movie-making is not too different from manufacturing airplane motors."
(WIDE WORLD PHOTOS)

WALTER MATTHAU AND ALEXIS SMITH
"This is not makeup you see—it's my arteries collapsing."
(REPRINTED WITH PERMISSION OF COLUMBIA PICTURES)

WILLIAM HOLDEN
"I'm at the age of male menopause, so why shouldn't I play it?"
(FROM THE MGM RELEASE *Network* © 1976 BY METRO-GOLDWYN-MAYER, INC.,
AND UNITED ARTISTS CORPORATION)

JIMMY COCO
"Just do it this time, God,
and I swear I'll never
ask for another favor."
(AUTHOR'S COLLECTION)

ROBERT EVANS (*with the author*)
"You've got to have guts to be a producer and I've got plenty of guts."
(PHOTO BY PAUL SCHUMACH/METROPOLITAN PHOTO SERVICE, INC.)

VALERIE PERRINE
"It's so much more fun
to be tacky."
(PHOTO BY ELLEN GRAHAM)

DIANE LADD
The warm, wacky dame
from Meridian, Mississippi.

JEFF BRIDGES
"I could throw up for you."
(WIDE WORLD PHOTOS)

ROY SCHEIDER
"There was nothing normal about making *Jaws*."

ELLEN BURSTYN
(*from the television series* Iron Horse)
"I have no time to sit down and do my crossword puzzles."

KATHARINE ROSS (*with the author*)
"I've always had a natural curiosity about life. I guess it's
not fully satisfied by merely being an actress." (AUTHOR'S COLLECTION)

MADELINE KAHN
"I guess I
must be funny."
(COURTESY OF TWENTIETH
CENTURY-FOX
At Long Last Love
© 1975 TWENTIETH
CENTURY-FOX FILM
CORPORATION.
ALL RIGHTS RESERVED)

GENEVIEVE BUJOLD
"I am like a
woman who is
always in labor."

GIANCARLO GIANNINI
"My goal is to find the strength to stop acting." (UPI)

DAVID BOWIE
Nobody can prove
he's not from
outer space.
(PHOTO BY
ELLEN GRAHAM)

ROBERT REDFORD
"I often feel I'll just opt out of this rat race and buy another
hunk of Utah." (PHOTO BY HOWARD BINGHAM)

Robert Evans

Robert Evans has everything. Except, maybe, happiness. But never mind. "Success," he says, paraphrasing an advertising gambit he invented for *Love Story*, "means never having to admit you're unhappy." After all, Robert Evans lives in Hollywood, where if you don't have happiness, you send out for it.

He has everything else. At forty-six, he looks like a tennis player, half the age of the guys he went to school with back in his New York growing-up days. As vice-president of Paramount Pictures in charge of worldwide production, he held in his sun-tanned hands the fates of the most powerful and creative talents in Hollywood's dying movie industry, where he was the only executive with an additional contract that allowed him not only to run the creative side of the studio but to produce his own films as well.

Now, with *Chinatown* and *Marathon Man* roaring to box-office history like a bonfire out of control, he's envied even more in a town where they swallow their jealousy with their morning melon. Robert Evans has the Midas touch. All the cigars and mink coats and hypoallergenic eyeshadows in

Hollywood hover around him daily, but he's clearly the biggest star in town.

He lives hard, plays hard, and works hard. He has cars, beach houses, hot and cold running women. He's been married to three beautiful actresses—Sharon Hugueny, Camilla Sparv, and Ali MacGraw—and has a hundred others ready to pop out of his Gucci phone book when he presses a button. He has a beautiful son, Joshua, who looks so much like his mother, Ali MacGraw, that when he stands up in the bathtub covered with soap and says "Daddy," Evans gasps at the likeness. He never wears ties or socks in a place where dressing up is part of the job. He lives in an elegant French Regency villa in Beverly Hills that would make J. Paul Getty jealous. Henry Kissinger is often in the guest room, where if you press the wrong button a special alarm rings in the Beverly Hills police station and you are surrounded by cops before you can turn down the Porthault sheets.

His house has sixteen rooms filled with Dalis, Modiglianis, Renoirs, Picassos and pre-Columbian art, a greenhouse, a tennis court, and a screening room where electric motors close the curtains and lower the screen from above the bookcases. He watches all the latest movies there, lying in a hospital bed because he has a bad back, and an invitation to watch them with him is more coveted in Hollywood today than a summons to San Clemente. And still it doesn't affect him. He rarely goes out.

He never attends banquets, luncheons, or charity benefits. He works sixteen-hour days, which leaves him little time for romance. "My work is my life," he says. "You have to be young to be an executive, and frankly, I like my success. Success is my companion. It burns up a lot of energy. But I am ready for it. There wasn't a day in my life that I didn't know I'd be a success."

But why? Why is Robert Evans such a success in an industry that watches executives come and go through revolving doors? One close friend, a Hollywood agent who loathes most Hollywood executives, says: "The business is run by ten idiots and Bob Evans. The ten idiots will say: 'You got a picture for Stanley Kubrick about a telephone booth? Sounds good to me. How about fifteen million dollars and

ten percent of the gross?' Bob Evans will say, 'Let me read
the script first.' That's the difference. He was an actor. He
was a businessman. Now he combines a business background
with a knowledge of the creative side of how the industry
works. It's an unbeatable combination and he's beating
everyone else in town at their own game."

Something else. He loves movies. He masterminded *The
Godfather, Love Story,* and *Lady Sings the Blues* to Paramount glory. Now, with his own films, *Chinatown* and *Marathon Man,* turning into gold mines, he's proved himself a
top producer, hard for the snipers to knock off. And he did
it all himself.

"It started off, once again, as a project for Ali," he grins,
memories of *The Great Gatsby* dancing like thorns in his
head, piercing him with pain. "I was having dinner two
years ago with Bob Towne, a writer who used to live with
Jack Nicholson, and I said: 'I'm looking for a good man-
woman story for Ali to do.' He said: 'Well, I'm looking for
something for Jack to do. I've got an idea and I'd like to call
it *Chinatown.*' It was based on a true newspaper story about
a divorce detective who got involved in a much more serious
case of political corruption just by following a woman
around. It was a good idea, so I gave him a little room and
some money and it took him eighteen months to write the
script. By the time it was finished, Ali had left me for Steve
McQueen, but we still had a picture. It was as simple as that.

"Now with Roman Polanski directing, we ran into problems. I had always had respect for Roman, but he goes way
off on tangents without proper control. He didn't want to do
it originally, he wanted to do something else. So he brought
over his last picture, called *What?,* which he thought was
terrific. I ran it in my screening room and it was the worst
picture I ever saw in my life. We had a terrible fight and
came within one degree of calling the whole thing off.

"During the picture, it was not easy. Roman is used to
working on his own and he felt tied down because I worked
so closely with Jack and Bob Towne. They didn't care about
money or time. They'd stay up all night just to work on a
certain smile or look for a scene. Roman resented that, because he's used to being an auteur. I, on the other hand,

wanted to be closely involved because it was the first time
I ever put my name on a film and I didn't want to just put
my name on it and walk away. It put my back out for six
months. I made myself ill over this picture.

"The reason directors are so much in control today is that
there are no producers. There are no Thalbergs, Sam Gold-
wyns, or David Selznicks, who can start a film, follow it
through, and know what to do after it's complete in the
cutting, dubbing, music, and finishing off. Producers today
are agents and packagers who raise money and walk away.
Real producers are a dying breed."

Most producers would argue that it's easy for Evans to
talk. Evans was, after all, in a unique position. Who was
going to tamper with his film while he was also running the
studio? "That's true, but I also know something about film-
making. It's a collaborative effort. The director is not the
only man responsible. A real producer takes chances, like
Darryl F. Zanuck did. I'll tell you an interesting story.

"Zanuck saw me dancing one night at El Morocco and
signed me to play a matador in *The Sun Also Rises*. Henry
King, the director, didn't want me. Ava Gardner, Errol
Flynn, Mel Ferrer, and the rest of the stars didn't want me.
Zanuck flew to Mexico from London, called everyone into
the bull ring where we were shooting, and in front of the
entire company, announced over a loudspeaker: 'This is
D.Z. speaking—the kid's in the picture and anyone who
doesn't like it can walk off now!' That to me is a producer!"

Evans feels the reason so many lousy movies are being
made is that too many directors are on an ego trip. "Before
the actors are picked, before the sets are done, looking at
dailies, making changes, not being happy with some per-
formers and replacing them with new ones—that should be
a collaborative effort. On *Chinatown* I wasn't happy with
the first two weeks' shooting and I fought Roman until I
made him fire the cinematographer. After the picture was
finished, I hated the music. A friend of Roman's wrote rinky-
dink music that harmed the film. We needed a lush, haunting theme. I fired the composer and hired Jerry Goldsmith.
Roman never even heard the new music. We fought bitterly, but the decisions I made helped the film. Roman is

very stubborn, argumentative, and difficult, but if chan-
neled properly, he is also brilliant. He's always had too many
sycophants around who flatter his ego and then his films turn
out badly. The best thing he can have is someone tough to
supervise him. Now, he's so happy with the changes I made
that we're going to do another picture together. You've got
to have guts to be a producer and I've got plenty of guts."

That's one thing he always had, even before money. His
father was a dentist, his mother a housewife. With no en-
couragement, he went out on auditions at the age of eleven,
appeared on radio shows like *Henry Aldrich* and *Archie
Andrews* in the Forties, and chalked up more than three
hundred roles by the time he was eighteen. Then his lung
collapsed and his family took him to Florida to rest. He got
his own disc jockey show for six months, then joined his
brother, Charles, as a partner in a ladies' pants company,
Evan-Picone. In 1956, he was sitting by the pool at the Beverly Hills Hotel selling pants, when Norma Shearer spotted
him, told him he looked just like her late husband, Irving
Thalberg, and asked him if he'd like to play him in *Man of
a Thousand Faces,* a picture about Lon Chaney that James
Cagney was shooting at Universal.

A few months later, in typical they'll-never-believe-it
movie fashion, Darryl Zanuck called him over at El Morocco
and said, "Hey kid, you an actor? How'd you like to play
opposite Ava Gardner?" Suddenly he was very hot for about
ten minutes. In *The Fiend Who Walked the West,* he killed
six men and raped two women. It was getting ridiculous.
"My brother finally gave me an ultimatum—either be an
actor or come home and run the pants business, but you
can't do both." Evans went back to the company and, two
years later, sold it to Revlon for "several million dollars."

Independently wealthy and bitten by the Hollywood bug,
he turned producer, peddling scripts instead of pants. "The
only way anybody would take me seriously as a producer
was if I had something nobody else had, so I hired a guy from
Publishers Weekly to find new books before they were published. I bought three properties and made some development deals and word got around. Charles Bluhdorn, who
was buying Paramount, asked me to head his European pro-

duction team in London. Six months later, in 1966, I took over the studio." After *The Godfather* and *Love Story,* he got his own producer's contract. Now he's a shark in a goldfish bowl.

It's cost him a lot. "There's no question *The Godfather* cost me my marriage. I insisted Ali make *The Getaway* when she didn't want to do it, then I was working eighteen hours a day on *The Godfather* and never had time to go down to Texas to see her. She was alone with Steve McQueen the whole time and it changed her life. It's all my own fault. My health is ruined. I've had acupuncture, I've had surgery, sometimes I can't get out of bed. But I feel younger than I did at twenty-eight, because of the pace. I've never belonged to a club. I've never had a group of friends. I've always been a loner. But I'd rather do that than go home to a boring life with a wife and three kids. I pay for my success, and now I'm very tired. Who knows? Maybe in ten years I'll retire. The movie industry outgrows everybody."

His friends laugh at the idea. They say in ten years they'll be making a movie about Robert Evans. And if you think it can't happen, you don't know Hollywood.

Valerie Perrine

1.

"I'm the kind of girl who's tried everything once," says Valerie Perrine, who plays a junkie-whore-lesbian-stripper in *Lenny*. But after being with her a few minutes, you get the idea she's tried a few things twice.

It's midafternoon in the hotel suite where she's doing interviews for the film, but Valerie Perrine gives the impression of always being on the verge of getting into or out of bed. She's wearing a see-through nightgown with most of the buttons and loops either missing or broken, revealing more than the usual safe amount of sun-tanned movie star cleavage. She's pacing the room barefoot, drinking white wine out of a bottle, trying to answer the ringing phones. "I'm having my fourteenth nervous breakdown of the day. I'm working my behind off. I've done twenty-one interviews in two days and I've got *Cosmopolitan* at three o'clock. Can I have some lunch?"

The press agent says to order anything she wants and charge it to United Artists, then find a low-cut dress for the *Cosmopolitan* photo session. She picks up the phone, tells the operator, "I'd like a low-cut dress, please," then breaks

up into a peculiar series of giggles that sound like the hic-
cups. "Oh, my God, I'm losing my goddamn mind. I mean,
I'd like room service." She orders a salad, then lies down on
the sofa with her head in the interviewer's lap for another
round. "Ask me about playing a junkie-whore-lesbian-stripper," she sighs, with her eyes closed. "Everyone else has."

Actually, she was a stripper herself, so at least part of the
role in *Lenny* came naturally. "Strippers are not all whores,
though. That's a myth. Most of the girls I knew would rip off
their clothes, do a bump and a grind, then go out in the
lounge and hustle for chips. I never did that. And I didn't
know any girls in the line who put out. You work so hard
there's no time between shows to be a hooker. I went to the
University of Arizona for a year, majoring in liberal arts,
then to the University of Nevada. I wanted to be a psychologist like my brother, who practices in a hospital in Glens
Falls, New York. Daddy lives in Scottsdale, Mommy lives in
New Jersey. It's a perfectly normal family. Mommy saw
Lenny and said, 'Are those nude scenes necessary?' They
always worried about me when I was a showgirl, until
Mommy came out to Vegas and met the girls in the line and
saw that I came home between shows and cooked dinner
and led a normal life. It was something to do for money. I
always knew I'd be a star."

Lenny is one of the most controversial films ever made.
People who loved Lenny Bruce hate it because they claim
it makes him look like a degenerate. People who hated
Lenny Bruce hate the movie because they claim it makes
him look like an angelic rabbi. Valerie just shrugs her shoulders and grins. "It's hard to say. The man is dead and everyone has a different memory. Bob Fosse did enough film for
five different movies, and it's sketchy because he just
couldn't use it all. We filmed twelve hours a day for four
months. Lenny's wife, Honey, came and visited the set, but
she never said anything. We never delved into any real
feelings or emotions and she never gave me any pointers on
what it was like to be on heroin or how to be a lesbian or
anything like that. Most of the things I played, I've been
there myself, honey."

"You never actually took heroin, did you?" I ask naïvely.

She roars with laughter, says "No," pointing to the tape recorder, while shaking her head up and down affirmatively. "I did all the things Honey did out of experiment. Not because I was a Vegas showgirl, either. Most of the narcotics I tried in Europe. But it's not true that you get addicted by trying things once. All these people putting the fear of God into everybody about heroin is the same thing as the church telling everybody they'll go to hell or their noses will turn green if they have sex before marriage.

"That's one of the things Lenny was fighting—the hypocrisy of society. People are always frightened of things they know nothing about. They always told me marijuana was addictive, too, but I've been smoking grass since I was eighteen years old and I stopped because it was giving me the munchies and making me sleepy. It also makes you boring. But it is definitely not habit-forming. I also know people who sniff heroin or smack just to see what it's like. They don't get hooked on it. Only one person out of a million gets hooked immediately.

"Most of what I played came from this boy on the set who had been hooked on heroin in Vietnam. We called him our dope advisor. I don't really know anything about shooting up, although I've watched people shoot up and it made me sick at my stomach. I didn't really get to know Honey or Lenny's mother. I've heard Honey isn't too bright. I didn't identify with her. She was a masochist who would do anything for a man even when he beat her up. I don't understand that kind of woman. I was like that when I was a kid, but as you get older you begin to realize you can have as many loves as you want, so why not pick one who is good to you instead of putting up with all that sadistic crap."

Valerie has never been married, but she has a lot of guys on the hook. "Each man in my life fulfills a different function. Between all of them, I've got the perfect man. Wit and intelligence on Monday, a good time in bed on Tuesday, career advice on Wednesday, the chauffeured limousine on Thursday, and that's how my week goes. I don't believe in Women's Liberation. Men have always been on top, and that's where I want to keep them. I've never been to a shrink, either. I freaked out after *Lenny*. It was like getting a divorce from sixty people when I finished that movie, and I was advised to go into analysis, but instead I hung out in the mountains in Aspen in my Levi's and rode bikes and went camping and hiking and got back to normal in a week. I worked so long on that movie that when it was over I had no outlet for my creative impulses. It was like getting fired. It had nothing to do with the low-life I played in the film. I only lived a low-life for three minutes during a scene. I'm the kind of person who can giggle and laugh and play Scrabble and carry on and do a tap dance before a heavy dramatic scene, get myself in the mood in two minutes, do the scene, come out, giggle and laugh and do a tap dance again. Push a button on any emotion you want and I just do it. I'm like a robot."

She's never had an acting lesson. She's just very open and uninhibited. She came out of the line in Las Vegas, a topless dancer at the Lido de Paris, and broke into acting by accident, playing Montana Wildhack, the nude starlet in outer space in George Roy Hill's *Slaughterhouse-Five.* From there to *Lenny,* with a brief stop between in the highly praised but sparsely attended *The Last American Hero,* is her total acting trip. She played trashy broads in all three movies and it doesn't worry her a bit. "Show me a good role that isn't trashy. Look at Marsha Mason in *Cinderella Liberty* or Jane Fonda in *Klute.* They just aren't turning out the old Kate Hepburn–Bette Davis roles for women anymore. Men control the industry and that's what they think women are like. The more strides women make, the less men respect them for it. I don't think it's terrible. I'll do anything if it's a good part. The only thing that freaks me out is total nudity. I'm fine as long as I can keep my G-string on, but without my G-string I get nervous.

"I guess my Vegas background prepared me for a lot of freedom in movies. I'm a very happy-go-lucky person. I get very down sometimes, but my depressions never last more than two or three hours.

"I don't diet. I eat bread and butter and grease. I'll eat anything. That's why I don't mind playing sexy roles, because they like me a little bit more voluptuous on the screen. When I'm not working, I move around. I live in an apart-

ment with a secretary and six Great Danes and I've only
been there six weeks this year. I only cook about four times
a year. I just send out for Chinese food. I'm not career-
aggressive, I'm not fighting for roles, I have no career structure or motivation. I just go where I want to go and do what
I want to do. Money is freedom and I'm free. I won't do a
play, because who wants to do the same thing night after
night? That would drive me nuts. So far I won't do TV
because there's so much trash on TV that nothing good has
been offered to me."

The worst thing about sudden success, she says, is "doing
dumb interviews. One guy asked me, 'When did you first
develop your phenomenal bust?' Look. I made a movie that
is obviously not about Lenny Bruce according to the critics,
I did not study Honey Bruce, I did not study Lenny Bruce,
I really know no more about them than I know about anybody else, and suddenly they're coming out of the woodwork to ask me what are your measurements, what do your
parents think of your nude scenes? It's all such bull.

"I hate talk shows. Johnny Carson just stares at my boobs.
But when I'm not working, I can be myself. I don't date stars,
I date investment counselors, lawyers, real estate brokers,
starving artists, and a couple of bartenders in Aspen. I don't
know anybody in show business. I'm one of the last contract
players at Universal. I like being loaned out. I get a salary
every week whether I work or not. So mostly, I just don't
work. My old friends are still showgirls in Vegas. I'm the only
one who made it. I'm the luckiest person I ever met. I guess
I'm just a vulnerable tramp. But I can't go on being a tramp
in the movies. I'm getting a sagging chin and I'm too old to
be showing my boobs all the time. They've offered me the
life story of Janis Joplin and the role of the nympho movie
star who gets kidnapped in *The Fan Club*. I don't want to
be a tramp anymore, but what else is there?"

Valerie Perrine shoves her salad away and stares blankly
out of the window. Then she shrugs, crawls up on the sofa,
puts her head in the interviewer's lap once more, pretends
to doze off before the next interview, and mutters: "Oh,
well, maybe just one more junkie-whore-lesbian-stripper
won't hurt. Some of my best friends are."

2.

HOLLYWOOD—On the hottest day of the summer in a rented Spanish adobe villa in Pasadena, a sweltering Hollywood film unit is stripped to its underwear, making a movie about W.C. Fields. In typical movie style, the real house Fields lived in is in fine shape but too small to move the camera around in. So the folks at Universal have moved everybody to the hottest part of the San Fernando Valley, where only the cactus plants breathe without oxygen. The actors have brought their own portable oxygen tanks to keep breathing.

The movie is called *W.C. Fields and Me.* It is based on the book by Carlotta Monti, the late comedian's mistress, and it is the latest in a sudden myopic craze for nostalgia that is taking the place on the current production charts of new films in preparation that are taking the place of cops, gore, violence and two-headed insects that ate Las Vegas. This fall we'll be seeing movies about Clark Gable, Carole Lombard, Errol Flynn, Amelia Earhart, Ernest Hemingway, Irving Thalberg, Marilyn Monroe and Rin Tin Tin. In *W.C. Fields and Me,* the cantankerous curmudgeon is being played by Rod Steiger. Carlotta Monti, who stood loyally by him from 1932 to his death in 1946, is being played with Catholic convent-bred dignity by none other than Valerie Perrine. The role is killing her.

Steiger is cooling off under the weight of a gigantic rubber stomach and a hot plastic nose in a baggy-pants costume complete with wool cardigan sweater and two-tone wing-tip shoes. Valerie has collapsed in an upstairs bedroom, away from the hot lights, with her dress above her tightly gartered thighs and an electric fan blowing air across a bowl of ice cubes into the space between her legs.

"I'm falling apart but my hairdo's fine," she groans, pointing to her marcelled wig, which is pinned in place by a straw pillbox Claudette Colbert hat. "I only took this film because it's the first chance I've ever had to play dress-up. You know how I always look so t-r-a-s-h-y . . ." She brings out some Polaroids showing her Carlotta Monti-look in hats and chiffon print dresses. "See, I look like Myrna Loy. Didja believe you'd ever see the old whore in lace gloves? Now I gotta wear pantyhose, girdles, bras—my god, bras!—garter belts, slips, panties. It is murder in this heat. It was easier just to wear a G-string."

Arthur *(Man of La Mancha)* Hiller yells up the stairs he's ready for Valerie in the scene. "Oh, Christ, that just means I've gotta stand around. My stand-in could do it. But Rod Steiger wants me there even if I'm not in the shot. It's got something to do with method acting. How did I ever get into this? I could be at the beach getting a suntan."

She takes out her chewing gum, parks it in an ashtray and staggers downstairs. The scene is the one in which Carlotta, a would-be actress, comes to Fields's house for an interview in the middle of a poker game with John Barrymore and Dave Chasen (who made Chasen's a world-famous restaurant during the silent-film era and remained one of Fields's best friends until his death).

Somehow, Carlotta, who is very elegantly dressed to make a good impression, is ignored and relegated to the kitchen, where she ends up making lunch for everybody. Jack Cassidy is Barrymore, comic Milt Kamen is Dave Chasen and Bernadette Peters is featured as Fields's first wife. The windows are closed, and the air conditioners are turned off to eliminate sound. It is so hot the actors are sitting in pools of sweat.

The scene begins. Suddenly, in the middle of the poker scene, an outside klieg light shines through a windowpane, causing a concentrated ray of light on the poker table, and the furniture catches on fire. The room is filled with smoke. The actors run around the room, clutching their throats. Extras and grips fan the air to drive the smoke from the room. A nurse is called to administer first aid while the set is repaired.

Valerie Perrine climbs the stairs to her bowl of ice, spreads her legs on the bed and turns on her fan again. "I wish I was dead," she moans. Then she opens her purse and takes out a joint, lights up and fans her breasts with her Myrna Loy hat. "If I can just get stoned enough to get through this day, it'll be time to go home and sleep for thirteen hours. Do you believe what just happened down there? And nobody laughed, man.

"I am telling you, this picture is not fun. I'm not having any fun doing this picture. On *Lenny,* I was always clowning around with Dustin Hoffman and Bob Fosse. We were always going out to dinner together and laughing a lot. Nobody kids around on this thing. Rod Steiger won't even let me borrow his car to go to the supermarket during lunch. I asked him, and he said no. The whole thing is a drag, baby.

"I'm bored, I'm tired, I'm hot, I'm sleepy. But most of all, I'm bored. I'm probably in this movie more than I was in *Lenny,* but there's nobody to pal around with. I've got an air-conditioned trailer outside, but it's too far to walk. I guess everyone in Hollywood would like to be playing this part, but it's dopey. I'd much rather be getting laid."

"Did you watch any W.C. Fields movies to research the part?"

"No. I saw one with Mae West once. I don't remember which one. They were all alike, anyway. Mae West was going to have a part in this one, but she threatened to sue them if they used her. She despised W.C. Fields."

"Well, did you read the Carlotta Monti book?"

"No. I'm doing it again, Rexie. Just going in there stark raving unprepared. Just like *Lenny.* I didn't know anything about Honey Bruce, either. I'm not an actress. I've never had an acting lesson in my life."

"Well, why did you do this one out of all the things offered you after *Lenny* and winning the Best Actress prize at the Cannes Film Festival? You had your pick of roles, and you turned them all down."

"Well, uh, I just got plain tired of not working. I hadn't been on the screen for two years, and this was the total opposite of anything I've ever played before. Quiet, well-dressed Catholic lady. The truth? Well, it is so B-O-R-I-N-G." She makes the mock wail of a baby yelling for its bottle. "I wanna play a whore again. It's so much more fun to be tacky!"

She dips into her purse again, unwraps a cookie sealed in aluminum foil, explains it's a hash brownie from Morocco and eats the whole thing, spilling precious crumbs all over the satin sheets at about $45 a crumb. "I don't even get kissed in this movie. No bed scenes, no nude scenes. . . . I have a lot of energy when I feel excited, but there's nothing on this film I feel like doing, so I spend my time sleeping. I'm not playing a strong lady, either, which drives me bananas."

"Have you met the real Carlotta Monti?"

"No, but she's coming to the set next week. I hear she's kinda weird. She was with him fourteen years, and when he died, all she got was twenty-five dollars a week for ten years and his old eight-cylinder Cadillac, which she still drives down Hollywood Boulevard.

"To tell you the truth, this Carlotta is just plain stupid. Who would live with W.C. Fields for fifteen minutes? This woman was a total slave to a man I'd like to rap right across the side of the *head!* I'm doing the strongest acting job I've ever had to play just to keep from kicking the hell outta that guy. He made fun of her in front of his friends, refused to let her have her own career, treated her like shit! He doesn't beat her up or anything—I mean, there's no violence, no sex, no nothing! Just a polite relationship. They don't even touch."

"How boring."

"Z-z-z-zzzz." She pretends to fall off the bed in a snore at the thought of her role. "Oh, we yell at each other a lot." She opens some more food.

"Is that lunch from home?"

"Oh, no. This is more hash from Amsterdam. By the time they hit, it'll be five thirty and I'll be through for the day. I don't have much to do today. Crying is the easiest part. Every time I have to cry, I think of my fiancé dying before we got married when I was still in the chorus line in Vegas, from which I've never really recovered, you know. Or I think about the bad scene with my family. Or I think that I have never had anyone in my life to take care of me. I think of all those things and bawl. I have to cry a lot in this picture. It keeps me from falling asleep on the set."

Valerie may not be career-driven, which is perhaps why the juicy roles keep falling into her amply endowed lap, but she does have a reputation for getting along with her crews and co-workers. By her own admission, she's also had a love affair with at least one person on each of her three previous films.

"Not this one, baby. It's driving me crazy. George Roy Hill, Michael Sacks, Jeff Bridges, Bobby, and Dustin—they were all pals. I don't have any pals on this film. Everybody is so goddamn serious. I can't get through to Rod Steiger at all. It's very odd to come onto a film about W.C. Fields and see a man all dressed up like W.C. Fields who is deadly serious about everything.

"I'm not an ambition-burning, career-mad female. I just want to have fun, and I'm not having any. All I have is my wardrobe, which I am keeping. It's outrageous Thirties and Forties. The clothes are fantastic. Just a trim of the hat or a cut of the hem, and I can wear them in public. I have one Marlene Dietrich one that really looks dikey. That's my favorite. I'll wear that in New York."

"What scene is that for?"

"I don't know. I haven't read the whole script. I have no idea what I'm doing until I get out there on the set and do it. I do know one thing. I have three and a half acres and lots of two-hundred-and-fifty-pound mastiffs and Great Danes, and they all sleep in my bedroom and the landlord's hassling me to get rid of them, and instead of being at home taking care of them, here I am, playing some jerk who's in love with W.C. Fields. It's not worth it. I'm moving out of Hollywood where I can get my whole act together again and take off this goddamn bra."

She flushed the remains of her psychedelic New Hollywood lunch down the toilet, repaired her wig and at 5:30, when they told her she could go home, she somehow made it, hardly noticing the car, the freeway or the traffic cops who might have taken her in for impersonating a Boeing 707. Somebody up there likes Valerie Perrine, and so do I.

Glenda Jackson

LONDON—Glenda Jackson is a savage when she's working. If her star dressing room at the Pinewood Studios near London looks like an army barracks latrine, she doesn't notice. She's too busy pacing the cold floor in her bare feet, chain-smoking from boxes of foul-smelling English cigarettes, and scratching the black roots of her dyed red hair, which looks badly in need of a shampoo. Her scalp itches with perspiration from wearing too many wigs, her face has erupted with zits from the nervous strain of film-making and the private trauma of a rather nasty front-page divorce in her personal life, and her hands flutter desperately in the air like dying birds. It is not a good day for an interview.

She is currently completing the gargantuan job of playing the legendary Sarah Bernhardt, a role once planned for Greta Garbo, in a multimillion-dollar epic called *Sarah*. The film begins in 1923, when the French actress is dying at the age of seventy-nine, flashes back to age eighteen and ends when she's thirty-five, before she became an international success. It's a role worth playing. Bernhardt collected lovers and animals, nursed the soldiers onstage at the Comédie

Française, which was converted into a field hospital during
the Siege of Paris, slept in a coffin, attended public execu-
tions by hanging and guillotine, performed *Camille* three
thousand times to sold-out audiences from Russia to the San
Quentin prison without ever learning to speak English and
invented the unisex look by being the first woman to wear
trousers. "You need a great actress to play a great actress,"
says director Richard Fleischer, "and in my opinion Glenda
is the greatest actress of our day."

She is also one of the most exhausted. "I've been in every
scene and on call from 7 A.M. until long after nightfall every
day for fifteen weeks," she sighs. "I'm certainly not tired of
Sarah Bernhardt, but I am physically exhausted from the
work and ready for a vacation." In the film she's worked
with chimpanzees, French poodles, a pair of lizards, a vicious puma, and a fleece of white rats. She has forty costume
changes, takes six hours to be made up and plays thirteen
scenes onstage in various Bernhardt roles from Joan of Arc
to Phaedra. "It seemed too good a chance to miss. It's an
immense challenge, but not because she was an actress. I
mean, we're not making a documentary about her. I'm not
attempting to reproduce the way she acted, because I don't
know how she acted. Greatness in acting is a very subjective
thing. What I think Sarah had was a charismatic appeal for
an audience, and that's a very magical, mysterious thing. I
mean, Christ, even Oscar Wilde was in love with her. It's an
important woman's role, and it's interesting to do, but what
is more interesting is making her a human being instead of
simply fulfilling—pardon me for burping—the myth of the
'Divine Sarah.'

"I don't know much about her, really. She was probably
the apocryphal actress. Ask anybody on any street corner in
the world, and they've heard of Sarah Bernhardt even if
they've never been to the theater. But the books about her
are conflicting, and I don't think facts, in the sense of dates,
times and places, are particularly of use when you're acting.
One of the most valuable things was a story told to me by
someone who had actually seen her perform, and the thing
he remembered most clearly was that she was the only

member of her company who had the guts to act with her back to the audience. That told me more than any book."

The day after Glenda won her second Oscar for *A Touch of Class*, she was invited to lunch at Claridge's by Helen Strauss, a respected literary agent for thirty-five years and the newly appointed head of production for Reader's Digest's film division, the group responsible for such family-oriented movies as *Tom Sawyer, Huckleberry Finn,* and *Mr. Quilp.* Ms. Strauss asked her if she would be interested in playing Sarah Bernhardt on the screen. Without a blink, Glenda said yes. Seven scripts and several million dollars later, they were ready to go. Glenda wanted John Schlesinger, George Cukor, or Billy Wilder to direct. They were busy. So they ended up with Richard *(Dr. Dolittle)* Fleischer and a film so vast in its magnitude it required 134 speaking parts and 500 extras per day. "That represents quite a logistical problem," says Ms. Strauss. "You have to wardrobe them, wig them, feed them, and transport them. But I think it's all worth it. We've got enough material left over for a sequel."

Outside Glenda's dressing room, the mob was assembling on streets that looked like an accurate reproduction of the city of Paris. Just beyond the Notre Dame cathedral you could see the prehistoric monster from *One of Our Dinosaurs Is Missing,* which the cameras were careful to avoid, and if Sarah Bernhardt's house looks familiar, don't wrinkle your brain. It was Robert Redford's Long Island estate in *The Great Gatsby.* All of which must seem rather like Disneyland to Glenda, an actress renowned for her moody, introspective portrayals in dark, somber films.

"I won't say it's the hardest thing I've ever done because everything you do is the hardest thing you've ever done while you're doing it," she said, stabbing the air with her cigarette butt. "Acting isn't easy. But this is certainly the most lavish film I've ever done. The sets and costumes are immensely impressive. The theater sets especially. They don't feel like sets; they feel like theaters. One of my first scenes was an audition, and the set was so real I got as nervous as I did when I really did my first audition in a live theater. I hasten to add, I never got the job."

Despite her protests that Bernhardt was "quite different emotionally," there are interesting comparisons between Glenda and the woman she's playing. Both have been called eccentric, both had an extraordinary energy that drove them like demons, and both had unhappy marriages. Sarah married a Greek actor with no talent who resented her success. Glenda married Roy Hodges, whom she met when he was a director in Bristol in her struggling days. She blazed to stardom early in the Royal Shakespeare Company's *Marat/Sade* when she was making only $50 a week. Now she has two Oscars and her first accumulated million, which her husband is suing her for.

During her recent American tour in *Hedda Gabler,* she fell in love with Andy Phillips, an electrician who did the lights for the show. Bernhardt had a child by a man she refused to marry. Glenda now faces the responsibility of raising her seven-year-old son, Danny, and remaining a working mother at the same time. When she talks of Sarah's marriage, it's almost as though she's talking about her own.

"I don't think marriage is a redundant institution, but I don't think it should be a sentence to solitary confinement in which you must stay forever and ever, either. And that's what most marriages turn into. There is some weakness in some people that requires them to constantly fail. In that kind of relationship, I don't think you can blame one person more than the other. People are what they are. I think Sarah Bernhardt's husband would have been a failure no matter who he married. What increased his tragedy was that he married such a flamboyant person, a publicly marked success, which must have made his own failure seem even greater."

Here the resemblance ends. Glenda has never been flamboyant. The day after she won her first Oscar, for *Women in Love,* she was photographed in the backyard hanging out the wash. "Nobody would ever hire me for my beauty," she says, and there are no arguments. She has bad teeth that require removable caps in front of the camera, spotty skin, and eyes that disappear "like tiny raisins in unbaked dough."

Yet a love affair with the camera occurs when she's on the screen that nobody can explain. Despite her militant refusal to be labeled a movie star, she is one.

She's come a long way from the homely country girl who daydreamed about being Esther Williams (she once almost drowned doing an impression of the MGM bathing beauty smiling underwater), but she still does not give a damn about money or glamour. "I can truthfully say money has never been a primary objective in my work. That probably sounds patently absurd since I am obviously paid a great deal of money, but I've never done anything because the money was right and the part was wrong. All the money in the world can't make me do something I'm not interested in."

She has never made a film in Hollywood. "One has to have a reason for going there. If you have a job there, it's like a passport or a visa, and you can always get out. But I should think to be stuck there all the time you'd go mad." Her next film, *The Abbess of Crewe*, a black comedy by Muriel Spark, about a group of nuns battling for the position of mother superior, will co-star Ingrid Bergman and will be filmed in Philadelphia. If she ever accepts the movie star label, she hopes to be compared more to Bette Davis than Raquel Welch. "I've long since outgrown the crushes I had on film stars as a child, but Davis is still impressive, even more so as a human being. The more I meet and chat with her, the more remarkable she becomes on the screen. When you think of some of the rubbish she actually managed to invest with style and intelligence, it's amazing."

Most people think of Glenda Jackson as a contemporary Bernhardt, cementing forever distinguished performances in costume dramas about queens and tragediennes, but she would give anything to play a modern girl for a change and get out of those corsets and wigs. "I've been working steadily in films for the past six years, and the depressing thing is the scripts they send me don't get better. Nine out of ten scripts I get are rubbish, and you're lucky if one out of ten is even readable." The prospects for an actress with her range are grim. That's why she keeps playing classics like *The Maids* and *Hedda Gabler*. They don't make money, but they flex her muscles.

"There's modern stuff around, but it's difficult to get anyone to finance it. Producers are afraid of modern women. It's partly the fault of Women's Lib. Instead of making people aware of the roles women play in society, they've frightened and confused people. I want to play contemporary roles, but they're not being written."

Curious. Glenda Jackson talking about the paucity of women's roles, when most actresses cite *A Touch of Class* as the kind of thing they long to play. "Well, I admit I've been lucky. I've scooped the pool over the past few years as far as prominent female characters are concerned. But this is entirely fortuitous. The majority of roles I'm offered are appalling. They're the same old functional, obligatory females. You've got to have one around to prove the hero isn't queer."

Jeff Bridges

The door to Jeff Bridges's hotel suite is opened by a girl in a white bathrobe. "He's got a hangover," she smiles wanly. Inside, the star of MGM's *Hearts of the West* has stuffed his six foot two, 175-pound hulk into a brown-striped bathrobe. The wheat-colored hair, neatly cropped in the film, is long and standing on end. The clean-shaven, all-American good looks that caused one critic to compare him to a young Gary Cooper have been replaced by a scruffy goatee that he sometimes strokes with caution, the slightest movement causing dizziness and pain. His pallor is turtle-soup green, and his blue eyes are poinsettia-red. Jeff Bridges is a mess.

"I was up all night drinking Wild Turkey," he moans, as two other girls who are not dressed in bathrobes dash in and out of the room administering hangover remedies brought by room service. "I'm really sorry, man." He clutches his stomach, glances with horror toward the bathroom, tries to sip some orange juice, turns from green to white. "This is only the fifth hangover I've ever had in my life. I've already thrown up twice before you got here."

While he tries gamely to pull the bathrobe around his

naked kneecaps and pull himself into a sitting position, facts reassemble themselves to remind the interviewer he hasn't wandered into Boys' Town by accident: His father was Lloyd Bridges, who gave Jeff his first acting job on the old *Sea Hunt* TV series. His older brother is Beau Bridges, who is more versatile and accomplished but who hasn't achieved the same degree of stardom as his kid brother, Jeff. His godfather was Larry Parks, who, along with Lloyd Bridges, was blacklisted by the House Un-American Activities Committee during the McCarthy witchhunts.

He went to a psychiatrist when he was sixteen, enrolled in a high school drug program when he was seventeen, ran away from home and worked in *The Last Picture Show, Halls of Anger, Fat City, Bad Company, The Last American Hero, Thunderbolt and Lightfoot,* and *The Iceman Cometh.* His favorite actor is Marlon Brando. He writes rock songs and likes gardening. He also obviously likes Wild Turkey.

There's a groan from the side of the room where he's collapsed. The interview, or what's left of it, can proceed. "In *Hearts of the West,* you play an idealistic young writer of western fiction who lands in B pictures. The movie is about disillusionment in Hollywood. Have you ever been disillusioned in Hollywood?"

"Yeah, you'll do a movie and disagree with the director a lot, and I'm always disillusioned when I can't do it my own way."

"Did you always have an ambition to be an actor, or did you fall into it by accident like the kid in *Hearts of the West?*"

"I appeared as a baby in some show of my dad's. He said, 'You wanna do somethin' and make some money?' and I started acting so I could buy toys. I was eight years old."

"Did your father help you with acting?"

"Yeah, he was my first teacher. He'd go over all the scenes with me and help me keep it simple. I never studied or anything."

"Did you and brother Beau ever act together?"

"We did some scenes for the Lions Club. I'd play my guitar and sing Bob Dylan songs and he'd read poetry and my grandfather would put us down for wearing long hair. It was a very confusing show."

"Was there much sibling rivalry in your childhood?"

"No, Beau was nine years older so it wasn't a big competition deal. He was more like an uncle. He would baby-sit and teach me sports. I left home at seventeen and joined the Coast Guard reserves, so I didn't see him much."

"There's industry talk that this film will put MGM back on its feet. Do you care, or are you interested in these corporate matters?"

"I don't care about MGM. I just think good movies mean good publicity for the movie industry as a whole. It's like Academy Awards. I don't care if I win one or not, but it's all good publicity and helps to promote movies."

"What do you think about critics? One of them said about *Hearts of the West* that you were the only talented member of the Bridges family. How did that make you feel?"

"I guess I like critics when they like me, but I don't like them when they're mean. That was a mean thing to say."

"With so much happening to you so fast, have you thought about how you might go about avoiding the pitfalls of self-destruction that so many talented people like Garland, Monroe, Kim Stanley, and Monty Clift fell into?"

The question, on this inappropriately ironic hangover morning, produces a guffaw that shatters his head with pain. "That's funny, but it hurts to laugh. I consider myself only mildly self-destructive. I dunno. I just have a lot of really dear friends who love me for what I am, man." The girl in the bathrobe removes his orange juice and replaces it with tomato juice.

"In 1972, *The New York Times* ran an interview in which you said you were full of self-hatred. Do you still feel that way?"

"We talked about a lot of things and hate came up and this chick took my observation that we hate our parents and children because we hate ourselves and played up that angle. It made me sound like I was ready to dig a hole in the ground and crawl in it. I don't feel that way anymore."

"What about future plans? Are there any roles you'd like to play?"

"I dunno. I've got a buncha scripts I'm reading now."

"Are you interested in broadening your scope by taking on classical roles?"

"Yeah. I'm tired of playing the same youths all the time. I gotta picture coming out in March called *Stay Hungry*, directed by Bob Rafelson. I play a Southern aristocrat."

"If sophisticated Cary Grant comedies ever come back, would that interest you as an actor?"

"Um—possibly. It depends on my mood. I have no long-range ideas of what I want to do."

"Are you and Beau close now that you've matured?"

"I don't see him much."

"What about the years when your father was blacklisted? Were times hard for the family when he was struggling to get work?"

"I don't really remember much about it. I was only two or three years old."

A lady press agent breezes in with an Alka-Seltzer, makes motherly chicken-soup clucking noises, ends up eating his lunch. He can't get up, says he might make it as far as the bathroom, have a cold shower and a nap before his flight back to Los Angeles. The "interview" has obviously chugged to an end.

"I don't have any more questions."

"I could throw up for you," he winces.

And that's the New Hollywood.

Diane Ladd

"I am not related to Alan Ladd any more than I am related to Lad, a Dog, and I wish people would stop asking me that question." Fortunately, there was no time to make that mistake. She volunteered the answer before I got the chance to get that far. "Why do people assume that? Do they ask Audrey Hepburn if she's related to Katharine Hepburn? Do they ask Leigh Taylor-Young if she's related to Elizabeth Taylor or Robert Young? Why can't I just be my own person? I am a distant cousin of Tennessee Williams, but nobody ever asks that."

Diane Ladd is quite her own person. In fact, there's plenty to go around for more than one. A flaxen, pioneer blonde with eyes big as sunflower hearts and a voice like dripping molasses, this warm, wacky dame from Meridian, Mississippi, is the one to watch in the overcrowded market of newcomers scratching for attention on the big and little screens.

Last year, she copped an Oscar nomination for her portrayal as Flo, the salty Tucson waitress in *Alice Doesn't Live Here Anymore*. NBC-TV just signed her to guest-star in a whole patchwork quilt of new shows, and her latest film, *Embryo,* is set for fall release. Although it might be remembered best as the film in which Rock Hudson parades across the screen stark naked, *Embryo* will not be restricted to Hudson's attributes alone. Diane Ladd could upstage a palomino playing "Humoresque." She was in town for a few days last week, attending a séance, getting a divorce, and trying to sell her New York apartment. She managed to get her licks in.

"The Oscar nomination instantly changed me from an actress to a movie star," she said modestly, "and I can really feel the difference."

How does it feel?

"Competitive. You've got to be the best there is. I'm trying to view it as a game. If you win, you've got a right to be smug. If you lose, there's always a next time. Like the Oscars. It would have meant a lot to me to win. We should not be taught to be ashamed to want to win. There's something very bad about pretending we don't want to win. That's baloney.

"I went on the Johnny Carson show and said, 'I bloody well want to win,' and later they told me I was the first actress who had ever really come right out and admitted it. The danger is in taking the loss seriously."

Last year's Academy Awards are history now, and Diane, of course, went home empty-handed. Ingrid Bergman won. "I love Ingrid Bergman," Diane said. "She has always been an idol of mine . . . *but* . . . at the Oscar ceremonies I happened to find myself seated directly behind her, and I decided it was the perfect opportunity to meet her. So, I tapped her on the shoulder, and she wheeled around immediately and in the most intimidating voice imaginable, she simply said, 'YES-S-S???'

"I was a bit startled, but I regained my composure and said, 'I'm Diane Ladd.'

"All she said was '*Yes-s-s??*' again in the same tone of voice.

" 'Well, I'm one of your fellow nominees, and I've always admired your work and just wanted to tell you so.'

" 'Ooh, Thaaahhnk youuuu!' she said and wheeled right back around.

"Now I'm a very loyal fan of Miss Bergman's. However, the only thing that riled me a little was when she accepted the award. She implied that she didn't think she deserved to win. Now, honey, if you don't think you deserve to win, you should decline the nomination! And on top of that, to single out Valentina Cortese as the one who should have won . . . well! The old Southerner in me began to rebel. My toes literally curled under in my shoes, went through the soles and clawed the carpet. I almost raised my hand like a schoolgirl and came to my feet, protesting, 'Wait just one goddamn minute, Miss Bergman! Talia Shire, Madeline Kahn, and I aren't exactly chopped liver!' I really had to stop myself, honey, I'll tell you that."

Diane has a tendency to talk a blue streak, and when she does, it's easy to see all the natural tabasco sauce that made the Flo character simmer and burn. But Diane is anxious as a turkey on Thanksgiving to lose that Flo image. She had, in fact, turned down various offers to continue in that shtick for the same reason Shirley Temple turns chartreuse when asked for a snappy chorus of "On the Good Ship Lollipop."

"I never want to see another waitress uniform, but that doesn't mean I didn't love that character when I was playing her. When I hear people describe her as a slatternly flirt, I get hopping mad. Flo never flirted. She handled people. She made the customers want to come back. She made them feel at home. When they got out of hand, she put them in their place. She was trapped with a husband who wasn't communicative, and she was terribly tough and lonely, but she was never unfaithful. She was a good broad."

Diane was never a broad. She was an exceptionally bright, scholarly teenager who graduated high school in three years. But since she was more interested in acting than anything else, she declined a scholarship to study criminal law at Louisiana State University and took off for New Orleans, where she enrolled in a finishing school, "which almost finished me."

She sang with a local orchestra, modeled some, and finally

escaped the South when she landed a part in a touring company with John Carradine that eventually ended up in New York. She became a Copa Girl at the old Copacabana, and while this was hardly the big time, it was still miles ahead of the Rockettes. Pounding the pavement paid off with a tour of *Hatful of Rain* and loud praise from the Actors Studio. She is still one of Lee Strasberg's favorite pupils, and her wedding picture is given its own testimonial in his private study next to one of Marilyn Monroe.

In 1959, she was cast in an off-Broadway production of Tennessee Williams's *Orpheus Descending.* "We did it as part of an acting group, and at first Tennessee refused to give his permission to move the production off-Broadway. So, I got on the phone and called him, explaining I was a long-lost relative and the least he could do for kin was to just see the show. So, we gave a special performance for him in a friend's apartment, and he was so impressed he gave us the go-ahead. It got great reviews and turned out to be the only production of that play that ever turned a profit. I was on my way."

Another member of that cast was Bruce Dern, who, like Diane, has moved on to bigger and better things. They were married for eight years, and their daughter, Laura, is now their fondest memory of those years. Diane later married William Shea, Jr., whose father built Shea Stadium. She was once listed in the social register but was dropped when she refused to pay the $15 for the listing fee.

She has never been on very close terms with pretentiousness. She's a member of the Pentecostal Catholic Church, which must be some kind of first in Hollywood, and is feverishly interested in astrology and parapsychology. She even claims to have some capacity to perform psychic healing. A strongly devout believer in reincarnation and fate, she has had several psychic readings for her future. "The psychics all say 1976 will be my big year," she says, shrugging. "The year 1975 was only a preparation for brighter things to come."

One of the "brighter things" might or might not be *Embryo,* in which she gets chased by Rock Hudson and a pack of vicious Doberman pinschers. She liked him, hated them.

"Honey, you never saw anyone move so fast in your life! I moved so fast they couldn't even get it on film! I don't quite know how to tell you about *Embryo*—it's either going to be very good or very weird. You can't really call it science fiction, because it's based on things they are really doing in laboratories today—experimenting with human fetuses in incubators."

Whatever the outcome, it is doubtful that Diane Ladd will go unnoticed. She has talent, drive, ambition and an ego that shines sweetly through the cornpone. Shelley Winters loves to tell the story about how Diane used to introduce herself to everyone at the Actors Studio so they wouldn't forget her.

Diane says she can't remember names. "I just naturally make the mistake of assuming they have the same problem with mine," she says in bemused bewilderment. She met Shelley five times and each time she saw her, she always said, "Hi, I'm Diane Ladd." On the fifth occasion, Shelley (no shrinking violet herself, hey) threw up her hands and said, "I *know* who you are! If you tell me your name one more time, I am going to scream! Not only do I know who you are, but I happen to think you are one of the three best actresses in the country!"

Diane, taken aback, said, "Who are the other two?"

Shelley, taken aback, said, "Well, honey, you're lookin' at one of 'em!"

Diane Ladd, part-Cherokee, ex-Copa Girl, almost-socialite, soon-to-be-star, blinks innocently. "I never did find out who the third one was." Ingrid Bergman, eat your heart out.

Marvin Hamlisch

He's not just another pretty face. In fact, he looks, at certain angles, like a cheeseburger with all the ingredients oozing awkwardly out of the bun. But Marvin Hamlisch, thirty-one, is rich, talented, and as much in demand as Robert Redford. In Hollywood, Hamlisch is practically a household word in the houses of people who make movies and pray for hit scores to go with them. Two of his hits, *The Way We Were* and *The Sting*, sold so many records he stopped counting. They just send the residual check to the bank without passing go.

Now he's taken the theater by storm with his dazzling score for *A Chorus Line*, a show that started modestly off-Broadway and became historic overnight. Later, *A Chorus Line* moved to a real Broadway house with all the klieg-light festivities accorded the legendary musical hits of show business. Marvin Hamlisch might have to buy the bank. That's the only way he's ever going to know where all the money is.

"Most people think I'm a Hollywood type who came to New York and got lucky," he says with amusement. "It's just

the other way around. I've always been a New Yorker. I
went out there and got lucky."

He's not taking over Broadway with finger-snapping, Hollywood, "I'll-show-'em" vulgarity. He was born in Manhattan. His father played accordion at Viennese parties, and
young Marvin (who'd make up a name like "Marvin Hamlisch"?) hummed along. At the tender age of five, he showed
a remarkable talent for reproducing melodies from the radio on the piano. At seven, he auditioned for Juilliard. He
couldn't play Bach, but he could play "Goodnight Irene" in
six different keys.

At sixteen, he wrote a hit song for Lesley Gore called
"Sunshine, Lollipops, and Rainbows." At eighteen, a publisher kept him waiting two hours to audition another song.
"I was so humiliated, I decided never to write another song
without being commissioned," he says. So he got a job as the
rehearsal pianist for *Bell Telephone Hour,* where he accom-
panied everyone from Peggy Lee to Leontyne Price.

This led to a job doing dance arrangements for an ill-fated
show called *Henry Sweet Henry.* The director of that lox was
George Roy Hill (who later hired him for *The Sting*) and the
choreographer was Michael Bennett (now the genius behind
A Chorus Line). Sometimes in show-biz, it seems like they
do it in mirrors.

"But my career really started with a cocktail party at
producer Sam Spiegel's penthouse," says Marvin. "I was going to school at Queens College and doing these musical jobs
on the side. Another musician couldn't play for the party, so
he called and asked me to fill in. I said very arrogantly, 'I
don't play for parties, and besides, I've got homework.' My
friend said, 'But this one's for Sam Spiegel.' I said, 'I'll be
there in ten minutes.' "

Spiegel liked the way he played "Blue Moon" and hired
him to score a Burt Lancaster film he was producing called
The Swimmer. "The picture was a bomb but the score was
gorgeous. It led to regular employment," Marvin says.

Marvin gave up his dream to write a Broadway musical,
moved to California and wrote Las Vegas acts for Liza Minnelli, Ann-Margret and Joel Grey between scores for films
like Woody Allen's *Bananas* and *Take the Money and Run,*

The April Fools, Kotch and *Save the Tiger.* It was *The Way
We Were* and *The Sting* that won him Oscars and cemented
his success. But even those blockbusters caused him a lot of
strife. The first one provided a 2-million single for Barbra
Streisand, and now that Gladys Knight and the Pips have
recorded it as a rock tune, it's a hit all over again.

"It was one of Barbra's biggest hits, but I had to beg her
to sing it. She never wanted to do it. She said it was too
simple. I said, 'So is "My Funny Valentine"; don't you like
that?' She said, 'I hate "My Funny Valentine." ' Everybody
in the picture had to vote before she'd sing it. We all out-
voted her. Now I'm afraid to go near her with a new song.
She scares me to death."

The ragtime theme from *The Sting* was an even bigger
nightmare. It sold 3 million, but Marvin was attacked vi-
ciously for taking credit for a song that was actually com-
posed by the late Scott Joplin. He is very defensive about it.

"Let me set that record straight. I did what a tailor does
—bring him the material and he tucks it in. The Scott Joplin
songs were public domain. I only adapted them for the score
of the movie. On the record, where I played the piano, I only
got paid as a performer. I could've claimed credit for arranger and made double money. My agents tried to talk me
into it, but my ethics and morals wouldn't let me. I've always
given Scott Joplin credit for writing the song. The Oscar
went to the score, so naturally I got it. But we all know it was
the song they voted for."

In fairness, it must also be underlined that Hamlisch went
out of his way to credit Joplin in his acceptance speeches for
both the Oscar and Grammy awards.

"I didn't steal anything. The theme was there to be used
by anybody. All I did was integrate it into the film. The
Oscar rules state the music award must go to the man who
adapts the music, not the one who wrote it. There's nothing
I can do about that."

The thing that makes him mad as a ruptured hornet is the
way some critics, even in rave reviews, passed lightly over
the score of *A Chorus Line.* It's his most serious work to date,
and he's proud of it. So proud, in fact, that he caused a furor
when he recently announced he hoped Stephen Sondheim

would produce a new musical score next season in competition with *A Chorus Line* so Marvin could beat him and win the Tony award.

"Some critics complained there weren't any hit songs. The problem was to write theme songs for sixteen people so you'd know the lives of every chorus gypsy in thirty-two bars. If I had written hit songs, the audience would root only for the people with the hit songs, and it would throw the show off balance. I sacrificed like hell for the sake of the show.

"But every song can be played a different way with a bit of rock rhythm, and it's a hit. The best example is 'What I Did for Love,' which is already on the charts. Two weeks before we opened, there was pressure to cut the song because it was such a standout, so I had to devise a non-rock way to get into it. I was so subservient, I even played down my own hit song just to make the show, instead of the score, a success."

Now "What I Did for Love" has been recorded by Jack Jones, Tony Bennett, Johnny Mathis and Andy Williams, and is lighting up radios and juke boxes everywhere.

"One thing I know. Critics don't know anything about music. They react to a whole show and write a review in one hour, but I think they should be required to listen to a score twice before reviewing a musical. There are new things to hear each time. This show is the first totally fresh, inventive, imaginative work of love I've ever done. I turned down a million-dollar tour and changed my whole work schedule for a whole year to write *A Chorus Line*, and I only got nine hundred dollars to write it. My New York apartment costs more than nine hundred dollars a month. Nobody did this for money. We did it for love."

Love is the one thing few people get a chance to show in today's tasteless musical meatmarket. "Music today is trash. You have to write for an idiotic mentality just to get a song played on the radio. To write for films, you have to do a song two different ways. They call me uncommercial because I keep refusing to prostitute my songs in that way. In Hollywood they don't think sophisticated; they think commercial. I fight them, but when the producer says, 'Your song is

beautiful, but throw in some boom-chick soft-core rock behind the lyrics to make it a hit, or I'll get someone else,' you
have to make your decision then, on the spot. That's why I
did *A Chorus Line* for no money because it offered me the
challenge to write classical, ballet, rock, jazz, and Broadway
music all in one show."

You'd think being hot as a pistol would make Marvin the
boss, but he says his head is still "a Ping-Pong ball."

"I bounce between writing for mass appeal in Hollywood
and sophisticated music like *A Chorus Line* that pleases
myself. I'm miserable because I cannot write everything the
way I want to write it, but on the other hand, it's good for
my ego to be popular. I get criticized from both sides. People who have good taste attack me for writing commercial
hits. Then I write something first-rate, and Clive Barnes says
he didn't hear any melodies he could hum.

"I'm not a hack writer, but I'd be lying if I said I am
completely happy with my success. I've got a hundred hit
songs in my piano bench that will never be recorded because they're not trashy rock. So I compromise by using
beautiful melodies and doctoring them up with today's
rhythms. I've made enough money now so I can afford to
have it both ways."

With *A Chorus Line*, he has finally hit the jackpot, creating a revolutionary score that is both an artistic triumph and
an exciting crowd-thriller. It took fourteen films and three
Oscars to get him to Broadway, but this time he didn't compromise. He knows the meaning of that hit song. Some of it
Marvin Hamlisch did for money. But *A Chorus Line* is what
he did for love.

Roy Scheider

Hollywood has its own built-in grapevine, telegraphing news of forthcoming box-office bonanzas faster than a flu epidemic sweeps through an elementary school. Right now the word is out. From the stars to the electricians to the girls in the typing pool, the smash hit movie for the summer is going to be *Jaws,* and the hot new actor to watch is going to be Roy Scheider.

Roy Scheider might be a new star, but he's not exactly a new face. He's played so many tough guys in action thrillers, such as *The French Connection* (resulting in an Oscar nomination as Gene Hackman's sidekick), *The Super Cops, Klute, Stiletto,* and *The Outside Man,* that people forget how adept he's been at Shakespeare on the New York stage working for Joseph Papp or how sensitive he was in the disastrous *Sheila Levine.*

In person, he doesn't seem the type to knock people around. He shows up for our interview in collegiate blue jeans, a white Oxford button-down shirt, sneakers and a gray wool crew-neck sweater. He could have just come from jogging in Central Park, flying a kite on Fire Island, or working on a graduate thesis at Columbia. Off screen, he looks half the size of his Humphrey Bogart image. And he's twice as nice.

"I knew *French Connection* was one of the best cop films ever made because we really broke our backs to make it authentic. We didn't pull any punches in the scenes where we slapped people around. It was practically a documentary. But the bad thing was, it was so good, I got inundated with cop scripts after that. It was the same role over and over, and every cop movie was a cheap imitation. I'd get this script and every one had a chase sequence, every scene was either set in a garage or a vacant lot or a warehouse with everybody getting gunned down. This has been going on for three years, and now the public is tired of it. So I hope actors will be offered something different for a change. I know I don't want to do any more cop movies.

"I tried immediately to get out of the cop mold, but unfortunately the projects I went into were flops. I liked *Sheila Levine* because it reinforced my position as a leading man. I played a doctor. I didn't shoot anybody; I didn't muscle anybody. It was strictly a light, romantic comedy. The hardest thing about that one was working with Jeannie Berlin. You don't do a picture with that one unless you've got a personal stake in it. She's very disturbed, and it was hard for the director."

The offscreen clashes of neurotic temperament took their toll, because there was a blank emptiness of cross-purposes that showed up on the screen. The film was a disaster for everyone but Scheider, who came out of it with a deluge of fan mail, a new leading-man reputation, and an elevated salary. Now if you want Roy Scheider, you gotta pay.

They paid. The result, in *Jaws,* will probably do more for him than all the previous years of hard work put together. But if Roy Scheider is suddenly a star, he's not leaning laconically on the word. He's still full of the boyish enthusiasm he exhibited back in Orange, New Jersey, where he grew up, joined the Golden Gloves boxing competition to protect himself in a tough neighborhood, and got the famous broken nose that is his current trademark. And he's never learned how to lie. There were rumors, hushed up in the press, of the catastrophic conditions in Martha's Vineyard during the filming of *Jaws*. Scheider doesn't hide behind studio diplomacy. He comes right out and tells it like it was.

"It was hell, man," he says, rubbing his eyes. "It started out to be a seventy-eight-day shooting schedule, budgeted at three and a half million. It went to six months and six million before we finished. None of the scenes were filmed in sequence. We were driven crazy by the logistics—bad weather, building permits, posting bonds, battling tourists— and we were given only a week to shoot on any one location.

"If there's a hero out of this whole ordeal, it's Steven Spielberg. It's amazing that he's only twenty-six, but he never lost his cool. The worst thing that can happen on a film is when the director loses his dream, that wonderful fantasy in his mind of what he wants the picture to be. Spielberg never lost that. He had to make compromises, but even when things got tense—the cast and crew started looking at each other and wondering, 'What are we doing here?' and, 'How did we all get into this nightmare?'—Spielberg was a rock.

"Nobody had taken into consideration that Martha's Vineyard is the home of every big yacht and sailboat on the Eastern Seaboard. At some point in the summer, everyone comes there. So on the horizon line, the regattas were going constantly. In the climactic scene, when Richard Dreyfuss, Robert Shaw, and myself go out to capture the shark that's been terrorizing the town, we're supposed to be in a boat at sea miles offshore and totally alone! And here are all these damn boats all over the place. First, we tried to shoot in between the sailboats. That didn't work. Then we tried getting up at five A.M. to get out there before the yachts did. That didn't work, either.

"Finally, we decided we'd simply have to reshoot when the regatta season was over. You can imagine how many days and weeks, not to mention the expense, that wasted. After we shot everything on land and were in our third month, we decided to go back and try to get some of those retakes in the boat. But the water was too choppy, with

five-foot waves washing over the side of the boat. So we took
the boat into the harbor for close-ups and got hit with a
northeaster that lasted six days.

"The money is going down the drain and people are just
standing around, and that's when things went bananas. One
night at dinner, I just looked over at Spielberg and poured
a plate of fruit cocktail right on his head. That's when it
started. Dreyfuss immediately reached over and threw his
wine in my face. And then I took a big wad of pâté that was
sitting in the middle of the table and smeared it on Spielberg's coat, and all hell broke loose. Ravioli went all over
Dreyfuss, and the table was bedlam. Fourteen people
started throwing food all over the place. The cook and the
staff loved it. The tourists just thought we were typical Hollywood riff-raff."

Despite the conditions and the dangers of working with
the sharks, Scheider only got hurt once, when he cut open
a toe and developed a huge infection, closing down the film
for three days until he could walk again.

"I did all of my own stunt work, not because I wanted to
—hell, I'm no hero, it's dangerous and there are experts paid
to do that stuff, let them do it—but because we were working on a boat in tight spaces and really had to show the
danger in the shark hunt. There was no way a stuntman
could do it without being shown full-face in the close-ups.

"There's the time the shark literally leaps out of the water
and crashes into the stern of the boat and splits the boat in
half. There was no time to work out all the special-effects
stunts. You just pray a lot, and you don't know what the hell
is going to happen.

"Well, what happened was that the damn shark did split
the boat in half. I was up to my shoulders in water, and I got
out of there like a torpedo. The fear just drove me right out
of that cabin like I had been shot. Things like that constantly
happened, since there was no way to test those stunts in
advance. We got a lot of marvelous things on film, at the
expense of a lot of people's necks and a lot of people who got
hurt. Under normal circumstances, this wouldn't happen,
but there was nothing normal about making *Jaws.*"

Scheider never actually worked with real sharks. For the

sections of the film in which the actors had to tangle with the killers, a specially constructed mechanical shark was used. "But I read about the real sharks, and I was ready to swim like hell. They're unpredictable and even the experts on the film admitted that the more you learn about them the less you know. They are natural eaters. They will attack anything that moves—men, animals, tires, license plates, orange crates. They will eat anything. The mechanical shark was very difficult to work with because you can't keep the camera on it too long. The special-effects guys did a terrific job, and it looks very frightening, but we still had to have real sharks to cut to. Every reporter in the country was up there, but the producers asked them please not to dwell on the mechanical shark, because this wasn't a Walt Disney movie. It's real.

"And it is true. Nothing that happens in *Jaws* is exaggerated. Our mechanical shark is twenty-six feet long; there are white sharks that are thirty-six feet long. Our shark leaps out of the water and destroys a boat—that's nothing. It's done all the time by sharks. So naturally, these reporters went down to the shed where we stored the mechanical shark, took a lot of photos, and wrote stories about it. One woman came up from *Time* magazine and said she would only research for a story that wouldn't come out until the picture was released. Two weeks later, she runs a whole article in *Time* with a picture of the mechanical shark.

"Finally, we just said, 'This is impossible,' and banned the press from the set. But it's amazing how many people came up to Martha's Vineyard and gave us a line of bull about really being interested in the production when they really just wanted to expose the fact that we were having difficulties with the mechanical shark. And what really hurt was that these people were taken in and made comfortable and taken into our confidence, and then we were terribly betrayed. It sure gave me a nasty picture of the press in this country."

It wasn't all bad, though. Spielberg rented a log cabin in the woods and showed old movies to the cast at night. Scheider got to meet Thornton Wilder, one of his idols, and even watched while he drove a Thunderbird through a telephone pole trying to park in front of the post office. When the *Jaws* company left, the local people forgave them for all the disruptions and bellyaching by throwing a big party to say good-bye.

"They were sad because we had become a part of the community by then. We were something a little different than they had ever seen in any other summer."

And Roy Scheider is something a little different than we've ever seen in any film. His clean-cut, Ivy League appearance and his Stillman's Gym nose provide a new, fresh fantasy for movie stardom.

"I don't know what's next. The camera changes you, finds out things about you that you didn't even know about yourself. The first few times I ever saw myself on film I was very upset. I looked so sinister. I'm really just a pussycat."

Remember the name Roy Scheider because the growl is getting louder.

Ellen Burstyn

Ellen Burstyn is the hottest thing since aluminum siding. She's burning a hole through the screen in *Alice Doesn't Live Here Anymore,* playing a middle-aged widow with a son to raise as she wafts her way across America trying to make a fresh start as a song stylist and ends up slinging hash. On Thursday, March 13, she opens on Broadway in a new play, *Same Time Next Year,* described as a "serious romantic comedy" about a couple happily married (but not to each other) who have been having an illicit affair once a year for twenty-five years. Each scene takes place five years later, which gives Ellen forty seconds to age five years at a time. She doesn't choose the easy way out.

Right now she's in her rehearsal blue jeans on top of a shabby, X-rated Forty-second Street grind house that shows porno sex films. You walk past the popcorn machine, take a small elevator that creaks to a gasping sigh, and step out onto a small rehearsal stage. Here, in the old days, Florenz Ziegfeld gave the opening night parties for his *Ziegfeld Follies,* and the cream of New York *haut monde* paraded through the gilt-edged cupolas and mahogany halls to make show-biz history.

Today, the splendor is gone. The diamonds and ostrich plumes have been replaced by New World actors like Ellen Burstyn, who sits on the creaky stage with a rag tied around her head while a guard wards off muggers who might come up from the cauldron of filth on the street below to knife her while she's being interviewed.

In a way, it's a perfect counterpart. Ellen Burstyn is as big a star as it is possible to be at this chaotic time in movie history, yet she shuns the glamour that goes along with it. Until *Alice* came along, she refused all interviews, even when she won the New York Film Critics award for *The Last Picture Show,* even when she got rave reviews for *The Exorcist.* She's agreed to see the press now, she says, because "This is the most important film I've ever made and I believe in it with all my heart. So I'll do anything to make it a hit."

The reason she always hated interviews is because "it is hard to split my concentration and do my work at the same time, and my work comes first. Also, I'm very private. Unless you're careful, it's easy to start caring about the wrong things. I don't think you can care about fame and fortune and still do good work. The minute you start worrying about your hair and clothes you're already spending too much energy in the wrong direction. So I forget about images, concentrate on the truth of the part I'm playing, and let the chips fall where they may."

She hasn't even read the glowing reviews she got for *Alice.* She doesn't much care what critics think. "The first review that came out on *Alice* was in *Variety.* Some guy named Art Murphy. He said it was boring and terrible and awful, but what bothered me was he said it was a film about little people that made you hate little people. It was such a repulsive thing to say and I said, 'I don't know who this man is or anything about him, but he's a terrible snob!' And that tortured me for weeks.

"A friend said the next time I read a good review it would make me feel twice as good as normal. So I started thinking about that and decided 'No, because that means I have to get up and read the papers to determine how I'm going to feel that day. Am I in a good mood or a bad mood? Let me see my reviews!' There's something wrong with that. So I don't read reviews anymore. I don't think critics have any more important opinions than anyone else and I refuse to let them affect my life in any way."

She's strong-willed now. But it wasn't always so. There are hair-raising parallels between Ellen and the character she plays in *Alice* that are more than ironic. Although she says it is not a Women's Lib film ("I'm not an affiliate of any movement except the people's movement—we should all be able to do whatever we want to do; whether we're male or female should have nothing to do with it"), it is certainly the story of her life.

"Now I know I could've been a good scientist, but nobody ever told me a girl could be a scientist. I was totally ignorant. Born Edna Rae Gillooley in Detroit, I was poor and uneducated and everybody laughed at everything I ever wanted to do with my life. I never even graduated from high school. I was president of the student council and a lead cheerleader but I didn't know one fact kids in the fourth grade knew. I flunked everything, never did homework or cracked a book, and finally dropped out and got married.

"When I was eighteen, I set out to educate myself. I started reading the encyclopedia and taking notes. I still have pages and pages of notes on the history of bridges. I know everything there is to know about bridges. And the history of architecture in England. Then I memorized all the state capitals and the names of English kings. Then I saw somebody doing *The New York Times* crossword puzzle and that became my college education. One puzzle would take an entire week because it had to be completely researched. I'd look up all the words in the dictionary, then use the encyclopedia, *Bartlett's Quotations,* the world atlas, gazetteers, biographical dictionaries, every reference book I could find.

"I did that for five years while I worked as a soda jerk, short-order cook, a sign painter in a department store, a model, and a fashion coordinator. People would invite me away for a weekend and I'd take my puzzles with me. Nobody could talk to me. I'd leave dinner tables and sneak into people's libraries to look up words in their books. It took me a year before I could even do half of a puzzle. After five years, I could finally do them without reference books. And that is my whole education. That's how I learned to think. And there are thousands of women in the world who are vegetables because all they ever did was get married and play the roles men expected of them and only now are they beginning to realize how they've wasted their lives. That's the kind of woman I play in *Alice Doesn't Live Here Anymore* and that's why I think it has something to say to everybody."

There are other parallels: Ellen's son, Jeff, is the same age as Alice's son in the film. He lived with her on location in Tucson, contributing much of the dialogue and many of the situations that appear in the film. She wrote some of the scenes, brought the script to the attention of Warner Brothers, cast seven of her friends from the Actors Studio in supporting roles, and saw it through from beginning to end. Jeff plays Harold, the boy with the guitar next door. "He's been on all of my locations with me. He goes to school in the back of a bus in the morning and hangs around on the set in the afternoon playing poker with the crew.

"He's got a movie camera and he's produced, written, directed and edited two movies already—the first one was a Frankenstein movie he shot at Paul Mazursky's house. I played an extra in it. Then he and the boy Alfred Lutter, who played my son in *Alice,* made a Western in Old Tucson where they killed off the whole cast and each other. The editor on *Alice* taught him how to loop and splice. So he's learned a lot and he's quite gifted. He's also my best critic. He gave me a good review on *Alice.* When we saw it the first time, he said, 'It's just like us, Mom.'

"We live away from the limelight in Rockland County on the Hudson River and I try to keep his life as normal as possible. We've all known people who have gone from rich to poor. I've been very poor in my life. Now I've got money, but I don't consider any condition permanent and I certainly don't want Jeff to. Every now and then he gets a little drunk on my success and I cut him down quick. He occasionally forgets and says, 'Send a car and chauffeur for me at school.' I look him in the eye and say, 'You'll take the bus!' He takes the bus."

Ellen plays a woman in *Alice* who has to start all over again in a man's world. She's been there. Three marriages and a lifetime of hostile rejections taught her if she couldn't lick them she might as well use her talent to try to change things while joining them. When she arrived in New York she held up billboards for Old Gold cigarettes on the Jackie Gleason show, and modeled under the names Edna Rae, Edna McRae, Erica Deam, and Keri Flynn.

As Ellen McRae she finally got into a soap opera called *The Doctors,* and made two abominable movies, *Good-bye, Charlie* and *For Those Who Think Young,* which she hopes nobody remembers. While she was living in Rome with her third husband, writer Neil Burstyn, she landed a part with Rip Torn in *Tropic of Cancer* and decided her years of studying with Lee Strasberg had given her enough courage to try all over again. "I just killed off Ellen McRae and became somebody else. I've been Ellen Burstyn ever since."

Ellen Burstyn is now forty-two. She drives a Volkswagen, invests her money wisely, turns down more scripts than most actresses read in a year, never goes to parties or premieres, refuses to live in Hollywood. Every night she goes home from the theater, makes dinner for Jeff, and lives a simple life not unlike *Alice Doesn't Live Here Anymore,* except she doesn't have to sling hash.

She has directed one movie for the American Film Institute and plans to direct more. She chooses all of her directors. They don't choose her. "I can't work except under good conditions. If there's any temperament or hostility or anger, I just fold." Next month she might even win an Academy Award for *Alice Doesn't Live Here Anymore.* Meanwhile, she'll be on Broadway, where everyone can get a look at her phenomenal, liberated talent in person instead of on a movie screen.

All of which leaves her little time to act like a glamour queen even if she wanted to. "I have only one regret," she says, pulling on her blue-jean jacket and heading for the rusty elevator that will lower her to the noise and violence of the carnival street below. "I have no time to sit down and do my crossword puzzles. I still do them every morning with my coffee. Even in California, I spend a fortune having *The New York Times* mailed every day just for the puzzles. My education is continuing, see, and I'm finally very good at it. If I ever give up acting, I guess I could go into business making up crossword puzzles." She winks and heads off to her Volkswagen. "I may be uneducated, but I've got a doctorate in crossword puzzles."

Katharine Ross

The timing was bad. I had the flu, it was pouring rain, and my doctor said if I left my sick bed he wouldn't be responsible. But the press agent on the phone was adamant. "Katharine Ross is only in town for the day, she's leaving on a six o'clock plane to Rome to make a TV movie about the Mafia, and if you'll just spare a few hours she'll show you a rough cut of her new movie *The Stepford Wives* and you can talk to her about it and then go home and get back in bed." I wore galoshes. Besides, Katharine Ross is prettier than my doctor.

The Stepford Wives was not bad. In fact, I rather enjoyed it. It's an eerie, macabre tale about suburban housewives in Connecticut who get turned into robots by a man who used to work at Disneyland. And it's always a joy to see Katharine Ross, on the screen and off. It doesn't much matter what the movie is. She's always the best thing in it. She's beautiful, intelligent, liberated, warm, and one of the few girls in films today who can really act.

Why she isn't the biggest movie star in Hollywood remains to this day a mystery unsolved by the morons who run the picture industry. It's pretty much of a riddle to Katharine Ross, too. "God knows, I'm willing," she grins in Technicolor after the movie is over. "Every time I make a movie, I think maybe this will be the one. I guess it's my own fault."

She's had enough chances. After *The Graduate,* she was a household word. But she wouldn't play the Hollywood games. She thought the cigar-smoking moguls were silly, she refused to play the parts they tried to stuff down her throat, she didn't go to the screenings or the parties where they sit around and eat Chasen's chili and talk about grosses, she wouldn't date movie stars or give stupid interviews to gossip columnists to keep her name in print. The press slammed her, the Hollywood hostesses called her a snob, and she moved to the beach to raise horses.

"I guess everyone finds a way to survive in Hollywood. Mine has always been to walk away, ignore the stupidity and the waste, and live privately away from it all. I came in at the end of the studio system, when the stars were signed to long contracts, and I suffered from that. I was signed to Universal and they never gave me anything to do but trash.

"After *The Graduate* I got sent every script in town, but Universal wouldn't loan me out, so I kept saying 'No!' to everything and they put me on suspension. I couldn't work in any of the good things I was offered, and eventually people gave up on me and thought I'd retired. It cost me a lot of money and a long legal battle to buy my way out of that rat hole. I look back and I think I did it all wrong. The only thing I gained was a bad reputation of being difficult. I kept holding out for something important, something I could be proud of, talk about, feel good about. It just never happened."

She poured tea, ordered hot chicken soup from the hotel room service, and gave me an aspirin. It was better than afternoon television. Every flu victim should have Katharine Ross for a nurse. And she was in a rare, talkative mood. Rare for her. She hates interviews. "I don't refuse interviews because I hate the press. It's just that they are so dumb. You hope when somebody writes an article about you it will reveal something, or at least be interesting. But it never is. Most writers already have a point of view. You end up providing the ends of sentences. All they ever ask me about is what it was like to kiss Paul Newman."

She means *Butch Cassidy and the Sundance Kid,* a dumb movie that was probably her biggest commercial success but that she has nothing good to say about. Her fondest memory of it is working with Conrad Hall, the genius cameraman with whom she lived for several years. The last time I had seen her, they were madly in love and writing a film together based on William Faulkner's *The Wild Palms.*

Now she's married to Tom Lisi, an aspiring director she met on *Stepford Wives.* He was working as a production assistant. "Conrad and I still own *Wild Palms* but you can't get anyone to do a serious film in Hollywood. We both gave up everything for three years and tried to make that film. We ran out of money waiting. You just can't sit around and wait for the perfect film to come along. Our private life just kind of fell apart waiting. I think we began to blame each other because we weren't working. So when I met Tom, I got married immediately. I'm not sure it was the right thing to do, but I was just tired of wafting through life alone. It hasn't sapped any of my independence.

"I turned down a lot of roles when Conrad and I were trying to have a personal life together. People got nervous. They thought I had given up acting. They have very short memories in Hollywood. Most of the people out there don't even remember *The Graduate.* They all started saying, 'Whatever happened to Katharine Ross?' They've even said it to my face. That's pretty hard to take."

Katharine Ross was an army brat. She moved around a lot as a kid, grew up in San Francisco, never wanted to be a movie star. But now that she is one, she's determined to swim instead of sink. "That's why I decided to get on with it. I really did *Stepford Wives* because it's the biggest part I've ever had. It's a huge role and I'm frightened to death to see it. Tuesday Weld was signed for it, but that didn't work out, so I knew nothing about it before it happened. It was not a script I actively sought out. They were ready to shoot by the time I read the script, and I only had a few days to make up my mind.

"We filmed it in Westport, Connecticut, and the house we

used as an exterior was owned by a suburbanite who looked exactly like the robots in the film. She was perfectly groomed at seven A.M. and all of her friends who came to the set were housewives who drove station wagons, had perfect lawns, and wore the same kind of clothes. I've never been a suburban housewife, so it was hard for me to imagine that kind of life, but I think the film has a statement to make about Women's Lib. I don't see it as a Women's Lib film, but it does prove you can make a film about women that is almost entirely populated by women and still have entertainment. I'm not a Women's Libber myself. I've always had my own independent life-style. But I saw plenty of women around that suburban set who could use some liberation. And the men are just as stereotyped in their way as the women. They rarely get a chance to be human or gentle or recognized as anyone you'd want to know.

"I hope I can make more films that break down these stereotypes, but the people in control, the men who run the studios, fall into the same traps. They think in clichés. I hope it's changing for women because it's been a long time since there have been any real women on the screen. I've been a decoration so long it's nauseating."

Complaining there's nothing to do and nothing to play in today's Hollywood movies, Katharine had to go to France to work before *Stepford Wives* came along. She appeared opposite Yves Montand in a film by a young French director, Philippe Labro, entitled *Chance and Violence*. It hasn't been released in America yet. "I got this call from Paris one day at the beach while I was feeding my horses. This director said he wanted me because Jennifer O'Neill wouldn't do a nude scene. I only got the part because he had seen *Butch Cassidy* in French. It's all a fluke. Everything that has happened to me has been an accident. The things I plan and pray for never happen. What the hell. I got a trip to the French Riviera out of it. It was shot in Nice. I have no idea how good it is. I spoke English and Montand spoke French and the whole thing was dubbed. I did learn something valuable in France. So many more women work in technical aspects of film there. There are female editors, producers,

directors and cameramen like crazy. The U.S. is years behind."

She's not career-driven. She's more interested in camerawork than acting because of her years with Conrad Hall.
While he was photographing *Butch Cassidy* he even taught
her how to shoot second-unit horse stampedes until director
George Roy Hill had her thrown off the set because she
wasn't a member of the camera union. On *The Stepford
Wives* she spent more time hanging around the grips and
technicians than the other actors.

"I've always had a natural curiosity about life. I guess it's
not fully satisfied by merely being an actress. I want a life,
a home, my horses, a family of my own—but I want to express myself through a career, too. I wish there was some
way to reconcile the two things. Maybe I'll always be restless." Katharine Ross helped me on with my raincoat. "I still
feel I'm going to do a terrific film that I'll be proud of the
rest of my life. I just wish it was sooner instead of later."

A nice way to beat the flu. Chicken soup, aspirin, and the
cooling hand of Katharine Ross on my feverish forehead. I
headed home, feeling better already.

Madeline Kahn

Madeline Kahn has a dazzle in her smile and a dimple in her voice. On the screen and in the stage roles she's created, the smile and the voice have been twisted into a grab bag of funny surprises. The Madeline Kahn who knocked everybody dead doing a parody of Marlene Dietrich singing Kurt Weill in *New Faces of 1968* is different from the Madeline Kahn who almost stole *What's Up, Doc?* right out from under the considerable nose of Barbra Streisand. And the Madeline Kahn who sends insomniacs searching for their *TV Guides* when she stops the late-night talk shows cold with her deadpan comedy is still another Madeline Kahn from the heartbreaking Miss Trixie Delight in *Paper Moon*.

Right now she's adding two more portraits to the confusion, with a five-minute guest appearance in the Ingrid Bergman movie *The Mixed-Up Files of Mrs. Basil E. Frankweiler* (she's the muddled schoolteacher with the group of moppet monsters on a tour of the Metropolitan Museum who steals the movie), and a starring role in Joseph Papp's production of *The Boom Boom Room* on the New York stage. Playing a tawdry go-go dancer with laughter and tears, she steals that one, too. The girl is unique.

Okay, so who the hell is the real Madeline Kahn? I ring her bell expecting almost anything. The girl who opens it looks like Tuesday Weld. She's pretty, she's stacked, she's wearing a bandana halter and tight jeans, and if I were a male chauvinist pig, I'd call her a dish. There's a big stuffed Raggedy Ann doll in a wicker chair surrounded by Raggedy Ann babies, a Diana Lynn coloring book, a Magritte painting of a naked woman with a vertical smile, and a framed song sheet of "It's Only a Paper Moon." "Those are some of my play-toys," she grins. She's shy, bright, sensitive and unaffected, and there's not a sign of vanity. In fact, she seems surprised that anyone would want to interview her at all and says so. "I just can't believe that little part in that movie would result in an interview! I made it ages ago, way before I did *Paper Moon,* and I thought it would never be released!" I compliment her on the announcement in the columns that Peter Bogdanovich will star her with Cybill Shepherd and Ryan O'Neal in his new Cole Porter musical *Quadrille.* Her eyes widen. "Oh, I keep reading that I'm in that and seeing it on Rona Barrett, and I don't know whether to believe it or not. But I'm taking tap-dancing just in case."

Things just keep happening to her because she's so talented, but she's more surprised by her success than anyone else. The girl simply has no ego. She's worked with some egos as big as housing developments (Streisand, Danny Kaye, Lucille Ball, to name a few), and it just hasn't rubbed off yet. "I guess I'm still too impressed by these people to compete with them," she says. "I was petrified of Streisand when I did *What's Up, Doc?* It was my first movie and every single thing about it was new. I was petrified of the palm trees! I had never heard of Peter Bogdanovich, but I knew about Streisand cutting Anne Francis out of *Funny Girl* and I didn't want to do the film. My agent talked me into it. I had an interview with Peter and told him what I had heard about what happens to other girls in Streisand movies and he assured me that wouldn't happen. It was a movie about

three people and there's only so much you could cut out of
it and still have the movie make sense. So I took a chance
and it turned out fine. I really liked her and we had some
good talks and I thought we could really be friends, but she
has so many pressures, and she's unavailable a lot on the set,
and we never became close or anything. I got a glimpse of
what it's like to be a really big superstar. I don't think I'd like
that."

Working for a year with Danny Kaye in the Richard Rodgers musical *Two By Two* was less entrancing. "I needed the
work very badly. I was broke. So I did it without even reading a script. And it started out to be a really good show.
Danny Kaye can be a really fine actor. He's very moving.
But it turned into the Danny Kaye Show. He reached a point
where he just didn't think the audience wanted to see him
play Noah on the ark and he chickened out or something,
and it turned into burlesque. I think it was fear. I think he
felt people wouldn't like him unless he made them laugh. It
amazes me to see people that established—you know, really
big stars—with such insecurity. I guess it isn't really so amazing. I guess you just never feel the way people think you feel.
Everybody in show business wants approval. You never feel
like a king—you just want to know, 'Is it all right, am I good
or am I coming across?' I've been amazed a few times by
stars who have no self-confidence, but now I'm not so
amazed anymore."

The biggest blow to her own personal career happened
last year, when she was fired from the movie version of
Mame. She had been signed to play Agnes Gooch. Lucille
Ball took one look at her curves; the next thing she knew,
she was standing in line for unemployment insurance. "I'm
not exactly sure what happened. They showed Lucille Ball
What's Up, Doc? and she liked me in it, but then I walked
on the set and I guess I don't exactly look like frumpy Eunice
in the movie.

"It was just a part. I mean, you can see I don't look like
that in real life. But I thought that was what the movies were
all about. Hey, nobody walks around Hollywood looking the
way they really look. I can look like forty different people
with makeup and padding. I didn't think it was a problem,

but I think when Lucille Ball met me, she thought, 'What kind of casting is this?' And I must admit I'm no Agnes Gooch. But I planned to play it differently from the way Jane Connell played it on Broadway and I thought they wanted a different approach too. The problem was do we go in a new direction or do we do what's already been done? They got Jane Connell and there's your answer. But I didn't take it as a personal insult or rejection. That's just show business."

Madeline still doesn't like Hollywood, but she says it's getting easier. "At least when I go out there they know who I am now, so I feel like I've got a right to be there." She's never been to one of their A parties. She's not even sure she's been to a B party. "I think the people I know are more like B-plus." For someone so hysterically funny in the roles she plays, there's nothing frivolous about her, and she insists the reputation baffles her. "Most of the time I'm not trying to make people laugh—I'm just trying to get a point across. But they laugh anyway, so I guess I must be funny.

"I don't do talk shows anymore, because they give me headaches. When I first started doing Dick Cavett I'd go in and they'd ask my opinions on things and when I started talking they'd laugh. I don't know why they had me on time after time, and finally, I started searching for funny things to say so they'd keep laughing. One day I found myself standing between two subway cars, trying to be funny, and people were looking at me like I was crazy. So I knew it was time to stop. I realized that was the only reason I was on. I hadn't done a terrific part or a movie or a book or anything. I didn't have an act, I wasn't Joan Rivers, I was just there because they thought I was funny. And I never wanted to be one of those girls who walks out and makes a fool of herself. So one night I watched myself on Merv Griffin and there I was, sandwiched in between George Jessel and Marty Allen, and just being treated like a dumb kook for them to bounce their jokes on, and I said that's it. Where did I ever say I had to do that? What's happening to me? So I just stopped doing talk shows."

Which proves what a special predicament Madeline Kahn is in. She's following in a tradition of Martha Raye–Carol Burnett comedy that assumes comediennes have to be ugly to be funny. Femininity has always been a stranger to the comic tradition. Now here's Ms. Kahn—intelligent, funny, and attractive—and she's unwilling to be self-deprecating. She won't play dumb, she won't do pratfalls. What's left? "I guess I'll just look for quality in the roles I play and try to keep from getting type-cast. My standards are high, there are things I want that I haven't done yet, but I haven't finished it all.

"I'm a terrific dancer, I studied to be an opera singer. When I was a kid, I fell in love with the fairy godmother in *Pinocchio.* She made me crazy, knocked me off my seat. I didn't want to be Ann Miller. I never even heard of Ann Miller. I just wanted to be Cinderella. I was very advanced musically. I could hear something and play it by ear immediately. The fact that I'm good at mimicry and imitating voices surprises me every time I do it. The Southern accent in *Paper Moon* just came out of me like a ghost. I don't know where it came from. I just do these voices. Now I just finished a Western, called *Black Bart,* with Mel Brooks, and I'm doing my first really big dramatic role in the play *Boom Boom Room,* and that's a side of me nobody has seen before and I'm just waiting to see what happens next.

"The thing is, I have less philosophy as I go along. I'm not as sure of anything as I used to be. I hate the show business life, I hate parties, I don't like hanging around with actors, I don't like packing up and moving to temporary lodgings. On the other hand, I like to work." The clown with the face of an angel sighs. "I think I'm talented. I just hope I live to someday be old and talented."

And famous too? "Uh-h-h . . ." With a little help from your friends, Madeline, with a little help from your friends.

Genevieve Bujold

HOLLYWOOD—"My place or yours?"

With Genevieve Bujold, the film industry's new mystery girl, it's a moot question. By her own admission, she's "a woman without a country, without an address, without roots, with no place to go," and she's determined to keep it that way. Producers can't find her because she has no phone number. Directors plying her with scripts go mad with frustration because she has no agent. The press is ready to sue her for nonsupport because she won't do interviews.

When *Swashbuckler,* the adventure spectacle in which she gets kidnapped by pirates, opened at Radio City Music Hall, Bujold gave in to studio pressure and flew to New York to make personal appearances. One hour after she checked into her Manhattan hotel, she grabbed her unpacked bags, fled down a back elevator, and whipped back to Hollywood, leaving behind the excuse that her father was dying of a heart attack. Jennings Lang, the producer of *Swashbuckler,* was understandably furious as he wiped egg off his face and explained bravely: "She's a very selfish, very complicated girl. She certainly wasn't forced into doing publicity to help the picture, but why did she have to lie about it?"

Mrs. Lang, who is the former actress-singer Monica Lewis, is even more outspoken: "I think she's crazy. One day she wants me to arrange fencing lessons, the next day she wants dancing lessons, but the instructor has to be black. I spend hours on the phone, and then she doesn't show up for the appointment. Once she phoned and said, 'I have finally found the center of my life, the first step toward finding myself,' and I expected some major revelation. It turned out she had purchased an all-purpose vacuum cleaner. I said instead of a vacuum cleaner, she should find a good psychiatrist."

After much persistence, she has finally agreed to meet me. It has to be "my place," which turns out to be a suite at the Beverly Hills Hotel. She arrives on time, carrying a bottle of red wine in her tote bag. She is radiantly rebellious: There is to be no interview, she prefers to just talk. We order a corkscrew from room service and she munches a McCarthy salad. Her freshness is winning, despite her protests that she slept over at a friend's pad and looks terrible. Her hair is shiny and gleaming as a stallion's mane, her eyes big and brown as chocolate jawbreakers, her tiny mouth a rosebud of surprise.

Packed into her five-foot, four-inch doll's frame is an intriguing mixture of purloined innocence, succulent sexuality, and guerrilla warfare. Tufts of hair grow wild from her armpits, wrecking the fragile china image. The rebellion grows.

"I think I've earned the right to be whatever I want to be," she offers proudly. "I grew up in Montreal in the strictest kind of Catholic society, went to convent schools where the discipline of the nuns was a heavy number. My father was a bus driver, my sister was the beautiful, perfect one. From the ages of eight to sixteen, I spent my time staring out of a window wondering how I would get away. My family was bewildered by my restlessness and even more by my acting. I shocked them when I married a WASP the first time, then I shocked them even more when I divorced him a year and a half later."

Then she married director Paul Almond and starred in three of his films—*Isabel, The Act of the Heart,* and *The Journey.* They were Canada's leading theatrical couple. They were divorced in 1973 after seven years of marriage. "We were more than a marriage. We were a team. We were partners. Paul built a magnificent house in Montreal out of a monastery with a view of the St. Lawrence River. I'm the one who walked out. I felt very guilty, but I was in love with someone else, and I wanted to live for myself. There comes a time when you must decide between your responsibility to someone else and your responsibility to yourself. I followed my heart. I have always lived my life by instinct, and I have paid dearly for the privilege, but I would rather be alone than be two people and still alone."

She wandered around Russia and France with an acting troupe. Alain Resnais saw her and launched her international career with a small but vibrant role in *La Guerre Est Finie.* This led to *The King of Hearts* with Alan Bates, which has now become a major cult film among movie buffs, and *The Thief of Paris* with Jean-Paul Belmondo. Searching for a female star to play the ill-fated Anne Boleyn opposite Richard Burton's Henry the Eighth in *Anne of the Thousand Days,* Hal Wallis remembered her from *Isabel* and made about a thousand phone calls before he tracked her down. She got an Oscar nomination and won a Golden Globe award as Best Actress of 1969. You'd think her fame and fortune would be cemented at Grauman's Chinese. But Bujold had other plans.

"Hal Wallis then wanted me to do *Mary, Queen of Scots* for Universal. I said, 'Look, Hal, I don't want to play any more queens. Give the part to some other actress who wants the job and would be very good in the part. With me, it would be the same producer, the same director, the same costumes, the same me!' Well, Hal Wallis said, 'If you don't do this, they'll put you in some piece of crap!' I had innocently agreed to do three more films for Universal, and now they were suing me for seven hundred and fifty thousand dollars, and I was completely washed up in Hollywood. I had a son to support, and I couldn't work in America, so I went to Europe and did *Trojan Women* with Katharine Hepburn and another film in Canada.

"Then I wandered back to Hollywood, and they threatened to put me in jail, and that's how I ended up in *Earthquake* and *Swashbuckler* for practically no money at all, just to erase the old debt. I take no responsibility for those films. I just do the best work I can, and then it's somebody else's responsibility. My work is finished. I will watch the rushes when I'm working, but I rarely go to see a film I've done because the girl on the screen is somebody else and it all happened yesterday and there is nothing I can do about it.

"I don't regret doing anything. I found some little piece of reality in *Earthquake,* and made the most of it. I played a woman whose child was in danger, and I identified with that. Also, I had a lot of hard physical work to do, and I love that. I love it when I sweat until I'm ready to faint. On *Swashbuckler,* I got a free trip to Mexico out of it, and I learned to fence. Robert Shaw was such a madman that my arm was black and blue from the way he shoved me around. He's a wild, talented, passionate actor, but a madman. I haven't seen the picture, but I didn't mind doing it. However, I don't see why I should give out interviews to promote it, either. I have nothing to say. If *Swashbuckler* is a flop, it's because the public doesn't want to see it. I can't do anything about that. If you try to talk people into seeing something they don't want to see by peddling yourself, then you become a saleswoman and a prostitute, and I am neither."

She's more enthusiastic about two other new films: *Obsession,* an eerie, haunting thriller in which she comes back from being presumed dead to tantalize her own father, played by Cliff Robertson; and *Love and Other Crimes* with Jack Lemmon.

"I did *Obsession* because I like the director, Brian De Palma, and I'm pleased that it is a success, but I understand they've changed it a lot. When I did it, I actually married my own father and slept with him, then when he woke up the morning after the wedding I had gotten my revenge and disappeared.

"It was fun playing a girl who was really a bitch underneath all that sweetness. Now they've cut the wedding scene and the love scene because it was too shocking for the studio executives and their wives and given it a happy father-daughter ending. That's what I mean about not caring. If I became involved in every aspect of film-making, I would go mad.

"The other film is supposed to be a comedy. Jack Lemmon plays a bail bondsman who gets involved with a wild gypsy, and there is nothing very funny about gypsies, so I think there will be more pathos in it than originally planned. I did a lot of research with the gypsies for that one, and it's the closest I've ever come to really finding a family. They dance, they tell fortunes, and there's always a pot of stew on the stove.

"I lived with the gypsies, I followed Bob Dylan around on his tour, I will now make a film in December with Claude Lelouch which will be filmed in Arizona and Paris. Who knows what will happen between now and then? I have no plans. I am like a woman who is always in labor. Every day I have a new contraction, and my whole life changes. That's another reason why I do not give interviews. Whatever I tell you now will be obsolete by next week. I know where my child is at this moment, but I don't know where life will take us tomorrow. I live each day at a time and make each minute work for me until the minute is over. Then I go on to something else. I am totally alone in this world."

She's tough as a little green apple, but the sensitivity shines through the defensive veneer like a ray of sun. Her son, Matthew, now eight, is the only man in her life. She moved him to a beach house in Malibu, enrolled him in a school there, then gave up the house when her ex-husband moved in three doors down the beach with his new girl friend. Now she plans to take another beach house from September to December, then take Matthew with her on location when she does the Lelouch film.

"My little son and I are like the gypsies. We move when the spirit moves. I know absolutely nothing about raising a child, but we raise each other. We are growing up together. Just the other day he said to me, 'It's too bad they don't have a hotel on the beach so I could go to school and you wouldn't have to worry about me.' He is very intelligent, speaks two languages, and gives me constant companionship. I'm his mother and his friend, and I'm always there if he needs me, but I will not raise him by any rule books. We have no possessions because I don't want to be owned by anything. I rent a car, a TV, a house. I have no friends, no money, no agent and no plans. But we survive, and we've got each other."

She stands, waiflike in the door, with her arms full of balloons I've given her for Matthew, an enigmatic blossom shrinking from the light. A brief kiss good-bye, then she's on her way to the next contraction.

Giancarlo Giannini

Giancarlo Giannini is the new noise in movies. People outside Rome and New York have probably never heard of him. Even in New York, where his consistently volatile performances in the cynical, comic, explosive films of Lina Wertmuller have made him the most talked about international star since Belmondo, there are people who have never heard of him. But the people who mold opinions and influence the arts are talking a lot, and the sounds they're making are loud, clear and exuberant.

They call him the new Marcello Mastroianni—dynamic, appealing, and sexy. In person, he's more like the old James Dean—frayed, intense, arrogant, bristling with moody intelligence and energy. The bags under his eyes challenge his youth, but there's a wild shock of Kennedy hair and a taut, lean body to prove he's only thirty-three.

In New York to publicize the new Wertmuller film, *Seven Beauties,* he became the toast of the town. He moved from party to party in casual sweaters and blue jeans, charmed the press with raging discussions about movies, dined with everyone from Francis Ford Coppola and Joseph Papp to

Anita Loos and Comden and Green, danced till 5 A.M. with Marisa Berenson and dragged himself home to Italy in a state of exhaustion. His huge, piercing green eyes recoil in horror at the mention of stardom, but he knows what to do to get it.

On screen, he's bigger than life, swaggering his way passionately through Wertmuller's films playing lustful, raging chauvinists, virile Communist laborers, and assorted pimps, assassins and murderers. ("I don't believe in heroes," he says with authority, "especially in films!") In his suite at the Hotel Pierre, he collapses in an overstuffed chair surrounded by his press clippings, like a child waiting for his nurse to turn the bed down.

He is small and boyish (the camerawork carefully conceals his five-foot-nine-inch height and adds weight to his hundred and forty-three pounds). His eyes are bloodshot. He hasn't shaved for days. An interpreter works hard to translate every comma while he munches a chicken sandwich. His English is good, but he fears it. My Italian hits a red light after "Arrivederci!" We laugh together at the silliness of interviews, then plunge ahead with one.

In *Seven Beauties,* Giancarlo plays a Neapolitan mafioso who abuses women, murders his sister's pimp, rapes a female patient in an insane asylum, and ends up in a Nazi concentration camp, where he survives because he seduces the swinish lesbian camp commandant. Back in Naples after the war, he is a broken man, but he has lived by using and destroying others.

In Italy, the critics attacked the film because it says Italian men will always survive no matter what the cost. In America, the film has been praised because it raises the question of whether survival is worth it if the cost is greater than the humanity that is paid. There have been so many different interpretations of the film you'd think it was seven movies instead of one.

Giannini smirks contentedly at the furor *Seven Beauties* and his powerful portrayal have caused. "I learned a long time ago not to read what they write about me. Success pleases me. It's a great compliment. And it amuses me to see the film viewed in so many different ways. Each critic has a right to see a film the way he feels it to be. Even if they don't agree, they're talking. Besides, it is very difficult to be specific today because society is so complex. But if the public understands the man I play at the end, I am happy.

"He says he's alive, yet his eyes are dead. He's a dead man. It's very simple. Italian men are simple-minded. To love and eat spaghetti and live is the most important thing to Italian men. But what Lina's films say is that there is more than one way of looking at something. There are infinite ways of molding clay. If to live means to live by betraying everything you believe in, then it's better to die."

He says he plays dramatic, combustible characters because "they are much more interesting than I am." In his own life, he has gone from a degree in electronics engineering to the make-believe world of acting "to feed my fantasy." He enrolled in a three-year acting course with no experience, and halfway through he quit to play Puck in *A Midsummer Night's Dream* at the age of nineteen. A year later, he shocked the Italian critics by playing Romeo in Franco Zeffirelli's stage production of *Romeo and Juliet* by unzipping his fly onstage. Five years ago he shocked them again by playing Hamlet as a hippie who danced the boogie-woogie and played football with the skull of Yorick. The critics murdered him. "They didn't understand it," he shrugs bitterly. "American critics are much more intelligent."

By this time, he was tired of the stage anyway, and movies were calling. Although he has become famous to American filmgoers in the Wertmuller films—*The Seduction of Mimi, Love and Anarchy, Swept Away,* and now *Seven Beauties*—he has also made a series of Italian farces that never crossed the Atlantic. In one of them, called *Mad Sex,* he played ten different characters, all totally different. He says his ambition is to play a woman.

"I never do anything easy. If I had to play characters close to me, I'd be ashamed to do it. To play characters different and weird is to act upon my fantasies. This allows me to speak in a more direct way to my audience. Each man feels a need to communicate. Acting is the way I do it. Deep in myself are facets of all the characters I play. But to bring

them out is a complicated thing that causes me much agony
I can't turn it off. I go home and drink coffee and play with
my kids, and my mind is still on my work. When I dragged
the woman across a deserted island in *Swept Away,* I did not
go home and beat my wife. But I thought about it."

He says he acts because he loves it, but the "buts" are
infinite. "I take photographs, I paint, I'm a good cook. But
it's better to do one thing well than many things badly. I'd
rather make a big mistake at the thing I do best than have
a series of small successes. When I do a film, I'm involved in
the daily rushes, editing, camera angles—every aspect of
film-making. Yet I rarely look like myself on the screen. I
like to hide what I am. Actors used to wear masks. I like that
even better."

And who is the real Giancarlo Giannini when the cameras
are silent? "Nobody. Just an ordinary man. I have all the
problems all fathers and husbands have. The difference is, I
arrive home one night with red hair and curls, the next night
with blond hair and a moustache. My family is used to my
life. When I did *Hamlet,* my oldest son was in the wings in
his playpen looking at me like I was a madman. That is a jolt
for a man. But they got used to it. Now they just say, 'What
is Papa playing tonight in those funny glasses?' "

His older son, Lorenzo, is eight; the baby, Adriano, is four.
When he came to Lina Wertmuller's set to visit Papa on
Seven Beauties, she had the brainstorm of casting him in the
role of Giancarlo as a child in the flashbacks. The four-year-
old took one look at the Thirties' wigs and underwear, and
said, "I will not play a *pagliaccio* [clown]—not even for
Papa." Luckily, the eight-year-old was there to step into the
role. "I think he liked it too much," frowns Giannini. "I don't
want him to be an actor." Mrs. Giannini is an ex-actress now
studying to be a child psychologist in Rome.

When he isn't acting, Giannini dubs American films into
Italian. Unlike most stars, he doesn't mind the work and says
it teaches him hidden aspects of his craft while he earns
good money for doing it. Currently, he is the voice of Jack
Nicholson in Antonioni's *The Passenger* and the voice of Al
Pacino in *Dog Day Afternoon.*

"I've learned a lot from dubbing Americans into Italian.

Only a genius can be a born actor. I am not a genius so I learn all the time. I love Chaplin and copy his walk all the time. I get very emotional in films. Fatally, I see actor's flaws and tricks, but if the film is good I can have just as much fun as the average person.

"I don't do it for the money. Money is only important to eat and sleep. I don't care much for material things because I wouldn't know how to use them if I had them. I could buy a motorboat, but I get seasick. I could buy a car, but then you have to have it waxed, so I ride in other people's cars. I don't have a very commercial mind, but I would like to make American films. I'd have to work very differently, learn to think differently. Anything is possible, but I have no desire to make musicals or cowboy movies. Most of the films in America are not worth making. And I might not have the control over everything I have with Lina."

After so many films with Wertmuller, he has now made a new one for Luchino Visconti. "I had to work differently. I trust Lina. I even tell her how to photograph my eyes. But I'm very stubborn with other directors in order to defend myself. The actor is always the victim. Visconti was no problem. He cares about actors and says little but listens to everything. He leaves his actors free to establish their own responsibility to the film."

The new one is called *The Innocent*. He plays a man with a wife and a mistress. When the wife has another man's baby, he murders the child, then himself. Not exactly a million laughs. "The story is very banal, but it shows how men who try to bend everything to their way of thinking end up destroying themselves. It's another anti-hero."

Like Jack Nicholson, Giannini has come along at a time of sexual confusion, when men on the screen are getting a fresh look at themselves and are not afraid to cry. "There are two factions to work for—the critics and the public. I work for the public. In Italy, I have the public. In America, I have the critics *and* the public. You can be a good actor, and nobody comes to see you.

"I've been lucky. If I try to analyze my success, I say Women's Lib has done it. Men are frightened; there is chaos everywhere. We wait to see what will happen. Women have always had the upper hand. Now they see what their power is doing to men in the characters I play—I knock them around, but they always do me in at the end. Men identify with the characters I play, and women feel sorry for them. This gives me power, and I love that."

The momentary elation subsides. He scratches his stubble of beard, and his voluminous eyes fill with tears of self-pity. "Power is another fantasy I live in. The truth is, I am weak. My goal is to find the strength to stop acting. It's not a profession for a real man. I find myself on top of a woman making love, and I am really on top of a chair. The actress has gone home and the camera is shooting me making love to a chair. It's an insane profession."

But it buys a lotta pizza.

David Bowie

David Bowie's Fleetwood Cadillac lunges through the rainy night forty miles from Los Alamos, past atomic bomb sites, solar furnaces, Aztec ruins, inactive volcanoes, and discarded Coors beer cans. In the back seat, the androgynous rock star who is making his spectacular movie debut as a creature from a distant planet in *The Man Who Fell to Earth* lies in a crumpled heap of black kamikaze silk, drinking straight Tequila Gold from a paper bag. He's wearing a space suit and a Crimean war hat. His bare, prehensile feet are stretched out over the bar, and he peers inquisitively at me, while I try to interview him, through pink aviator glasses. His flaming orange hair turns lemon-yellow around the widow's peak like Elsa Lanchester in *The Bride of Frankenstein,* and his milk-white, anemic-looking skin tone occasionally turns baby-pink when he laughs.

With him are his chauffeur, a burly ex-hood in a ten-gallon Stetson named Tony, and Corinne Schwab, his buffer-secretary-traveling companion who keeps the wolves away. Corinne was born in Bloomingdale's basement. "I found her in a want ad. I rang her up and asked her, 'Do you want to work for me?' "

"I never heard of him," says Corinne. "I hate rock and roll."

So do I. In fact, I don't know what I'm doing here. I guess I thought I was coming along to meet a rock freak who made good. Instead, I am amazed to discover that David Bowie is astoundingly literate, fantastically well-read, creative and professional. He has written nine screenplays, a book of poems and essays, a novel, and a collection of short stories. He carries around a 16-mm newsreel camera, which he uses to photograph everything around him.

He's been a Buddhist, he studied music with a Dalai Lama in Tibet, he plays the tenor sax beautifully, he's into mysticism and numerology, and he's very knowledgeable about everything in movies before 1933. "Then I stopped going. I've been most influenced by Keaton and the German impressionist films of Fritz Lang, Murnau, and Pabst." He wants to direct films and get out of the rock music business forever. It's hardly what I expected.

"I have never considered myself a rock freak," he says. "In fact, hitting the rock scene was just a way of becoming enough of a force to say what I wanted to say. I always felt I would make a quick flash, like a comet, flare, shine very bright, then fade away and never be seen again. Otherwise, it becomes a career, and who wants a career in rock and roll? I'm not a rock musician. It was only a grand means to an end. I've always wanted to be a film director.

"All of my concept albums, from *Ziggy Stardust* down, were ideas for films, but I couldn't get anyone to perform the stuff I wrote, so I did it myself. To keep from getting bored on tours, I always made my acts as theatrical as possible. The whole bisexual chic, which I'm credited with originating, started five years ago as an answer to an impertinent interviewer about my sex life. I've always been an original, sort of a rock-and-roll guinea pig. But I was an actor first.

"I was a mime artist for two and a half years with Lindsay Kemp, and that's how I became fascinated with Genet. The androgynous, the neuter, the Everyman theme—I used all of that mime experience in rock music the way Buster Keaton did in films. I've finished with it now. I don't always wear green eyelashes, glitter pants, and feather boas. Sometimes I wear Kabuki samurai robes and platform boots. Sometimes I wear entire wardrobes purchased from Sears-Roebuck. I can be a hundred different people. I've always been an actor. I've never been David Bowie, the person, in front of an audience. That would be scary!"

Because he guards his private persona so aggressively, he avoids interviews like the plague. "I'm terribly self-conscious. And the ignorance of journalists amazes me. They're rude and dumb, and it's a waste of time. I don't travel in the rock world. They are tiresome people. Mick Jagger and John Lennon are the only friends I have in rock. My records are very diverse. I own very few rock recordings.

"My real friends are very loyal, and they're there for me, and they know how to be with me even if I don't know how to be with them. I'm not trendy. I will do anything to avoid so-called fashionable people. So they think I'm a tight-lipped little bastard. Not only do I not care, but I don't know what they're writing about me, because I don't read anything that is even vaguely in the rock press. I am actually quite down to earth as a person, really. See these pink glasses? They're just an effect. I have one good eye and one bad eye. Don't get me confused with Elton John, though. I can't stand him."

So many bizarre things have been written about his past that nobody knows who David Bowie really is. But tonight, in this wild car ride through the mesas of New Mexico, he's in a talkative mood. "I grew up in South London. It was like Harlem. I was very butch in those days. I was in street brawls and everything. My father was a gambler and a drinker and a layabout for most of his life. I have one brother and one sister that I know about. There may be more. We're all illegitimate. After I was born, they made it legal, and my father went straight. He worked in a children's home.

"But I was really out of place as a child. I've literally wiped that whole period out of my life. It's like a nightmare. One reason I've never been in analysis is that I've always been afraid of what I'd find out. My brother is in a psychiatric hospital, and madness has always run through our family. I have a terrible fear it's genetic." The equally dangerous game of submerging himself into too many fake disguises for the public doesn't seem to bother him. "It's okay if, after you play all the roles, you're happy with the person you take home at night." Then he adds with an evil giggle: "Some nights are better than others."

The person he does not always take home at night is his wife, the equally outrageous Angela Bowie, whose escapades often share space in the gossip columns with David's. "She's remarkable, funny, totally independent, decisive in her love-hate tastes. She was born in Cyprus. Her father ran a mine. What is it he mined, Corinne?"

"Whatever it is they mine in Cyprus," shrugs Corinne.

The Bowies have a five-year-old son named Zooey Bowie, named after J. D. Salinger's *Franny and Zooey*—"super and ever so funny and very precocious"—but continue to live distinctly separate life-styles. "I'm not a leader of the Gay Liberation movement or anything like that," says David. "But I have nothing to hide. It's in my music. I like men, I like black girls, I can be a hundred different people in a hundred different scenes."

He says his tours have never made money because they're so expensive ("seventy people in the company and sets and lights by Jules Fisher"), but he's still rich. "I'm moving to Bhutan to escape the British taxes, so I'll have more. I don't own material things, except for books, video tape machines, tools and machines, which I am fascinated by, and a Jeep and the Fleetwood, which I take on tour. I never drive. I never bothered to get a license. I can't put my hands on any of my money, but it's there. I've got to have money to afford my wife."

"Home" at the moment is a reconverted brownstone across from an 1830 church on West Twentieth Street in Manhattan. "I store my costumes in New York. I have about seven thousand costumes in storage trunks. I love New York because I'm anonymous there. I've come to love the gang fights in the street, too. Makes me feel like I'm a child again in the London slums. I hate Los Angeles because it's not a city and not a town, and I can't abide anything that can't make up its mind about itself. You know where you are in New York."

I express surprise that he is able to walk the streets of New York without being recognized by screaming fans. "I've never had any trouble walking down any street in the world unrecognized if I plan it that way. Except Tokyo. You can't go around with orange hair in Tokyo without looking different."

He once toured through Russia on a train and was the first person ever allowed to take a camera to Siberia. "I've written a novel about it which I am publishing this year. They thought I was a circus clown. You can get away with murder in Russia if you have orange hair." His great ambition is to give a rock concert in China. He's working on it. He's also been promised an exhibition of his paintings and sculptures by the Metropolitan Museum of Art.

Although *The Man Who Fell to Earth* is his first film, he says with supreme self-confidence that it will not be his last. "I never read the script. I never had any anxiety about my songs, concerts, or acting ability. I have total self-confidence. Is that awful?" The producers of the film originally wanted Peter O'Toole. "If we'd hired him, he'd have been forced to act it. It was much easier for David to be it. He's weird enough already. Nobody can prove he's not from outer space."

In the film, David has no fingernails or toenails. He has cat eyes covered with a membrane to look human. "The hardest part was the makeup. It took five hours to remove the sex organs, navel, and ears. I walked into a hotel lobby in Santa Fe, and grown men screamed. The hours and hours of work and pain involved were incredible. People who go expecting a science fiction movie with super hits will be disappointed. To me, it's a love story. I don't feel like a creature from outer space. I felt very romantic.

"Some really freaky things happened. We shot in the Aztec burial grounds, where no white man has ever been and certainly no movie crew has ever shot a film before. I knew from my years as a Buddhist that something was wrong. One day I was drinking a glass of milk, and I tasted something bitter. I looked into the glass and saw some gold liquid swimming around in shiny swirls inside the glass. Suddenly the pain in my stomach was incredible.

"Corinne rushed me to the hospital, and they said I had been poisoned. They gave me an emetic and I vomited everything up and was out of the picture for two days. They sent the milk to a lab in Albuquerque to be tested and no trace of any foreign element in it could be found. Six people saw this eerie mess in the milk, so I know I'm not crazy. Also, Steve Schapiro, the photographer, had his cameras jammed and nothing come out on film. It was very bad karma."

For another scene, Bowie went to Carlsbad Caverns and saw the famous bat cave. "It was completely dark except for one hole in the top. Suddenly there was a whistling sound like rats screaming. Thousands of bats flew out from the rocks and up through the hole. They return every morning at four A.M. I'd love to do my next concert there, with thousands of vampire bats descending on the audience's heads."

Whether *The Man Who Fell to Earth* survives the critics or not, David Bowie will surely survive the movies with a fertile imagination and a healthy ego. "I get so much fan mail it has to be handled by a computer. I'm an instant star," he adds with a slug of tequila and a Dracula grin—"just add water and stir."

Robert Redford

Robert Redford, the hottest movie sex symbol since Clark Gable, looked as wholesome, stiff, and unshakable as a bowl of tapioca. His normally perfect strawberry blond hair stubbornly tufted about his head like the scarecrow's stuffing in *The Wizard of Oz*. A slight puffiness around the eyes betrayed an understandable early-morning sleepiness, but the sternly set jaw warned of heartfelt seriousness. Environment and American Indians have long been passionate concerns of this Cinemascope hero who often suspects his critics of thinking him handsomely vapid, and he had ventured forth into the dull humidity of a yawning New York dawn to pay tribute to both.

It was a strange time and place to encounter Robert Redford—9 A.M. in the Whitney Museum. But there he was— the star who wouldn't lift a finger to promote or publicize any of his multi-million-dollar movie extravaganzas, the man who fears and avoids the press like typhoid—holding a press conference to help a low-budget documentary he narrated called *Broken Treaty at Battle Mountain*, about the Shoshone Indians' struggle to regain their Nevada homeland.

The press seemed to sense the sincerity of the occasion. When the lights went on in the small, hot screening room there was a prevailing air of closeness, smelling like wet mittens steaming on a school radiator, which intensified as TV crews focused high-powered spotlights and cameras on the panel. No sighs of longing or slack-jawed stares of awe could be found on the faces of Redford fans. The Indians were stony-faced and silent. An occasional beaded head-band or protruding feather were the only hints of levity. A Presbyterian minister stood attentively throughout the proceedings, his small daughters holding his hands. Chic Vassar types passed around an infant whose bawling indicated it was suffering a self-induced dampness of its own. There was no rush to get closer to the most famous redhead since Rita Hayworth.

Even the questions were directed mainly to the members of the Battle Mountain Indian Colony. When Redford did answer a question he remained seated and spoke quietly: "Indians and the environment go together . . . an Indian's concept of land is different from a white man's . . . I would rather you ask the full-blooded Indian on my left what *he* thinks of those movies where Indians were inhuman savages only anxious to spill blood." The gentleman on his left stood and chuckled as he said today's Indian actors who take on these roles are referred to as "Uncle Tomahawks." They are also called "apples"—red on the outside, white on the inside. And so it went, until abruptly it was over and Redford left with barely a sidelong glance from the few museum spectators who accidentally found themselves riding in the same elevator with "Numero Uno." Outside, on an unexpectedly sunny Madison Avenue, Robert Redford ducked into a waiting car and it took a whole city block before a group of teenagers lunged at his passing all-too-famous face staring icily back at them from the rolled-up window.

Robert Redford hates being a star. He's the man most fantasized about by women (a fact that embarrasses him), the man who has everything (a fact he never brags about), yet fame has become a painful thorn, privacy a coveted luxury.

It's the old story. Robert Redford the superstar is experiencing the ultimate in growing pains. Room at the top is damned uncomfortable for a guy who styles himself a nonconformist, an individualist, a concerned member of society. Coping with success is making him cranky. "There are so many vital issues I could be a part of, but I honestly don't think anyone gives a damn," he says. "I recently worked with Ramsey Clark and here was a perfect example of what the press had been screaming for in a politician! A real Mr. Smith Goes to Washington. All we had were crooks in the government, Nembutal cases in the White House, guys who weren't qualified, limited people with limited scope. We needed Mr. Honest. But Ramsey Clark's race for Jacob Javits's seat in the Senate was a classic case of the good guys who always lose. His momentum crested, but when it came down to the wire, the smart-aleck *New York Times,* which is always crying for liberal candidates, endorsed Javits again. I went to Boston with Clark and prepared myself to overcome this fear of publicity so I could really talk to the people about something meaningful. But nobody would talk about him. They only asked me to show them my 'fast draw' from *Butch Cassidy and the Sundance Kid.* I don't think people care what really happens to them, and I often feel I'll just opt out of this rat race and buy another hunk of Utah to protect my privacy. I get very cynical. But I'm basically a happy man, so out I come again, still swinging."

Looking back at some of Redford's films makes *me* happy. He might have skyrocketed to superstardom, but he still shows enough desire to be an accomplished craftsman and enough style to always be a little off center in his choice of roles. He once did a screen test to prove he was *not* right for *The Graduate* when all of his financial advisors were begging him to do it. Before that, he sought the dangerous and possibly damaging role of the homosexual movie star in *Inside Daisy Clover* when all of his financial advisors were begging him *not* to do it. He doggedly persevered in producing and starring as the shockingly unsympathetic skier in *Downhill Racer,* and again in the cynical but prophetic Oscar-winning *The Candidate.* It was the iconoclast in Redford that made the mighty *Jeremiah Johnson* so appealing. Way back when Indians were still unpopular, he took a cut in salary to work with blacklisted Communist director Abe Polonsky on the ground-breaking *Tell Them Willie Boy Is Here.* His sunnier and more typical Hollywood epics, like *Butch Cassidy, The Sting,* and *The Great Gatsby,* have led many of his critics to consider him a star who plays it safe in sympathetic roles. Loudmouthed gossips on the inside track say he even changed the script to his heroic advantage in *The Way We Were,* throwing the movie off balance.

Rumors were even circulating that he refused to dye his golden hair to villainous brown in *Gatsby,* giving credence to the opinion that Mr. Clean was insisting on indulging his star prerogatives. (The truth is, he did dye his hair to offset his own "blondes are luckier" theory, which he felt was wrong for the character of Gatsby.) Redford is human enough, with a healthier-than-average ego, to be sensitive to these slanders. When they accumulate, he just runs away to the mountain he carved for himself in the wilderness of Utah.

Last year, he was standing in the flat plains of Texas, squinting through the penetrating rays of a sun that fried the Texas sky. He was all decked out in the romantically nostalgic duds of a World War I flying ace—high boots, jodhpurs, short leather jacket, flaring white satin scarf and skull-tight leather helmet. He was surrounded by local Texas townspeople playing extras in *The Great Waldo Pepper,* a movie about the barnstorming antics of an ex-Air Force ace trying to make a living in the 1920s. Somehow, the vintage airplanes, cars and costumes blended extraordinarily well with the rude Texas wind and sunshine. Redford grinned into the rough elements and said: "I have a good, solid feeling down here. It's comfortable. I like locations because they're real. But I don't like the idea of being real all the time.

"Reality is like an anchor. To work out our lives we have to deal with it, but I think laughing and goofing off are just as important as the serious things in life. Sometime I opt out. I don't think that's wrong. Locking yourself in a career is a lot like dealing with a tricky, beguiling mistress. Not everyone can be as lucky as the man who owns and loves all of these old Jennie planes here, and spends his whole life doing exactly what he wants to do. The other day I found myself out on the wing of one of those buggers—the wings are only made of nylon—and there I was, 'wing-walking' way up in the air, and I felt incredible freedom. Then I had to ask myself, 'What am I doing here?' and get back down to the reality of hard work."

This winter, Redford has been asking himself that question a lot about New York, where he has spent three long months playing a CIA agent in *Three Days of the Condor*. He loves New York, but hates the fact that he is more accessible to the army of journalists who hound him for interviews and the legions of fans who follow him into the men's room. He has amused himself by raising the evasion of silly questions to a fine art. Like, "How does it feel having a perfect marriage?" "The same way it feels to have a perfect divorce. There's no such thing." Only last week he complained: "Do you believe a major newspaper in this most sophisticated city in the world ran a story on me that read, 'Robert Redford is standing around the streets in a stocking cap!'? I ask you, is that news? Last week I attended a vitally important energy conference but not one paper printed a word about it. But my stocking cap gets into the headlines. Famous is not so great. I never knew famous was going to be like this."

Amid the debris of cheese Danish and used coffee containers that clutter his movie set, Redford gets almost misty when he talks about his next film, *All the President's Men*, which he bought to co-star himself and Dustin Hoffman as Pulitzer-Prize–winning Watergate reporters Woodward and Bernstein. "I'm very enthusiastic about it, but not for the reasons you might think. I'm excited about making a movie that will inform people. I never learned anything until I left school. I was like all the other kids in school. I wanted to be voted the most popular guy in the class. Now I've changed and it's the guys like Rockefeller who want to be the most popular guy in the class. I'm cynical but optimistic. I think the real leadership in this country is going to come out of citizen's groups, like Ralph Nader's, or the Public Interest Research groups, or Consumer Action Now, in which my wife, Lola, is active. And from the women in politics. That's another thing that bothers me. There are so few roles for women in films. I've already got my next film after *All the President's Men* and it's a mature western with a great role for a woman."

A curious statement from an actor whose career is studded with co-starring roles opposite men. But Robert Redford is always good for a surprise, and he's changing all the time. "I think we are all really motivated by change," he says reflectively. "If anything endures, it is really only change. Ralph Waldo Emerson once wrote, 'Even a hero becomes a bore at last.' Maybe I better watch it."